Clare

Past and Present

THE CONSTRUCTION OF ABORIGINALITY

Aboriginal Studies Press
Canberra, 1994

Past and Present

THE CONSTRUCTION OF ABORIGINALITY

EDITED BY JEREMY R BECKETT

First published in 1988 by
    Aboriginal Studies Press
    for the Australian Institute of Aboriginal Studies,
    GPO Box 553, Canberra, ACT 2601.

Reprinted in 1994 by
    Aboriginal Studies Press
    for the Australian Institute of Aboriginal and
    Torres Strait Islander Studies,
    GPO Box 553, Canberra, ACT 2601.

    The views expressed in this publication are those of the author and not necessarily those of the Australian Institute of Aboriginal and Torres Strait Islander Studies.

© *Australian Institute of Aboriginal Studies 1988.*
    Apart from any fair dealing for the purpose of private study, research, criticism or review, as permitted under the Copyright Act, no part of this publication may be reproduced by any process whatsoever without the written permission of the publisher.

National Library of Australia Cataloguing-in-Publication data:

    Past and present.

        Bibliography.
        ISBN 0 85575 190 8.

        [1]. Aborigines, Australian — Race identity. [2]. Aborigines, Australian — History. I. Beckett, Jeremy. II. Australian Institute of Aboriginal Studies.

    305.8'9915

Designed by Aboriginal Studies Press.

Typeset in Compugraphic Avant Garde.

Printed in Australia by Australian Print Group, Maryborough, Victoria.

1000 08 94

Contents

	Contributors	vi
1.	**Jeremy Beckett** Introduction	1
2.	**Kenneth Maddock** Myth, history and a sense of oneself	11
3.	**Jane M Jacobs** The construction of identity	31
4.	**Howard Creamer** Aboriginality in New South Wales: beyond the image of cultureless outcasts	45
5.	**Barry Morris** The politics of identity: from Aborigines to the first Australian	63
6.	**Gillian K Cowlishaw** The materials for identity construction	87
7.	**Deirdre F Jordan** Aboriginal identity: uses of the past, problems for the future?	109
8.	**Robert Ariss** Writing black: the construction of an Aboriginal discourse	131
9.	**Basil Sansom** The past is a doctrine of person	147
10.	**Tim Rowse** Middle Australia and the noble savage: a political romance	161
11.	**Lenore Coltheart** The moment of Aboriginal history	179
12.	**Jeremy Beckett** The past in the present; the present in the past: constructing a national Aboriginality	191

Contributors

Robert Ariss
Department of Anthropology, University of Sydney.

Jeremy Beckett
Department of Anthropology, University of Sydney.

Lenore Coltheart
Centre for Continuing Education, University of Sydney.

Gillian K Cowlishaw
School of Social Science, Mitchell College of Advanced Education.

Howard Creamer
Anthropologist, National Parks and Wildlife Service, New South Wales.

Jane M Jacobs
Department of Geography, University College, London.

Deirdre F Jordan
Department of Education, University of Adelaide.

Kenneth Maddock
School of Behavioural Sciences, Macquarie University.

Barry Morris
School of Social Science, Mitchell College of Advanced Education.

Tim Rowse
Department of Anthropology, University of Sydney.

Basil Sansom
Department of Anthropology, University of Western Australia.

1. Jeremy Beckett   Introduction

All but two of the papers in this collection were presented at the biennial meetings of the Australian Institute of Aboriginal Studies (AIAS) in 1986. The organising committee under the chairmanship of Robert Tonkinson had decided that one of the three day-long sessions should be devoted to the theme of 'Uses of the Past in the Construction of Aboriginal Identity'. The convener of the panel published a brief description in an appeal for contributions:

> There has been some tendency among anthropologists to regard Aboriginality as unproblematic. To do so is to ignore a process of cultural construction that is integral to the working out of relations between Aboriginal and European Australians.
>
> In describing Aboriginality as a cultural construction we are not suggesting that it is inauthentic. It refers to the ways in which Aborigines select from their experience and their cultural heritage to communicate a sense of identity to their young people, to Aborigines of differing backgrounds, and to other Australians. European Australians are also engaged in the construction of Aboriginality as 'experts', advocates and critics. The media devote considerable space to Aboriginal affairs, constructing Aboriginality for the many European Australians who have no direct experience of Aborigines. Aborigines themselves are exposed to these influences and have come to terms with them in their dialogue with European Australia.
>
> The principal currency in these exchanges is the Past. The memories of old people, anthropological writings, archaeological remains, documentary records, are all ransacked to give authenticity to competing constructions.
>
> The Committee invites contributions on the various aspects of this process, European as well as Aboriginal, local as well as national, past as well as present.

Nine papers were presented in response to this invitation, all of which, after revision, have been included in this volume. Tim Rowse, who was present at the conference, subsequently accepted an invitation to contribute. Robert Ariss's paper, originally written for another purpose, was requested by the editor as filling an important gap in the collection. In terms of disciplines, the contributors include one educationist, one historian, one geographer and eight anthropologists.

It is important to establish at the outset what this collection is and is not attempting to do. It does not presume to lay down particular criteria for the definition of Aboriginality; still less to define who is or is not Aboriginal. It is rather concerned with the ways in which Australian society and Aboriginal people have since the beginning of European colonisation maintained and reproduced the notion of Aboriginality, so that at any given time certain members of that society have experienced it as Aborigines. The idea of Aboriginality of course refers to the historical fact that there were people already living in Australia when the colonists arrived, and that they have descendants in the present population. But although the idea of Aboriginality as a continuing entity is based in the descent principle, it cannot be understood simply as the direct, natural consequence of biological reproduction. Some descendants of the original inhabitants of the continent have at various times been declared, and declared themselves, not to be Aboriginal—although such declarations may have been contradicted by the assertion that they were 'really Aborigines' after all. Moreover, the definition of Aboriginality has changed over the years, and at any given time has been ambiguous in certain respects and subject to dispute. In other words, the idea of Aboriginality has in a sense existed at a remove from the things which at any given time characterised it; its power residing in the assumption of continuity.

Aboriginality, then, is a cultural construction. It shares this quality with all other nationalisms, including the Australian (cf White 1981), being an example of what Ben Anderson (1983) has called the 'imagined community'. This definition does not imply inauthenticity (it is clear that nationalism, ethnicity and Aboriginality remain some of the most passionately felt forms of identity throughout the world), but simply that they are products of the human imagination. This is necessarily so because, as Anderson (1983, 15) observes, 'the members of even the smallest nation will never know most of their fellow-members, meet them, or even hear of them, yet in the minds of each lives the image of their communion'. This image is a cultural artefact, achieved by remembering things held in common, but also by strategic forgetting (Anderson 1983, 14–15). The 'imagining of communities' is not arbitrary, but, like all cultural processes, takes place under particular political and economic circumstances, within a particular cultural tradition and in terms of particular historical experiences. It is these conditions that give the construction its authenticity and also its fluidity.

The complexity of such processes can be illustrated by reference to the proposal by the Director of Western Mining Corporation to confine the status 'Aboriginal' to those who appear to be 'full bloods' and whose way of life is deemed to be 'traditional'. Hugh Morgan's opinions were evidently sufficiently newsworthy to be given space in several newspapers, creating the possibility that they may have influenced 'public opinion'. Tim Rowse's paper in this collection suggests that Morgan's opinions may have struck a chord in Australian public opinion. At the same time, the papers by Cowlishaw, Creamer and Morris reveal the existence of communities in New South Wales who, despite European genetic admixture and an apparent absence of traditional practices, have for generations been regarded, and have regarded themselves as Aboriginal. It is inconceivable that Mr Morgan's modest proposal can dissolve overnight the lifelong experiences of these communities and their non-Aboriginal neighbours—it is more likely to inflame the division between them.[1]

Australian writing on Aboriginality has, until recently, been meagre. Anthropologists have rather, as Cowlishaw notes, been part of the process of construction, sometimes knowingly, as advisors of governments; sometimes unknowingly as communicators of 'scientific truth' which has had unintended consequences. The politicisation of Aboriginal studies during the 1970s made such scientific detachment almost impossible, but the British influence on Australian anthropologists had led them to concentrate their efforts on local systems of social relations, so that they saw their role primarily in local matters such as land claims and community advising.[2] The wider issues they left to others, such as the political scientists and economists.

Ronald Berndt (1977, 5) was one of the first anthropologists to address the issue of Aboriginality in his introduction to a collection of papers presented at the 1973 meetings of the AIAS. Writing under the title, 'Aboriginal identity...reality or mirage', Berndt draws a basic distinction between the 'reality' of traditional Aboriginal life, which 'has to do with first hand experiences within it, and with particular kinds of idiom', and 'ideas or visions of it' by those 'outside the system'. The latter 'is a mirage in relation to traditional Aboriginal life as it existed in the past or continues to exist today in some regions', but 'as a viable view, believed in by those who wish to believe in it, it has a reality of its own'. Berndt (1977, 8–12) goes on to discuss the 'contrived task' of creating a pan-Aboriginal 'commonality', out of a 'selection of traditional elements' (in which anthropologists can help), combined with contact history—this would constitute 'the real Aboriginal identity'.

No one took up Berndt's proposal, at least as far as the written record is concerned. It remained for two North American cultural anthropologists, Delmos Jones and Jacqueline Hill-Burnett (1982, 216), to bring into focus what they called 'ethnogenesis', including 'the process whereby a "common culture" comes about and the manner by which it is defined'. Their paper, based on an Australia-wide survey in 1976, deserves closer attention than it has received. Of particular relevance is the conclusion they draw from the cultural diversity of the people who are becoming a group (Jones and Hill-Burnett 1982, 216):

> As to the degree to which past cultural tradition potentially provides the boundaries and norms of an ethnic group, we argue that the common culture of diverse subcultures is not 'given' in a situation that is culturally diverse. Commonalities are first conceptualized and then 'constructed'.

They go on to offer the general observation that (Jones and Hill-Burnett 1982, 238):

> in many cases ethnic ideology is primarily the property of an ethnic elite, a condition that makes it possible for a national government at times to ignore the existence of diversity at the local level but at other times to use it as a mechanism to manipulate that elite structure. The explanation for this paradox is simply that insofar as a group-wide identity exists, it exists among the elite. An ideology at this elite level may indeed reflect the aspirations of the local population...or may on the other hand reflect goals moulded by outsiders.

In contrast to Berndt, Jones and Hill-Burnett emphasise that Aboriginal people are not free to construct their Aboriginality as they please. Others have a close interest in the process of ethnogenesis, not least the state. Sally Weaver makes a similar point in her comparison of developments among Canadian Indians and Australian Aborigines. She has drawn a useful distinction between the 'private ethnicity' which is 'practised by groups or networks of aboriginal minority members in their daily lives', being 'defined and rationalized by the aboriginal groups, not the nation-state', and the 'public ethnicity' which is 'part of the *political culture* of the nation-state', being 'determined in the public arena of *relations between* the nation-state and the aboriginal minorities' (Weaver 1984, 186). I would add that while, as Weaver says, private ethnicity has 'a space and legitimacy of its own within aboriginal groups', the enormous power of the state and its ability to harness the mass media ensure that private ethnicity exists in the shadow of the public. However, the two are not simply unequally competing loci of construction, but contrasting milieux. Weaver (1984, 185) writes:

> Unlike private ethnicity, which is behavioral, situational and heterogeneous, public ethnicity is symbolic, global in application (to all or specified members of a minority) and uniform in concept. It is generalizing from, and for the most part either ignores, or is highly selective in its use of private ethnicity.

All these writers recognise that the process of construction is not achieved through some kind of communal consensus, but in a number of different loci whose output may coalesce, but equally may be in contention. Indeed, competing constructions may well be the vehicles for competing political and economic interests, Aboriginal and non-Aboriginal.

Australia has manifested an intensification of 'public' and 'private' interest in Aboriginality from the late 1960s to the present.[3] This cannot, however, be understood in isolation from developments elsewhere. A full analysis cannot be attempted in a short introduction, but it seems necessary to relate the Australian situation to the re-emergence of ethnicity in much of the developed world, and the politicisation of indigenous minorities in colonies of settlement, such as the United States, Canada, Mexico, Australia and New Zealand—what is sometimes called the Fourth World. Large and well publicised campaigns, such as that of the black civil rights movement in the United States, both provided models for others to emulate, and created a political arena in which others were forced to participate in order to survive. Thus, for example, the Black Panthers of the late 1960s in New York, gave rise to the 'Jewish Panthers' and the Jewish Defence League (Dolgin 1977). Again, the massive movement of labour across national boundaries, particularly during the 1960s, brought into existence first generation immigrant 'communities', which became units of economic and even political competition during the subsequent recession. Governments were forced to respond to these developments, which required revision of the national ideologies and doctrines of citizenship by which their nation states were constituted. In states with a long tradition of immigration, the response was to locate ethnicity at one level and nationalism at another. Dolgin and Magdoff (1977, 353) argue that in the United States, the metaphors by which ethnic groups are 'concretised' (eg blood and land) are potentially substitutable, and that the assumption of the equality of any individual and any ethnic group provides a foundation for the substitutability of most ethnic groups. Australia's official 'multiculturalism' of the 1970s was built on similar assumptions, as was its fostering of Aboriginality.

For the bearers, however, ethnicity is founded on a sense of uniqueness, so that the homogenising influences of the state are met by contrary tendencies. In this respect aboriginality generically speaking, is at an advantage, for although it must be considered as a form of ethnicity, it retains distinctive features, particularly occupation of the country prior to colonisation and the lack of a mother country beyond the seas. Settlers may contest the claims to autochthonousness contained in much aboriginal mythology—'Where did the Aborigines come from?' was one of the first questions British settlers in Australia asked (see for example Cunningham 1827)—but they cannot deny prior occupation.[4] Thus it becomes possible for Aboriginal people to substantialise their identity by asserting primordial rights over the land which settlers 'own' and which in other modes—for example through the idea of cultivation—substantialises settler identity.

The identity and rights of contemporary Aboriginal people depend on them being recognised as in some sense 'the same' as those who occupied the country when the settlers arrived. One way of doing this, which carries a considerable credibility in European cultures, is the notion of descent, concretised in the metaphor of 'blood'.[5] Less certain is the notion of cultural heritage, which may distance people from their ancestors rather than bringing them together. Here the position of the Australian Aborigines is complicated by the presence of 'the past in the present', which is to say the existence of Aboriginal people who live in ways that are regarded as in some sense the same as those followed before the arrival of Europeans.[6] This presence simultaneously validates the cultural claims of Aboriginal people, and calls into question the status of those whose way of life differs from it. Marcia Langton (1981, 16–22) has pointed out how in Australia, anthropologists moved easily from recording the absence of Aboriginal cultural traits in 'detribalised' communities to denying the members any cultural difference from the majority, in some instances even denying them culture. Similarly, several contributors to this collection point up the bitter contradiction between this denial and imposition of a distinct Aboriginal sociopolitical status through repressive laws and social discrimination. Solutions to this predicament have included the rediscovery of traditional culture by various means (see Creamer Chapter 4) and the assertion through the revision of racist theory that certain qualities and capacities are transmitted with Aboriginal blood. Alternatively, Aboriginality has been constructed in terms of the experience of being Aboriginal under colonial conditions—an experience that Aboriginal people are often urged to forget or revise for the sake of national harmony. Sansom in his chapter, argues that such a view constructs a 'past populated by reified agents', though one might add that the view of Aboriginal people as bearers of unchanging tradition is scarcely less depersonalising.

Nations and ethnic groups, including aboriginal peoples, define themselves and are defined by reference to a past which becomes their 'Past'. Whether this is made up of a remote past enshrined in mythology and legend or uncovered by archaeology, or to a past still fresh in living memory, or to the two articulated as a history, events that involved particular individuals in particular localities have to be accepted as standing for the collectivity. In some states a national academy is assigned the task of writing the official history, which is then institutionalised through the erection of public memorials, the ceremonial commemoration of historic events and the syllabuses of schools. Berndt seems to have had something of the kind in mind when he proposed that a 'real' Aboriginal identity should be constructed by Aborigines making choices from a range of possibilities presented by anthropologists. But after ten years there are few signs of any such collaboration, at least at the national level, and in retrospect it seems improbable that such a collaboration could have succeeded. The processes by which the ruling culture transforms a subject people's lives into scientific fact cannot easily be reversed. Such people, who live for the most part outside the domain of science and written history must find some means of reappropriating the past experientially if it is to release its potency. This is what some of the Aboriginal writers, examined in Ariss's chapter, seem to be attempting, but for the majority it is probably easier to work with such fragments of the past as remain theirs. Discussing the effects of the conquest of 'primitive' societies and the colonial decomposition of their religions, Michael Taussig (1984, 88) writes:

> The 'bits and pieces' that remain of these religions are thus *not* testimony to the tenacity of tradition, as the historicist would argue. Instead they are mythic images reflecting and condensing the experiential appropriation of the history of conquest, as that history is seen to form analogies and structural correspondences with the hopes and tribulations of the present.[7]

Instead of an authorised version of Aboriginality in Australia, there has been a medley of voices, black and white, official and unofficial, national and local, scientific and journalistic, religious and secular, interested and disinterested, all offering or contesting particular constructions of Aboriginality. It is likely to remain this way.

The chapters in this collection are, as I have said, not attempts to define Aboriginality. They share the assumption that there need be no one definition that is 'true' even for a particular period, still less for all time. Aboriginality, like other nationalisms, is in a constant process of creation and it may have many definitions that compete for acceptance, among particular groups of Aborigines or Europeans, or in the society at large. The contributors have set out to understand a few among the many moments in this ongoing process.

Most of what has been written about Aboriginal people constructing Aboriginality, and the European Other, for themselves derives from communities which have lived at close quarters with white people for generations. There are few examples of constructions in the traditional mode (cf Rose 1984, Beckett nd). Kenneth Maddock's analysis of some 'Captain Cook myths' are thus of particular interest here. The chapters by Jane Jacobs, Deirdre Jordan, Howard Creamer and to a lesser extent Barry Morris, are concerned with Aboriginal constructions of tradition under the constraints of political dealings with government agencies such as land tribunals, schools, national park boards and municipalities. Aboriginal town dwellers, however, in greater or lesser degree, construct their Aboriginality in terms of contemporary characteristics, as illustrated by the chapters of Morris and Cowlishaw. Ariss's chapter examines the unusual but nevertheless important situation of the Aboriginal writer, whose representations of Aboriginality must satisfy non-Aboriginal publishers and reach readers, the majority of whom are not Aboriginal, but who are nevertheless oriented toward other Aborigines. Sansom contrasts the construction of the person in a particular Aboriginal community of his acquaintance, with that in some scholarly practice. Also concerned with non-Aboriginal loci of construction, Coltheart addresses the problem entailed in historians writing Aboriginal history and Rowse analyses a recent instance of construction through an opinion poll that influenced political judgements. Finally, my concluding chapter attempts an overview of what Weaver calls public Aboriginality in Australia that deals mainly with European constructions, but also considers recent Aboriginal attempts to influence the process.

Notes

1. It is true that the Nazi regime was able to deprive German Jews of their Germanness, but only by employing the full force of state power and extreme methods.

2. An exception must be made in the case of AP Elkin whose anthropology derived from a tradition earlier than that of the structural-functionalists. His general study *The Australian Aborigines, How to Understand Them*, still in print after forty years, does address the issue of the Aboriginality of Aboriginal people in the southern half of Australia. However, his association with the assimilation policy resulted in his work being largely ignored by his successors in the 1970s.

3. It would, I think, be necessary to go back to the 1930s to discover a period of similar intensity. However, the activities of William Ferguson, Jack Patten and Pearl Gibbs were confined to southeastern Australia, while actions such as the Torres Strait Islanders' strike in 1936 (Sharp 1982), and the upheavals on Palm Island, were not such as to produce repercussions elsewhere.

4. The prehistoric 'movement of peoples' was a major scientific pre-occupation throughout the age of European nationalism and imperial expansion. It has virtually disappeared from mainstream anthropology and linguistics, though in minor mode it lingers in some

branches of prehistory and historical linguistics. Peter White has pointed out to me that the doctrine of descent from Adam entails the dispersal of his descendants throughout the world, and so prefigures subsequent scientific enquiry.

5. The ambiguous situation of individuals who are of mixed descent has been 'resolved' by various forms of folk genetics.

6. The situation of Aborigines in Australia differs from that of the Torres Strait Islanders, who regard their conversion to Christianity—conventionally dated at 1871—as separating them from Darkness Time.

7. Taussig's remarks, made in the course of an attempt to explain the magical potency of imagery drawn from and referring to the past in the practice of shamanic healers in Colombia, were in part inspired by Silvia Bovenchen's (1978) interpretation of the resurgence of witch mythology in European feminism.

References

Anderson, B.
1983 *Imagined Communities*, Verso Press, New York.

Beckett, J.
nd Walter Newtown's History, manuscript.

Berndt, R.
1977 *Introduction to Aborigines and Change in the 1970s*, Australian Institute of Aboriginal Studies, Canberra.

Bovenchen, S.
1978 The Contemporary Witch, the Historical Witch and the Witch Myth: The Witch Subject of the Appropriation of Nature and Object of the Domination of Nature, *New German Critique* 15, 83–119.

Cunningham, P.
1827 *Two Years in New South Wales*, Colburn, London.

Dolgin, J.
1977 *Jewish Identity and the JDL*, Princeton University Press, Princeton, New Jersey.

Dolgin, J. and J. Magdoff
1977 The Invisible Event. In J. Dolgin, D. Kemnitzer and D. Schneider (eds), *Symbolic Anthropology*, Columbia University Press, New York.

Jones, D. and J. Hill-Burnett
1982 The Political Context of Ethnogenesis: An Australian Example. In M.C. Howard (ed), *Aboriginal Power in Australian Society*, University of Queensland Press, St Lucia, 214–46.

Langton, M.
1981 Urbanizing Aborigines: The Social Scientists' Great Deception, *Social Alternatives* 2, 16–22.

Rose, D.B.
1984 The Saga of Captain Cook: Morality in Aboriginal and European Law, *Australian Aboriginal Studies* 2, 24–39.

Sharp, N.
1982 Culture Clash in the Torres Strait Islands: The Maritime Strike of 1936, *Journal of Royal Historical Society of Queensland* 11(3), 107–26.

Taussig, M.
1984 'History as Sorcery', *Representations*, 7, 87–109.

Weaver, S.
1984 Struggle of the Nation-State to Define Aboriginal Ethnicity: Canada and Australia. In G.L. Gold (ed), *Minorities and Mother Country Imagery,* Social and Economic Papers 13, Institute of Social and Economic Research, Newfoundland.

White, R.
1981 *Inventing Australia: Images and Identity 1688–1980,* George Allen and Unwin, Sydney.

2. Kenneth Maddock — Myth, history and a sense of oneself[1]

This chapter concerns Aboriginal myths of early or initial contact between Aborigines and outsiders. I have included all the stories I could find on the subject, with a view to seeing whether they convey a message about an Aboriginal sense of identity formed in reaction to encroachment. As the myths come from scattered parts of eastern and northern Australia, my approach is far removed from the 'micro-sociology' favoured by many anthropologists. I believe, however, that a pan-Aboriginal consciousness has been with us for some time, and that it can be misleading to treat particular examples of a cultural form (eg a myth or a ritual) as necessarily bound to neatly integrated local communities.

None of the myths were collected by me, and as far as I know such stories are not told in areas in which I worked.[2] Most sources say little or nothing about the context of narration—for example, by whom the myths are told, to whom, on what occasions or with what motives? These gaps in our information would be felt as crippling deficiencies by a micro-sociologist, but they are much less serious from my perspective.

In addition to analysing the myths and considering what they convey about an Aboriginal sense of identity, I make observations on their historical value. This seems an obvious move, for more than half the myths are centred on that indubitably historical character Captain James Cook. (Two other historical characters also make appearances.) The relation of myth and history is, of course, an anthropological pre-occupation of long standing, which many recent writers have discussed (see for example, Bilby 1984; Eliade 1965; Okpewho 1983; Simmons 1976; Willis 1980). In Australia there has been a tendency in the last few years to credit Aboriginal myths with historical veracity, to treat them as containing factual information about what happened where. Linguists and prehistorians seem especially prone to this view. My inclination is to scepticism, though I admit that it would be wrong to dismiss out of hand the possibility of a residue of past events having been orally transmitted in myth form.

Aboriginal stories about Cook provide a favourable opportunity to test the relation of myth and history as it occurs in Australia, for both Cook and the botanist Joseph Banks kept detailed journals during the voyage of the *Endeavour*. By setting their entries against episodes in myth, one can form a judgement on whether the 'documentary analogy' (ie the assimilation of oral traditions to written documents which have come to us unchanged from some past era), has any validity in the Aboriginal case. In other words, can Aboriginal history be written when the only sources are oral traditions about events before living memory? If the documentary analogy is invalid, what inferences should be drawn about the use of the past by Aborigines in constructing their identity?

Myth and the Cook problem

Aboriginal stories about Captain Cook have been reported from a number of places in the last thirty or so years. At first sight, they challenge the common opinion that Aborigines had short memories for historical events.[3] But when the stories are compared with relevant entries in journals kept during the *Endeavour's* voyage one is compelled to revise initial impressions that they might amount to a kind of 'oral documentation', supplementary to and contemporaneous with written records from the late eighteenth century. Nevertheless the possibility remains that the myths throw some kind of light on history.

Two of the six stories about Cook presented here are set on the east coast—up which he sailed, and along which 'relics' of his journey are pointed out by local Aborigines—but the others are from the southeast Gulf country in Queensland, the Victoria River district of the Northern Territory, and the Kimberleys in Western Australia. Cook was never near those parts, for after reaching Point Lookout the *Endeavour* turned northeast and left Australia behind.[4]

Have we, then, to deal with two sets of stories about Aboriginal contact with Cook? Are there, on the one hand, east coast tales in which oral tradition, dating back to 1770, has transmitted to us a folk memory of Cook; and, on the other hand, tales from the north which have become established in local lore, in spite of owing nothing to the real Cook? Or does the interest of the stories lie less in any help they can be in correlating myth and history, or in supplementing history, as in the prospect they offer of insight into Aborigines in crisis—a crisis provoked by contact and involvement with Europeans?

Aborigines had occupied Australia from time immemorial before Cook. Apart from fleeting glimpses of voyagers here and there on the coast, and intermittent relations with Papuans and Macassans in the north, Aborigines would have known nothing of other peoples and cultures until 1788, when British settlement began. The arrival of the First Fleet at Port Jackson, and the spread of colonisation from that and other coastal footholds, may seem of enormously greater import than the mere passage of the *Endeavour* along the coast, yet it is the latter which has found its way into Aboriginal mythology.

One may be sure that Aborigines made some sense of their first contact with outsiders. It is true that the Aborigines who underwent this experience died long ago without leaving written records, and it may be doubted whether oral traditions are reliable in the absence of corroboration. The conclusion might well be drawn that we are entirely dependent on observations and impressions noted at the time by observers. Many such notes were made (see for example, Reynolds 1981, 5–49), and they suggest that Aborigines strove to 'domesticate' what was 'alien'. For instance, outsiders were often taken for ghosts of dead kin. But the Cook stories offer something more—they are rounded narratives in which our Aboriginal contemporaries give accounts of contact with Cook in the form of reports contemporaneous with the events described. To all appearances the stories date from Cook's presence in Australia; they seem to be eyewitness accounts brought to us by oral transmission.

Cook on the east coast

My southernmost story is set at Bateman's Bay in New South Wales. A 'terrible tall' Aboriginal woman who lived to be more than 100 told it to Percy Mumbulla's father. Percy in turn told it to the poet, Roland Robinson (1970, 29–30). On this chronology the story is of considerable age, perhaps stretching back to at least the mid-nineteenth century.

> **Myth 1**
> The big ship came and anchored
> out at Snapper Island.
> He put down a boat
> an rowed up the river
> into Bateman's Bay.
>
> He landed on the shore of the river,
> the other side from where the
> church is now.
> When he landed he gave the Kurris clothes,
> an those big sea-biscuits.
> Terrible hard biscuits they was.

> When they were pullin away to go back
> to the ship, these wild Kurris
> were runnin out of the scrub.
> They'd stripped right off again.
> They were throwin the clothes and biscuits
> back at Captain Cook
> as his men were pullin away in the boat.

According to Cook's journal, Bateman's Bay was passed on 21 April. No Aborigines were seen and no attempt made to land. The first landing attempt came a week later between Lake Illawarra and Bulli, about 150 kilometres north of Bateman's Bay. Some Aborigines were seen, four of whom were carrying a canoe, but they took to flight as Cook's boat neared the beach. Heavy surf prevented a landing. Myth 1 is not at all like a recollection of this event.

Cook's first landing was at Botany Bay, a day after the unsuccessful attempt near Bulli. There the *Endeavour* spent a week, and Aborigines were met and given presents, including nails, beads, combs, mirrors, cloth and a bird which had been shot. The English received nothing in return. On one occasion they ate shellfish being prepared by Aborigines (who made off as the English came up), and on another took 'darts' from a camp where only small children were present. As for Aboriginal reception of gifts: the first to be made ('nails beeds &ca') were thrown ashore from the boats and picked up by Aborigines; strings of beads left with the children at the camp from which darts were taken were found lying in one of the huts when the camp was revisited next day; and the persons to whom the shot bird was offered would not touch it. Aborigines threw a stone and two darts at the English at their first landing, and darts were thrown on two other occasions. None of this is especially suggestive of the actions described in Myth 1. Straining to find a common thread, one can say that in each case Cook arrived from the sea, made gifts to Aborigines, and had things thrown at him.

The next Cook story is set at Cardwell, in Queensland, about 1,850 kilometres north of Botany Bay. Chloe Grant and Rosie Runaway, both Dyirbal women, told it to the linguist Bob Dixon (1983, 1–3).

Myth 2
All the tribe saw Captain Cook when he came into Cardwell. At first he seemed to be standing up in the sea. 'Man', he said, 'you want a smoke?' The Aborigines watched as Cook and his group smoked a pipe. 'What is that burning thing this man has stuck in his mouth? What is making all the smoke?'

Cook boiled a billy of tea to the incredulity of Chloe's ancestors, and offered them a drink. 'That's just dirty water', they answered. Then the white man said again, 'This good, look, I drink him, I drink him'. But the scalding liquid drew no takers. Then Cook said, 'I put cold water there, you drink him'.

Cook was now baking a Johnny-cake on the coals, turning it over—front to back, back to front, top to bottom. He lifted it up to see whether it was yet light and cooked, put it down to cool, and then cut pieces off which he handed around. It looked to the Aborigines like cakes roasted from brown walnut, one of their staples. But the Johnny-cake did not measure up to its looks. It smelt stale, and they threw it away untasted.

Beef, Cook's next offering, was better received. Never before had the Aborigines seen boiled meat, but it smelt well, its salty skin could be wiped off, and its taste was acceptable though new.

The explorers' preparation for departure aroused consternation among the Aborigines, who had concluded from their white skins that they were the spirits of ancestors returning to visit and advise their descendants. 'Father, father, come here, come back to us', the Aborigines wailed, beating their fists on the ground in desolate sorrow. But Cook and his party sailed off to the north.

It is doubtful that this charming tale about 'the first contact with Europeans', as Dixon calls it, has any connection with the voyage of the *Endeavour*. The journals of Cook and Banks mention no landing at or near Cardwell. As noted, the first occasion on which the English dealt face to face with Aborigines was at Botany Bay, far to the south. The second was at Cooktown on the Endeavour River, about 300 kilometres north of Cardwell. Cook and his crew spent seven weeks there, repairing damage caused by the *Endeavour* striking a reef. Apparently the English established closer relations with Aborigines than during their shorter stay at Botany Bay.

Not only were the Aborigines given things, but once they boarded the ship and tried to haul two of a number of turtle from the deck:

> being disappointed in this they grew a little troublesome and were for throwing every thing over board they could lay their hands upon; as we had no victuals dress'd at this time I offer'd them some bread to eat, which they rejected with scorn as I believe they would have done any thing else excepting turtle.

A few days after this incident a member of a shore party who had strayed from his companions found four Aborigines sitting by a fire at which they were cooking meat.

> [He] went and sit down by them and after he had sit a little while and they had felt his hands and other parts of his body they suffer'd him to go away without offering the least insult, and perceiving he did not go right for the ship they directed him which way he should go.

Myth 2 can no more be accepted than Myth 1 as an oral tradition relating events which actually occurred at the place given in the story. Each might, of course, be seen as imaginatively reworking a meeting between Cook and Aborigines at Botany Bay or the Endeavour River. But, if so, the events described would not have been witnessed at the places named by the ancestors of the persons who told the tales to Robinson and Dixon. Some such developmental sequence as this would have to be supposed:
1. events at Botany Bay or the Endeavour River were there embodied in oral tradition;
2. the tradition was diffused to Aborigines at Bateman's Bay or Cardwell (either directly or through a chain of intermediaries); and
3. there the tradition became localised, and its reception from elsewhere was forgotten.

At one or more stages in this process the original events would have been reworked, thus accounting for the discrepancy between journal entries, which have reached us unchanged since 1770, and myths which (assuming but not granting they originated in 1770), have come to us through many hands and with a change in locale.

An alternative would be to suppose that the persons who narrated the stories to Robinson and Dixon had made them up, or had learned them from recent forbears who were the true originators.[5] The stories would not be transmitted memories of Cook, but would have to be explained in some other way. They might, for example, be based on Cook stories which Aborigines heard from Europeans, or they could be memories of European explorers or pioneers who were really in the districts concerned (but a long time after the *Endeavour* was in Australian waters). In the latter case the events would have been recast in the telling, being pushed back to an earlier time, built around another character, and given a maritime emphasis, together (in all likelihood) with other changes.

If that is what happened there has been an assimilation of oral narrative about an historical character to the forms of the Dreamtime mythology through which traditional Aborigines made sense of their natural and cultural environment. Thus Myth 1 and Myth 2 show the character of mythological charters—they introduce the clothes, tobacco, tea, and staple foods which Aborigines acquired as a result of European contact. Through a kind of telescoping process the leader of the first white men to travel along the east coast is fittingly (in view of the common design of Aboriginal myths) credited with giving Aborigines their first exposure to these items. In each case he gives and they receive. There is no Aboriginal countergift; but Myth

1, in which Cook's presents are thrown back at him, contrasts with Myth 2, in which the Aborigines react in a more complex way by passing from incomprehension to refusal and finally to acceptance.

The Cook stories are not, of course, set in the Dreamtime, but at a time when Aboriginal society was already established. However, it is an Australia which would—as far as Aborigines were concerned—undergo a transformation as radical as that wrought by Dreamtime Beings. The first two myths are silent about the fateful future, but those of the next group go into explicit detail.

Cook in the north

The east coast people are not alone in putting Cook in myths which explain aspects of a new era. He appears also in stories set far to the west of his actual journey. In a tale told by Rolly Gilbert (1985, 168–69), a Kurtjar man, Cook is a murderer who paved the way for the cattle industry in the southeast Gulf country:

> **Myth 3**
> That Captain Cook, that Jew, he was travelling in the boat on the ocean. Then he came out to see Australia. A couple of blokes were in the boat and himself. He said: 'We go ashore in Australia' and they did come to shore, and saw these couple of Aboriginal people standing by the beach. They were going to do them over, like shoot them down, and another fellow said 'You had better not do that. They might give a good idea where the other people might be.' And so they did. They pointed out where the Aborigines had their main camping area. So they set off and found the tracks of Aborigines where they were hunting around the area. Then they went back to the boat and set up the people to explore and go down the countryside and shoot the people down, just like animal. They left them lying there for the hawks and the crows...So a lot of old people and young people were struck by the head with the end of a gun and left there. They wanted to get the people wiped out because Europeans in Queensland had to run their stock: horses and cattle.

Rolly Gilbert related this story to a conference of the Australian Academy of Science on 'Ecology and Management of the World's Savannas'. In the opinion of Athol Chase (1985, 167), who transcribed and edited this and other Aboriginal contributions to the conference:

> Mr Gilbert...has a keen sense of history, and his opening remarks provide a rare glimpse into the world of first contact with Europeans, from the Aboriginal side. While the history books put Captain Cook's route well away from the Gulf of Carpentaria, the explorer

has become synonymous in Aboriginal eyes with all first explorers. He is a mythic figure, like those in Aboriginal mythologies, who travelled around, made things happen, and who left their mark on the land and its people for ever. Captain Cook is an explanation for Aboriginal people here of why Europeans came, why they settled, and why they treated the indigenous peoples as they did.

Myth 3 is to be taken absolutely seriously, then, as a statement of an Aboriginal view of the past, in spite of its conflict with the record of Cook's voyages. It is no fireside yarn. The theme of Cook-as-villain also occurs among the Gurindji in the Victoria River district of the Northern Territory. According to a story collected by Hannah Middleton (1977, 7):

Myth 4
First there was water here and then it went back so that there was the Northern Territory. Then a thousand million Aborigines were here and lived on the land for a long time. The first cudeba (white man) who came was Ned Kelly and he brought with him the first horses, a stallion and a mare, which bred here and the first bullock, a very hairy one whose picture you can see on some rocks in Victoria River Downs country. Ned Kelly was a friend of and helped the Aborigines. The second cudeba who came was Captain Cook. He looked at the land and saw that it was very good and wanted it for himself. He decided to clear the Aborigines off the land. So he shot many of them and he shot Ned Kelly too and he stole the land.

Frederick Rose (1976, 141–42), who supervised Hannah Middleton's research, remarks that though the story may be nonsensical at first sight, it has a deeper meaning. Ned Kelly, active in the southeast of the continent, has found a place in white Australian folklore as a hero who robbed the rich. So the Gurindji, loath to adopt European success symbols, depicted the outlaw Kelly as a friend of theirs, and the celebrated navigator Cook as a thief and murderer. One might add that Myth 4 was recorded in 1970, the bicentenary of the *Endeavour's* visit to Australia. The anniversary was widely commemorated, but some Aborigines took the opportunity to protest against their dispossession, which they connected with Cook's voyage.

In fact, Kelly and Cook not only never set foot in the Territory but were so far from being contemporaries that Cook was killed in 1779, long before Kelly's birth in 1856. As it happens Kelly was virtually a contemporary of the first cattlemen in Gurindji country—they began settling there within a few years of his execution in Melbourne in 1880—but it is completely anachronistic to associate Cook with pastoralism anywhere in Australia.

From a recent paper by Deborah Rose (1984, 31–34), it is clear that a 'Captain Cook Saga', as she calls it, is widespread in the Victoria River district. Because her account is so long, I have made a short summary.

Myth 5
Captain Cook, thinking about acquiring more land, sailed from London to Sydney, where he admired the country, and landed bullocks and men with firearms. A massacre of local Aborigines followed. Cook then made his way to Darwin, where he behaved in much the same way. He sent armed horsemen to hunt down Aborigines in the Victoria River country. Cook was responsible for founding the cities of Sydney and Darwin, and he gave orders to Gilruth, the police, and the managers of cattle stations on how to treat Aborigines.

Considered as a charter, Myth 5 is more ambitious than the others. It portrays Cook as having virtually an Australia-wide significance. Like Myth 4, it is anachronistic. Indeed, as Gilruth was an administrator in the Northern Territory in the early twentieth century, he was even less Cook's contemporary than Kelly. Unlike Kelly he shares Cook's villainous character.

Cook is vilified in the Kimberleys, too, according to Erich Kolig (1980, 275), who reports the details in the form of a 'meta-story' containing 'the essence of Aborigines' reflections on the subject', rather than in the terms Aborigines would use.

Myth 6
When Captain Cook, the major culture hero of the Europeans, and his people landed in Australia they sighted Aborigines. Cook had some shot, thus setting a precedent for the white man's standard approach to Aborigines. On returning to his own country, Cook maintained that he had seen no indigenes; his affirmation of Australia as a vast and empty land formed the rationale for the settlers who came after him to claim it for themselves. In claiming the land and asserting cultural dominance over Aborigines the Europeans are relying on the Law of Captain Cook. But their claims are unjust and fallacious, for Cook's Law is less ancient—hence less venerable and true—than Aboriginal Law.

Kolig suggests that the ideas expressed in the tale may have originated with 'well-informed southern urban Aborigines', who had recently entered into dialogue with their remote and more traditional cousins. (Kolig's main observations were made in the early 1970s.) The southerners themselves would almost certainly have learned of Cook through Europeans, either directly or indirectly.

The Cook myths reviewed

There is an obvious division between myths in which Cook does great harm to Aborigines (Myths 3–6), and those in which he makes gifts to them—though his presents are rejected for no apparent reason in one of the latter group (Myth 1). This difference is correlated with some others.

Cook always comes from the sea, but in the 'doer-of-harm' stories he shows a pronounced interest in the land which is lacking when he is a gift-giver. It is in the northern myths that he does harm (though Myth 5 is partly set in Sydney), and in the east coast stories that he makes gifts. The gift-giver stories are from earlier settled, more urbanised districts, in which Aborigines have long been a small minority; the doer-of-harm stories are from thinly populated, more recently settled districts, in which Aborigines are relatively numerous, urban life is virtually absent, and rough and violent conditions are still within living memory.

In general, the myths suggest Aboriginal hostility to or resentment against Europeans in the person of Cook and his collaborators. Only in Myth 2—which is quite different in tone from all the others—is he shown in a favourable light, though the motif of the friendly and well regarded white man occurs in the shape of Ned Kelly in Myth 4.

The events and processes depicted in the myths—the coming of European goods, loss of land, loss of many lives, the introduction of pastoralism—were real enough in Australian history, and the characters who are named—Cook, Gilruth, Kelly—also existed. Where the stories go wrong is in tying Cook to those events and processes, and making him contemporary with Kelly and Gilruth. There is a quandary here for scholars who want to draw on the rich reservoir of myth to supplement their knowledge of what happened where.

Assume we knew that Aborigines had been dispossessed, cattle introduced, and so on, but were hazy about the details. Assume also we knew that such voyages as Cook had been on the Australian coast, but again lacked precise information (written records not having been made by them, or made but lost before much detail could get into secondary sources). As none of the Cook stories rests on inherently implausible assertions (as distinct from assertions which are factually mistaken), there would be a temptation to accept them as telling us where Cook landed and what he did. The result would be some totally erroneous pages of history.

My analysis may come as cold comfort to those writers who see historical value in Aboriginal myths. Dixon (1980, 46), for example, takes issue with modern anthropologists who are 'sceptical of the attempt to seek an historical basis of any kind in traditional stories and myths'. He believes that they deserve more credence than they usually get; thus the Dyirbal 'have legends that clearly relate to the end of the Ice Age, and to such geological events as volcanic eruptions that took place at least ten millennia ago' (Dixon 1983, 4). Unfortunately Dixon does not ask what credence his Cook story deserves, or why it should be accepted as originating in 1770 instead of much later.

The prehistorian Josephine Flood (1983, 11), is also inclined to a literalist view of mythology. She considers that 'oral traditions passed down as myths and legends about the Dreamtime' form one of our two sources of knowledge about the really distant human past, the other being archaeological evidence. Her opinion is that scientific investigation confirms much that these stories say. It can only be regretted that she does not enlarge on this corroboration.

Scepticism of the historical verisimilitude of myths leaves open the possibility that they throw interpretative light on the past through their treatment of themes and symbols. Their value lies less in enabling the past to be reconstructed as in giving a 'reading' of an Aboriginal sense of themselves, or of their past, in relation to the outside world ('an' not 'the' Aboriginal sense, because a solitary story from a community should not be conflated with its world-view). Taken individually or together the stories contain a sketch of a challenge to a scheme of life in which Aborigines were set, and of their response. The authors of these tales must have drawn on such sources as their own experiences, experiences transmitted from or through other Aborigines (including immediate forbears), and their sense of what it would have been fitting to do in the circumstances (eg throwing gifts back at the donor, or refusing to acquiesce in the loss of land).

The occurrence of the same historical character in all the stories, the broad scene-setting of some of them (especially Myth 5), and their reference to processes which affected Aborigines generally suggest that the myth-makers are expressing a consciousness belonging to a wider sphere than the limited local community. An awareness of being Aboriginal in Australia has broken through. But the Cook stories are not the only ones in which an Aboriginal sense of themselves is worked out in relation to outsiders. Consideration of this other material may help to show whether, and to what extent, the Cook stories are distinctive expressions of Aboriginal thought.

Macassans in Arnhem Land

Macassans visited Australia before the British by whom they were to be displaced. They used to sail to the north coast for *beche-de-mer*, but would leave at the end of the season without attempting to settle permanently. New items entered Aboriginal material culture, and new words into their languages, during this period. In addition, Aborigines made up myths about their contact with these outsiders. Warner (1937, 530-31, 536-37) reports three from northeast Arnhem Land, and Worsley (1954, 98-99) one from Groote Eylandt. I give Warner's first.

Myth 7
A Macassan who lived in the Kolpa clan's country in a house with doors and windows had clothes, blankets, and food stolen from him on several occasions by a member of that clan. Next the clansman stole matches and set fire to the grass near the house, which was destroyed in the blaze. Finally the Macassans left the country with their remaining belongings, having failed in their attempts to catch the thief.

Warner does not comment on this or the other Macassan myths, but it can be seen to stand in striking contrast to the Cook stories. An Aborigine acts so effectively against outsiders that they go away discomforted. Far from being given things by them, the Aborigine helped himself (compare Myths 1-2), and he did not lose his land (compare Myths 3-6)—at least in the long run, for the myth does not explain how the Macassan(s) came to be in Kolpa country. But Myth 7 is atypical, and Warner's other stories strike a more familiar note.

Myth 8
Dog kept close to the Macassan, but when spoken to merely repeated what was said. He refused tobacco, tomahawks, canoes, and other gifts. He also rejected an offer of a match, saying he had firesticks. So the Macassan said that Dog could be an Aboriginal, and that he should get off the mat on which he was sitting and sit on the ground instead. The Macassans took away a house they had intended giving him.

When asked why he rejected the things offered to him, Dog replied: 'I want you to be a Macassar man. I'm a black. If I get these things I'll become a white man and you'll become a black.'

A bark canoe which Dog made to cross Cadell Strait sank and turned to stone. Defeated, Dog sat on the beach, and also turned to stone.

Myth 9
The Macassans, who were black, worked for Aborigines, who were white. Dog suggested to his Macassan master that 'We better break this house down and throw him away and live without houses'. When asked by his master whether he wanted

something, Dog repeated the question. Next he refused matches, tobacco, tomahawks, and a sailing boat. So the Macassans kept these things for themselves instead of giving them to Aborigines. Aborigines turned black, and worked for the Macassans.

These stories are more 'mythical', less 'matter-of-fact', than any about Cook. Myths 1–6 read quite like accounts of actual happenings in which Cook (or other Europeans) and the forbears of the narrators (or other Aborigines) could have taken part. We might well give them factual credence if it were not for documentary evidence to the contrary. Myths 8–9, however, are akin to the general body of Dreamtime myth in their reliance on marvellous transformations. A key character is an animal who is able to communicate with humans (in spite of showing himself to be stupid or obtuse when he repeats questions instead of answering them), and whose actions are decisive for the Aboriginal future: skins change colour; a character and a canoe turn to stone; and role reversals occur between master and worker. Myth 7 is comparatively matter-of-fact, though even it has a mythical flavour absent from the Cook stories. (An additional detail mentioned by Warner is that a bird plays a part against the Macassans.) Worsley's Groote Eylandt myth is also marked off from the Cook stories:

Myth 10
A Macassan ship and a European ship from the south stopped at several places on Groote. When the native people were asked in Macassan who they were they repeated the words. The Macassans, who had to repair their ship, left part behind at Bickerton Island, where it turned to stone, but the European ship needed no repairs. The Macassans lit a fire after reaching Melville Island; the smoke, blowing over the mainland and Groote, turned Aborigines black.

According to information given to David Turner (1982, 44), who worked on Groote after Worsley, the piece of ship left behind by the Macassans turned to stone when the Aborigines tried to use it by putting it to sea.

Turner (1982, 42–50) has analysed the Macassan myths in a paper subtitled 'An Aboriginal Response to Domination'. He considers that they have a double focus. The one, more particular, is on the problem posed by the presence of Macassans among Aborigines; the other, more general, is on the problem posed by the existence of people different from Aborigines. The myth-makers 'solved' these problems by constructing a hierarchy out of such pairs of contrasts as lighter/darker in skin colour, superior/inferior in technology, and dominant/subordinate in sociopolitical standing. These contrasts are correlated: for example, in Myth 10, the Aborigines are turned black by smoke from the Macassan fire and the discarded piece of Macassan ship petrifies when they try to use it, while the ship belonging to the light-skinned Europeans needs no repair and remains whole; and in Myth 9 the Aborigines exchange roles as master and worker with Macassans as well as becoming darker than them. Aboriginal stupidity or obtuseness is noticeable in Myths 8–10, when questions are repeated instead of being answered, offers of more advanced equipment are turned down, and attempts to put to sea fail miserably. The actions and transformations described in these myths explain the position of Aborigines—as the dark-skinned and relatively immobile people of the land—vis-a-vis outsiders in the late historical period.

Myth 7 may seem something of an odd-man-out (compare Myth 2 among the Cook stories), but it confirms the identification of Aborigines with the land. The burning down of the house may be compared with its suggested demolition in Myth 9 and the Macassan decision not to give it in Myth 8, while the driving away of the Macassans—who are the source of superior equipment—may be compared with the refusal to accept such equipment in Myths 8–9 and the inability to use it as Macassans and Europeans would in Myth 10. At bottom, then, the main distinguishing feature of Myth 7 is that Aborigines outwit the Macassans and force their departure.

Cook and Macassan myths compared

If the Macassan stories are more mythical in flavour than the Cook ones, the explanation is likely threefold. First, they are probably older (Warner collected his material in the late 1920s), and reflect a more traditional cast of mind (northeast Arnhem Land in Warner's time, like Groote in Worsley's, was relatively remote and isolated). Secondly, the Macassan experience was already in the past when Myths 7–10 were collected, though still in living memory, whereas Europeans are omnipresent. Thirdly, Cook is a name to be reckoned with in modern Australia. Many Aborigines (like other Australians) would acquire a knowledge of him through such sources as schooling and the media; and he is commonly, though rather inaccurately, held out as an outstanding figure in the founding of Australia (see Robertson 1981). The details of the voyage of the *Endeavour* may be known only to a few among the more erudite, but Cook's fame combines with the penumbra of popular uncertainty around his doings to make him a most suitable hero for charter mythology.

The differences between the two groups of myths are underlaid by a shared property—each story is about contact between Aborigines (people of the land) and aliens (people from outside). We may understand the stories as Aboriginal reflections on intercultural relations, or, more specifically, as their responses to the challenge of alien impact.

In what terms have the myth-makers dramatised the relationship? Overwhelmingly they have invoked land and material things. Relations between Aboriginal and alien are treated as a medium for transferring property, yet anything like balanced exchange is missing. In both Cook and Macassan myths gifts are made, without being asked for, and thefts are committed (see tabulation below).

	Gift	Theft
Cook	Myths 1–2	Myths 3–6
Macassan	Myths 8–9	Myth 7

Not only are the gifts unsolicited, but often they are refused—either immediately (Myths 8–9) or with a delay (Myth 1). Myth 2 is more complex in its treatment of the gift theme—the Aborigines are bewildered by tobacco, find tea and Johnny-cake too unpalatable to take, but finally accept salt beef. Theirs can readily be understood as a human reaction to the unfamiliar (similarly with their initial impression that Cook was standing up in the sea).

Rejection of gifts is more mysterious in the other myths. Dog fears that acceptance would transform the relation between Aborigines and Macassans in Myth 8, but there is also a hint of self-sufficiency: having firesticks, Dog does not need matches in that myth; while in Myth 9 he suggests breaking down the house and living without permanent habitation. If rejection is critical in Myths 8–9 in setting Aborigines in their place vis-a-vis aliens, its function and motivation are obscure in Myth 1. Were the Bateman's Bay people afraid that they would change places with Cook, or were they rejecting aliens by the symbolic gesture of throwing his gifts after the departing donor, or were they expressing self-sufficiency? Could it even have been their way of expressing resentful disappointment that he was leaving them? (Compare with Myth 2, in which Cook is implored to come back.)

Although attempts to give usually end in failure, attempts at stealing always succeed, whether made by Cook against Aborigines (Myths 3–6), or by an Aborigine against Macassans (Myth 7). Cook's motive for theft is straightforward—he wants to clear the way for white settlement, and more particularly for pastoralism. The Kolpa clansman's motive is less obvious—was it to possess Macassan goods, or to drive out the aliens, or to transform the relation between them and Aborigines?

Alone among the myths, Myth 10 appears to have neither the gift nor the theft theme. But the Macassans did leave part of their ship behind, which the Aborigines tried to use by putting it to sea (in Turner's version), where it turned to stone. So even here, where Aborigines were willing to accept something originating with aliens, it remained outside their use as surely as if they had rejected it. (Compare Dog's rejection of a canoe in Myth 8, and of a sailing boat in Myth 9.)

A set of stories can be as significant for what is omitted as for what is included:
1. there is never a balanced exchange of advantages between Aboriginal and alien;
2. gift and theft never occur in the same story;
3. gifts are rarely accepted;
4. thefts are never foiled;
5. Aborigines never give to aliens; and
6. Aborigines rarely steal from aliens.

Such a degree of skew or bias can scarcely result from chance. If randomness were at play, one would expect gifts sometimes to be accepted, Aborigines to offer them to aliens, thieves sometimes to be foiled, and so on.

As it is, the obsession of the myths with actual or attempted transfers of property between Aborigines and aliens is concentrated on gifts by aliens (which Aborigines usually reject), or on thefts (usually by aliens, but which always succeed). Thus, in general, property passes from Aborigines to aliens, regardless of whether gift or theft is the mode of transfer. Not only do balanced exchanges not occur, but they are not even attempted by Aboriginal or alien.

Conclusion

The stories are clearly saying something about Aboriginal contact and involvement with the outside world. That they are so concerned is shown not only by the fact that Aborigines are on stage with people from outside, but also by the actual or attempted property transfers being between Aborigines and aliens, never between Aborigines alone or between aliens alone.

Contrary to the view some recent writers have taken of Aboriginal myths, there is no reason to see them as orally transmitted records of events in which the characters took part. That is so not only when the events described are patently mythical—skins changing colour, boats turning to stone, and so on—but when the characters are historical. The interest of the stories, from an historical point of view, has nothing to do with their telling us who did what, where, and when, but with their demonstration that some recurrent processes of culture contact in Australia have been assimilated by Aboriginal imaginations. Such personages as Cook, about whom the myth-makers would have learned from European sources, have been taken over and turned into symbols of what was real or possible in intercultural relations. Judged as history, the myths are inexcusably cavalier, yet they belong to an old Aussie tradition, as may be deduced from Jillian Robertson's (1981, 2) sardonic observations:

> Captain Cook has little more factual connection with Australian history than Romulus and Remus with that of Rome. Nonetheless, in the same way as the wolf-children, he has gradually grown into an almost legendary founder figure. Cook has come to be idealised and exalted in Australia, like Asoka in India, or George Washington in the United States, but lacks their historical pertinence. His popularity has increased as the population of the continent has increased. Since 1788 it has grown from a penal colony to a nation of middling importance. Without a Moses, a Napoleon, a Garibaldi to strike the collective imagination, inadequate folk heroes have swollen to fill the void. In the absence of a supreme hero or savior to preside providentially over the continent, we have had to create one. Cook, as it turned out, the working-class boy made good, fitted the ideal Aussie self-image perfectly.

The difference is that Aborigines have more often made Cook a villain than a hero.

When the myths, Cook or Macassan, are seen as symbolic presentations, the skew or bias to which I referred makes sense. Reality constrains myth, and the reality of contact in Australia is that by and large Aborigines emerged as losers, in both property and power. Hence, one might think, the absence of the reciprocity between characters which was traditionally the rule in the ritual, marital and economic spheres.

It might be objected that reality constrains myth only in the last analysis. Reciprocity between Aboriginal and alien could therefore have been shown as an original norm which, 'Fall-like', was lost at the end. If so, it seems significant that none of the stories begins in that way. (We cannot assume Myth 4 is an example, because although Kelly is friendly to Aborigines he is not shown as being in a relation of reciprocity to them.)

It cannot be merely an experiential or imaginative deficiency which explains the lack of balanced exchange at any point in the stories. Many Aboriginal myths (including some considered in this chapter) include transformations from one condition to another, so why not transformation from balance to imbalance? Can it be that the myth-makers were unable (or unwilling) to conceive of equality in relations between persons of different cultures, so that unavoidably a hierarchy had to be imagined? Or does equality presuppose that each has something of value to offer the other, as well as something of value to receive, and that the myth-makers were unable (or unwilling) to envisage what objects were required for such two-sidedness? Both would explain why the retrospective visions of alien contact in these myths are expressed in terms of theft or of unsolicited gifts.

Comparison might be drawn between contact and Dreamtime myths. The doings described in the latter established a scheme of life which, in principle, continued without change until disturbed by outsiders. Stories about the Dreamtime often include thefts or unsolicited gifts. Thus the contact myths could be seen to rely on pre-existing patterns of action, and their emphasis on lack of balance to result more from Aboriginal beliefs about primordial beings than from (retrospective) reflections on original dealings between Aborigines and aliens. But something extra seems to be breaking through, especially in the Cook stories. The Cook of Myth 2 is a father figure whom the Aborigines implore to return—that is they want to incorporate him. In Myths 3–6 one senses that the work of despoliation could be undone—Kelly personifies the possibility of amicable relations in Myth 4, and one of the motives for telling Myth 5 to Europeans is to appeal to their better feelings. We are seeing, I suggest, the emergence of political myths, which not only explain or refer to a state of affairs but envisage an alternative to it.

Notes

1. Versions of this chapter were read at the Universities of Edinburgh, St Andrews and Manchester after the AIAS conference. I am grateful for the comments received. For a more historically-oriented discussion of some of the Captain Cook myths dealt with here, see Maddock 1985.

2. The areas are southwest Arnhem Land (mainly Beswick Reserve), southern Gulf of Carpentaria and east from Tennant Creek. There must, however, be more such stories to be collected, and in view of the probable recency of many of them there is no reason why versions should not appear in areas from which they were absent a little time ago.

3. See for example, Maddock (1984, 23–25) following Stanner (1963, 241–50). The contrary view has been strongly urged by Dixon (1980, 46–47; 1983, 4), and Flood (1983, 15, 30, 74, 113). See also Charlesworth 1984, 383–86. Articles in the journal *Aboriginal History* provide material for assessing the time depth to be gained from myth and oral tradition in Australia.

4. The historian Beaglehole, whose editions of the journals of Cook and Banks are the best, discusses in close detail the progress of the *Endeavour* along the east coast. See Beaglehole 1962, 1967–69.

5. To accept this alternative entails rejecting the literal truth of the Aboriginal stories, even though Aborigines seem to regard them as literally true.

References

Beaglehole, J.C. (ed)
1962 *The Endeavour Journal of Joseph Banks 1768-1771*, Public Library of New South Wales, Sydney.
1967-69 *The Voyage of the Endeavour 1768-1771*, Volume 3, Hakluyt Society, Cambridge.

Bilby, K.M.
1984 The Treacherous Feast: A Jamaican Maroon Historical Myth, *Bijdragen tot de Taal--, Land-- Volkenkunde*, 140.

Charlesworth, M.
1984 Introduction to 'Change in Aboriginal Religion'. In M. Charlesworth, H. Morphy, D. Bell and K. Maddock (eds), *Religion in Aboriginal Australia: An Anthology*, University of Queensland Press, St Lucia, 383-87.

Chase, A.
1985 Aboriginal Perspectives: A Comment. In J.C. Tothill and J.J. Mott (eds), *Ecology and Management of the World's Savannas*, Australian Academy of Science, Canberra, 166-67.

Dixon, R.M.W.
1980 *The Languages of Australia*, Cambridge University Press, Cambridge.
1983 *Searching for Aboriginal Languages: Memoirs of a Field Worker*, University of Queensland Press, St Lucia.

Eliade, M.
1965 *The Myth of the Eternal Return*, Bollingen Foundation, New York.

Flood, J.
1983 *Archaeology of the Dreamtime*, Collins, Sydney.

Gilbert, R.
1985 Address. In J.C. Tothill and J.J. Mott (eds), *Ecology and Management of the World's Savannas*, Australian Academy of Science, Canberra, 168-69.

Kolig, E.
1980 Captain Cook in the Kimberleys. In R.M. Berndt and C.H. Berndt (eds), *Aborigines of the West: Their Past and Their Present*, University of Western Australia Press, Nedlands, 274-82.

Maddock, K.
1984 The Foundations of Aboriginal Religious Life. In M. Charlesworth, H. Morphy, D. Bell and K. Maddock (eds), *Religion in Aboriginal Australia: An Anthology*, University of Queensland Press, St Lucia, 23-27.
1985 Gli aborigeni australiani e il capitano Cook: quando il mito incontra la Storia, *Materiali Filosofici* 14, 57-70.

Middleton, H.
1977 *But Now We Want the Land Back*, New Age Publishers, Sydney.

Okpewho, I.
1983 *Myth in Africa: A Study of its Aesthetic and Cultural Relevance*, Cambridge University Press, Cambridge.

Reynolds, H.
1981 *The Other Side of the Frontier: An Interpretation of the Aboriginal Response to the Invasion and Settlement of Australia*, History Department, James Cook University, Townsville.

Robertson, J.
1981 *The Captain Cook Myth*, Angus and Robertson, Sydney.

Robinson, R.
1970 *Altjeringa and Other Aboriginal Poems*, A.H. and A.W. Reed, Sydney.

Rose, D.B.
1984 The Saga of Captain Cook: Morality in Aboriginal and European Law, *Australian Aboriginal Studies* 2, 24-39.

Rose, F.
1976 *Australien und seine Ureinwohner*, Akademie Verlag, Berlin.

Simmons, D.R.
1976 *The Great New Zealand Myth: A Study of the Discovery and Origin Traditions of the Maori*, Reed, Wellington.

Stanner, W.E.H.
1963 On Aboriginal Religion: VI, Cosmos and Society Made Correlative, *Oceania* 33, 239–73.

Turner, D.H.
1982 Caste Logic in a Clan Society: An Aboriginal Response to Domination. In M. Howard (ed), *Aboriginal Power in Australian Society*, University of Queensland Press, St Lucia, 32–54.

Warner, W.L.
1937 *A Black Civilization: A Social Study of an Australian Tribe*, Harper, New York.

Willis, R.
1980 The Literalist Fallacy and the Problem of Oral Traditions, *Social Analysis* 4, 28–37.

Worsley, P.M.
1954 The Changing Social Structure of the Wanindiljaugwa, PhD thesis, Australian National University.

3. Jane M Jacobs   The construction of identity

The main concern of this chapter is the construction of Aboriginal identity in the land rights process. Land rights has demanded that both Aborigines and whites develop and articulate definitions of a unique Aboriginal identity. Distinguishing a unique Aboriginal identity (and concomitantly a unique interest in the land) has been a crucial step in validating Aboriginal claims for land rights. It has also been an essential ingredient in the government's justification of its separate and often specialised treatment of Aborigines. Both sides of the land rights process will be examined here in the context of South Australia.[1] Of initial concern will be the constructions of Aboriginality made by those who are in power and thus control Aboriginal access to land. The land rights opportunities open to Aborigines as expressed in legislation and policy, are examined in this regard. The South Australian case suggests that government can not only grant or deny land rights, but intervene in, and control the land rights process.

The focus of the chapter then shifts to examine the way in which Aboriginal groups seeking land rights construct and articulate their own identity in the political arena. The land rights activities of the Adnjamathanha and Kokatha groups are dealt with in some detail in order to demonstrate this process. The analysis of land rights action shows that Aboriginal groups are not insensitive to the constructs of Aboriginality set by external agents. The Adnjamathanha and Kokatha groups have actively sought land rights and in this process have developed and presented to outsiders a public identity which works to differentiate their interests in land not only from those held by whites but also those held by other Aborigines. It is argued that success in gaining control over land is dependent upon the willingness of Aboriginal groups to articulate their Aboriginality, using procedures and symbols which are acceptable to those controlling access to land. The very processes by which an acceptable identity can be established in the political arena provide the mechanisms by which the government can not only grant or deny land rights, but intervene, and control the land rights process.

Simply put, Aboriginal land rights is a process by which Aboriginal groups seek access to resources now in the control of white Australia. Attempts to gain land rights operate within the limitations set by the attitudinal, political and legal constructs of those in power. This hegemonic framework is inequitable and the result has been that some Aboriginal groups have been more successful than others in gaining land rights. The legislation dealing with land rights in South Australia reflects both covertly and overtly the popular attitude that the only 'true' Aborigines are those who are overtly traditional.

Aborigines in the Northern Territory and in some parts of South Australia have been given special rights over land above and beyond those available to Aborigines in other parts of Australia. The body of legislation which provides for Aboriginal land rights reflects ingrained attitudes of white Australians toward Aborigines. Those Aborigines to receive the fullest rights (and to receive them first) have been those who are overtly traditional. This may be dubbed the 'noble savage syndrome' and has, as Tatz (1982, 10) points out, resulted in the adulation of the 'loin-clothed...idealised type' to the detriment of the 'non-traditional' or 'detribalised' Aborigines (cf Langton 1981, 16). Weaver (1984, 208) argues that the differentiation is an extension of past attitudes among white Australians who perceived 'real' Aborigines to be 'full bloods' (substitute 'traditional') and less 'real' Aborigines to be 'half-castes' (substitute 'non-traditional' or 'urbanised').

In South Australia, those Aborigines who are overtly traditional have benefited from the passing of the Pitjantjatjara Land Rights Act (1981) and the Maralinga Tjarutja Land Rights Act (1984). Both Acts confer special rights over specific tracts of land to the relevant Aboriginal groups. The Acts were loosely modelled upon the precedent-setting Northern Territory Land Rights Act (1976) but differ in that they are state-based and apply to specific areas and specific groups only. The Northern Territory Act establishes the mechanisms by which Aboriginal groups can claim land. In its original form and application it reflected a very limited notion of what constituted a valid claim. Gumbert (1981) and Maddock (1981, 1982) have illustrated how the model of Aboriginality embodied by the legislation was based on specific and often disputed anthropological reconstructions of traditional Aboriginal society. Through the claim process the Northern Territory Act has evolved to incorporate a broader and more realistic notion of the valid claimant and what constitutes a legitimate claim to land. The South Australian derivatives, in contrast, are not open to constant re-evaluation or broader application and stand as solid reminders to the rest of the state's Aborigines that the government has only been prepared to confer special rights to those who are overtly traditional and thereby fit the notion of 'authentic Aborigine'. An important ingredient in the general acceptance of the Pitjantjatjara and Maralinga groups as traditional is the degree of anthropological evidence to this effect. The traditional life of both groups has, in true reconstructionist style, been well documented.

In South Australia there are a large number of Aborigines who do not fit the limited notion of 'Aboriginality' underscoring the passing of the Pitjantjatjara and Maralinga Acts. Many of the state's Aboriginal population have been displaced from their traditional lands, live in towns, participate in the mainstream economy and, in short, do not display any of the characteristics which white Australia accepts as hallmarks of a tradition-oriented lifestyle. This is not to say these groups do not have a strong sense of Aboriginality based on culturally unique constructs; simply that they are not seen by outsiders as culturally pristine. Nor is it correct to presume that these Aborigines do not have an interest in land, whether cultural, social or economic. The existence of community-based action groups which work to achieve land rights attests the importance of this issue for such Aborigines.

The Adnjamathanha and Kokatha groups belong to this section of South Australia's Aboriginal population; they are not overtly traditional and yet they retain a strong interest in and sense of responsibility toward their country. A large number of each of these tribal groups now reside in the rural town of Port Augusta and would be perceived as 'urbanised'. Both groups also have members who still live in towns or reserves located in the heart of their 'tribal' areas. The Adnjamathanha people see the Flinders Ranges, located north of Port Augusta, as their country and the Kokatha see themselves as originating from and responsible for the area northwest of Port Augusta. Although these two groups share a broadly similar contact history, there are noteworthy differences between the experiences of the two groups.

The Adnjamathanha contact experience was characterised by movement onto the Nepabunna Mission, which is located in the heart of the Northern Flinders Ranges, the country which the Adnjamathanha see as culturally significant. The mission experience placed considerable pressures on them. By the 1940s male initiation had ceased as had most other ceremonial activity. Today there is only a small number of elders who are familiar with traditional matters, although the language and much of the mythology has been passed on in a fragmented form. Despite the impact of contact on the ceremonial and religious life, the closed mission environment provided a focal point for the emergence of a strong collective identity based on close kin and community ties. The Kokatha experience differs from that of the Adnjamathanha in that no single focal point emerged during the early contact phase. Rather, contact meant a fracturing of the Kokatha: some chose to live permanently on the Koonibba

Mission; some chose to associate sporadically with the mission located at Port Augusta; while others chose to avoid mission life as much as possible by travelling from one pastoral lease to another. Today large numbers of both Kokatha and Adnjamathanha people reside in Port Augusta. Their continued interest in and concern for their country is reflected by the emergence of two land rights groups; the Adnjamathanha Land Rights Committee and the Kokatha People's Committee.

Groups like the Adnjamathanha and Kokatha do not readily fit the image of traditional Aborigines. They have not benefited from special legislation like the Pitjantjatjara and Maralinga people. Instead they have been relegated to the political fringes and must attempt to gain recognition of their interest in land through the opportunities provided by piecemeal legislation enacted at both the state and federal level. In terms of acquiring control over specific tracts of land, Aborigines like the Adnjamathanha and Kokatha can rely on the options provided by the South Australian Lands Trust or the federally instigated Aboriginal Development Commission (ADC). Land acquired by these mechanisms can be held by perpetual or limited tenure lease, but is not freehold as with the land granted under the Pitjantjatjara Act.

The South Australian Aboriginal Lands Trust was considered to be very progressive when it was established in 1965. It was the first formal recognition of Aboriginal rights to land in Australia. In practice the Lands Trust has done little more than operate as a title-holding body for land already set aside for Aboriginal occupation as government reserves or missions. Lack of funds or power have meant that its capacity to purchase or acquire additional land has been severely limited. The other main alternative for Aborigines outside the jurisdiction of specialised legislation is acquiring a loan from the ADC to purchase land on the open market. However, the capacity of such agents to provide Aboriginal groups with access to land is limited. The ADC is not solely concerned with land purchase and much of its allocated budget goes toward funding other enterprises. Those Aboriginal groups seeking ADC funds for the purchase of land must make submissions stating their reasons for wanting funds to purchase a particular area. As ADC funds are limited the submission procedure is inherently competitive. Furthermore, the land acquisition occurs on the open market. The ability of the ADC or a similar body to acquire land which is of cultural significance to their clients is more often a matter of market default, the luck of the sought-after area being available for purchase, than deliberate planning.

The other major alternative for Aborigines in South Australia who are seeking to have their interest in the land recognised is the state's site recording program, operating under the Aboriginal and Historical Relics Heritage Act (1965).[2] Having sites recorded provides no direct Aboriginal control over them but does at least acknowledge an Aboriginal interest by providing legal protection for the sites. The limitations and pitfalls of such site recording programs have often been expressed (eg Dix 1978). There are problems arising from the transfer of traditional knowledge to external agents. There is a danger of the site recording program with its emphasis on discrete sites creating a disjointed and static picture of the Aboriginal landscape. And there are operational problems arising from limited resources and the lack of both adequate policing of sites and the enforcement of punitive measures on those who damage sites.

Both the land purchasing and site recording programs operate with limited resources. It is not possible for all groups to receive equitable attention from each of these agencies. Thus Aboriginal groups like the Adnjamathanha and Kokatha must seek land rights within an inherently competitive structure which pits one Aboriginal group against another. The competitive context of land rights action is exacerbated by the fact that much of the land sought by groups like the Adnjamathanha and Kokatha is either controlled or sought by dominant interest groups such as pastoralists and mining companies. Indeed, the success of the Pitjantjatjara and Maralinga claims (as in the Northern Territory) is in part due to the availability of claimable land; that is, land not sought by a wide range of interest groups. In the Pitjantjatjara case, there was the historical legacy of a large area of once economically marginal land which had since early in the state's history been reserved for Aboriginal occupation. In the more recent Maralinga case, it was a vast area of land so contaminated by British nuclear tests no one else cared to occupy it.

It is within this inherently competitive framework that Aboriginal groups like the Adnjamathanha and Kokatha have sought to gain land rights. Their efforts are overshadowed by the knowledge that in South Australia it is overtly traditional groups like the Pitjantjatjara and the Maralinga people who have received the best land rights deals. Their political strategies are shaped by the awareness that they must compete both against each other and against more powerful external interests. In such a context it has become imperative that the Aboriginal groups present their interest in the land in a way which will convince those who control the land resource, not only that they are deserving of land rights, but that they are more deserving that their competitors. A crucial ingredient in this political process is the articulation of a specifically Aboriginal interest in the land. The process has involved Aboriginal groups deliberately selecting aspects of their cultural inheritance which they know have become acceptable to external agents as proof of their unique and special interest in land. Aborigines involved in the land rights process are conscientiously structuring a public 'Aboriginality' which will validate their land claims in the political arena (cf Weaver 1984, see Beckett Chapter 12).

At this point I would like to turn to the political strategies of the Kokatha and Adnjamathanha. Both the Kokatha and Adnjamathanha people had land rights action groups which operated out of Port Augusta: the Kokatha People's Committee (KPC) and the Adnjamathanha Land Rights Committee (ALRC). The regularly participating core of both these groups were closely related Port Augusta residents. At the time of research neither committee was incorporated but they operated as the unofficial negotiators of land rights business on behalf of their respective tribal groups. Both the KPC and the ALRC began in 1979 in response to the heightening of the Pitjantjatjara lobby for land rights. From the very outset both committees looked to the political example set by the successful Pitjantjatjara claim.

In many ways the strategies adopted by these land rights action groups were similar. Both groups attempted to present their interests in the land in a manner which would convince external agents that they were deserving. In this process specific aspects of their cultural inheritance were stressed above others. For example, both groups selected chairmen (not women) from the small number of initiated men. This move had undoubted intrinsic value in that the active participation of these men in land rights politics ensured that the political action did not contravene internally relevant structures of dealing with land. However, it also had a purposeful extrinsic meaning; namely that initiated men have a valuable symbolic status not only respected by external agents but at that time almost expected as proof of the creditability of Aboriginal claims for rights over land.

A similar political point was often made by the land rights groups in meeting with government officials. Great efforts were made to ensure that the attendance at such meetings by elderly, male members was high. In one important meeting between the ALRC and the government at Parliament House in Adelaide a special bus was hired, Pitjantjatjara style, to bring the elders down from Nepabunna and Port Augusta. Once in the meeting the elders seated themselves in an intimidating and convincing line behind which all others stood. The elders were the battle front of the meeting and, while they did little talking, their white hair and headbands (worn especially for the occasion) dramatised the Adnjamathanha's link with tradition. By so presenting themselves the ALRC members verified their continuity with the past, their cultural uniqueness (see Morris Chapter 5) and consequently their special rights in relation to land.

Another common ingredient in the political actions of these two land rights groups was the stressing of a collective tribal identity. Each of the land rights action groups spoke not for their own individual interests but for the interests of all Kokatha people or all Adnjamathanha people. In principle this paralleled the way in which the Pitjantjatjara operated in the political arena, not as family or small community groups but an anangu Pitjantjatjara, 'one land, one law, one people' (Toyne and Vachon 1984). The Kokatha and Adnjamathanha emphasis on their particular tribal identity worked for them in two ways. Firstly it worked against the tendency of the government to lump all Aborigines together as one amorphous minority. By stressing that their concerns were Kokatha concerns or Adnjamathanha concerns, these two groups could successfully differentiate their specific needs and claims. This was essential when the system within which their land rights activities operated was competitive.

The emphasis on a collective tribal identity in the political arena had other important implications. In a very real way it became a means by which the land rights groups could validate their claims. Both of these land rights groups had a limited participating membership dominated by closely linked, Port Augusta-based kin groups. On a number of occasions the claims of the land rights groups were undermined by government agents who accused them of being a minority and not representing the interests of the whole tribal or community group. This challenge was especially levelled against the ALRC for the Adnjamathanha are so clearly split between those who live in Port Augusta and those who live on the reserve of Nepabunna. To counter this challenge the ALRC would ensure that in all meetings with the government there was representation from Nepabunna. If challenged about their representativeness they would call upon the Nepabunna people present.

The Kokatha faced different challenges to their land rights claims and this is reflected in the way in which their collective tribal identity was articulated in the political arena. The Kokatha expression of collective identity was not done solely through ensuring broad representation at meetings, rather it was actively constructed in press statements made by the KPC. The KPC used press statements frequently as the means by which they publicly indicated their position in the complex negotiations proceeding over mining at Roxby Downs. In almost all press statements made by the KPC, the extent of Kokatha country was defined as a bounded territory (cf Creamer Chapter 4, Jacobs 1986). The public articulation of Kokatha country as a bounded, continuous and culturally homogeneous territory operated to distinguish their right to be consulted with and speak over activities on specific tracts of land, including Roxby Downs which was the major concern of the KPC at the time. But the public articulation of Kokatha territory had another valuable purpose in the political arena. It ensured that outsiders knew who the Kokatha people were. Unlike groups such as the Pitjantjatjara and, to a lesser extent the Adnjamathanha, there has been little documentation of the Kokatha people. At the beginning of the Roxby Downs controversy, few people had even heard of the Kokatha let alone knew that they held interests in a particular area of South Australia. In contrast, white Australians had long known of the existence of the Pitjantjatjara people in the northwest of the state. The enormous documentation of the group by anthropologists and later the popular press saw to this. At the outset of the Pitjantjatjara land rights lobby the majority of white South Australians may not have been able to pronounce 'Pitjantjatjara', but they knew they existed and where they existed, and this no doubt assisted in the Pitjantjatjara struggle for land rights recognition. In contrast, when Roxby Downs became a public issue the Kokatha did not have a high profile. It was through Roxby Downs that most South Australians first read about the Kokatha, leaving them open to the ultimate challenge that they did not have any interests in the area until mining began. The procedure of repeatedly stating the broad region of Kokatha country provided them with a much needed spatial and cultural identity in the public arena. People could no longer ask 'who are the Kokatha and where is their country?'

As has been shown, both the Adnjamathanha and Kokatha campaigns were influenced by the example of the successful Pitjantjatjara. But it was the Kokatha who most consciously and completely embraced the 'Pitjantjatjara model' of land rights action (cf Toyne and Vachon 1984, 111–20). They saw it as tried and tested. During 1981 representatives of the KPC visited the Pitjantjatjara lands and sought advice on the difficulties they faced in dealing with mining interests at Roxby Downs. After repeated consultation with the Pitjantjatjara, the Kokatha decided to adopt the Pitjantjatjara model for dealing with mining companies. An essential principle of this model is that Aboriginal groups should not disclose the location of cultural sites to outsiders but instead mark out safe areas where mining activities can occur. The identification of sites and marking out of safe areas is done with the assistance of professionals in the employ of the relevant Aborigines and not the outside interests. The strategy is designed to protect Aboriginal interests by ensuring that knowledge continues to be controlled internally and that consultation with outside interests is ongoing. Retaining Aboriginal control of knowledge about the land is essential to Aborigines retaining the very basis of their unique identity. As Morris (Chapter 5) notes, denying or limiting outside access to such knowledge allows Aborigines to remain in control of how their Aboriginality is defined.

The Kokatha adoption of the Pitjantjatjara model in relation to Roxby Downs meant that they were reluctant to deal with a company-paid anthropologist and were not keen to disclose the exact location of sites. This strategy was unacceptable to both the government and the mining company and a prolonged impasse resulted. The Pitjantjatjara strategy did not work for the Kokatha. There were a number of underlying reasons for the failure including the lack of specific resources to see the strategy through. Another basic difference with the Kokatha application of the Pitjantjatjara model is that, since they had no legal title over the land at issue there was no real obligation for the mining company to comply with their preferred method of consultation. But perhaps the most significant reason for the failure of the mining company to accept the Kokatha strategy was that the company and government wanted specific proof of the group's interest in the land. In short, they wanted specific information on sites. The underlying logic seemed to be that it was acceptable for the Pitjantjatjara to use this strategy of not disclosing sites because they were traditional. (This is known from the vast amount of documentation to this effect and has been validated by the passing of the Pitjantjatjara Act.) The validity and acceptability of the Pitjantjatjara identity was recognised. In contrast, the Kokatha group have not been extensively documented and certainly have not been given popular documentation beyond their recent attempts to establish a broad tribal identity. Their Aboriginal identity was one of the casualties of dispossession and assimilation policies. As such they needed to prove their Aboriginality by the disclosure of traditional information before their interests in the Roxby area would be acknowledged.

The Kokatha commitment to the Pitjantjatjara model not only resulted in serious difficulties with the mining company. It also created conflict between them and those government agencies, like the Aboriginal Heritage Branch of the South Australian Department of Environment and Planning and the ADC, which provided the normal channels by which they could obtain land rights. The Kokatha adoption of the Pitjantjatjara model was an indirect statement of their dissatisfaction with these procedures. The government agents saw them as non-cooperative and dubbed them 'the dreaded Kokatha'. The Kokatha, however, had good reason to feel dissatisfied with these agents. They had not been funded by the ADC to purchase any land and had been largely ignored by the Heritage Branch, which until then had directed much of its resources to the Flinders Ranges and the Adnjamathanha people. The lack of options had forced them to adopt what they saw as the only realistic alternative, and the adoption of this alternative strategy further distanced the Kokatha from the conventional mechanisms for achieving land rights. Their unwillingness to conform to what they saw as unsatisfactory procedures has worked to deny them any substantial land gains.

The Adnjamathanha case stands in sharp contrast to that of the Kokatha. The Adnjamathanha have succeeded in gaining title to two pastoral leases and partial control of the Gammon Ranges National Park by way of a joint management plan modelled on that operating in Kakadu National Park. This success is not a case of the Adnjamathanha being more deserving than the Kokatha but a reflection of the Adnjamathanha having a public image which conforms more readily to the externally set notion of Aboriginality and deserving claimant. The ability of the Adnjamathanha to formulate and project this construct of 'Adnjamathanhaness' has been the result of a long association with external agents, who have—at times without the consent of the people—translated their culture into more popular or public forms. This process began with CP Mountford, who translated much of the Adnjamathanha mythology into popular stories for the local press. Of far more importance for the emergence of a culturally visible and acceptable Adnjamathanha identity has been their extensive and long association with the state site recording body, the Aboriginal Heritage Branch.

This association has significantly influenced the nature of land rights activities among the Adnjamathanha. The Aboriginal Heritage Branch began working in the Flinders Ranges with the Adnjamathanha people in the early 1970s. The relationship was instigated by the Branch and it was some time before the elders agreed to participate in the site recording program. The initial association was later consolidated by the appointment of a few of the younger Adnjamathanha as Heritage Rangers. Through their association with the Branch a vast number of cultural sites have been recorded, an extensive contact history of the group written (Brock 1985), a linguistic project undertaken and a comprehensive genealogy completed (Davis and McKenzie 1985). Aspects of the Adnjamathanha culture are taught in Port Augusta schools to Adnjamathanha, other Aboriginal and white children alike. In short, the relationship with the Branch has transformed 'Adnjamathanhaness' from an identity which was once maintained covertly (away from the eyes of the mission) and internally, to an identity which has a high local and state profile in the broader community.

Through this relationship the Adnjamathanha have conformed to the government endorsed procedures for expressing their Aboriginality. Their agreement to express their interests in the land and their cultural uniqueness through the structures and in the language required by the government has been 'rewarded' by their relatively substantial gains. In seeking funds from groups like ADC the Adnjamathanha can be assured that their interest in the land is not questioned—the sites have been recorded, it is in black and white, for all to see. The strategy also carries an inherent danger, however.

The Adnjamathanha reliance on the government endorsed procedures for expressing Aboriginality and their interest in the land have provided the mechanisms by which government could indirectly control the activities and power of the ALRC. An example of this occurred in 1981 when the Kokatha attempted to solicit the support of the Adnjamathanha in their adoption of the Pitjantjatjara model. The ALRC was keen to offer support and joined the newly formed Southern Land Council, a political collective representing a number of tribal groups in the area. The vast majority of Adnjamathanha did not however, endorse this move. Aligning with the Kokatha was seen to be too risky, for among other things it was felt that it might jeopardise their relationship with the Heritage Branch. It may have resulted in the loss of jobs and the loss of access to resources which had assisted in a cultural revival and substantial land rights. Above all, a shift away from the Heritage Branch was undesirable because it would mean relinquishing what Adnjamathanha control remained over the vast amounts of cultural information which has passed into the hands of outsiders (cf Morris Chapter 5). In effect, the relationship with the Branch has meant that adopting an alternative land rights strategy, especially one which conflicts with government preferred procedures, is virtually impossible.

Conclusion

This chapter has attempted to show that externally set constructs of Aboriginality and particularly the 'authentic Aborigine' have had an enormous impact on Aboriginal land rights efforts in South Australia. There is considerable pressure upon Aboriginal groups to prove the validity of their claims by displaying a culturally unique, and preferably traditional association with the land. The less a group appears traditional or is known to be traditional by way of popularisation of their culture the greater the pressure for them to prove their Aboriginality. Acceptable proof of Aboriginality, especially in terms of land rights, must be done in a language and by mechanisms endorsed, accepted and often structured by the government.

There is an immense pressure on groups who are not overtly traditional to disclose their cultural sites by way of the site recording procedure. As has been shown, groups who have done so in South Australia have had preferential treatment from the agencies controlling access to land. The inequitable allocation of land to Aborigines in South Australia does not accurately reflect varying need but the varying willingness of Aboriginal groups to present to outsiders an image of Aboriginality which conforms with what is expected. The Kokatha articulation of identity in terms of the collective tribal territory, rather than by site identification, was unacceptable; while the Adnjamathanha approach of specifying sites and disclosing cultural information to outsiders was acceptable. As the Adnjamathanha experience has shown, this strategy may provide the proof needed to gain land rights but it can also lock Aboriginal groups into a government preferred model of land rights action.

Notes

1. This chapter is based on fieldwork in Port Augusta, South Australia during 1981.
2. This Act has for some years now been under review and a new Act is currently being passed. At the time of fieldwork it was the 1965 Act which was operative.

References

Berndt, R.M.
1959 The Concept of 'the Tribe' in the Western Desert of Australia, *Oceania* 30, 81-107.
1976 Territoriality and the Problem of Demarcating Sociocultural Space. In N. Peterson (ed), *Tribes and Boundaries in Australia*, Humanities Press, New Jersey, 133-61.

Berndt, R.M. (ed)
1982 *Aboriginal Sites, Rites and Resource Development*, University of Western Australia Press, Nedlands.

Brock, P.
1985 *Yura and Udnyu: A History of the Adnjamathanha of the North Flinders Ranges*, Wakefield Press and Aboriginal Heritage Branch, Adelaide.

Davis, C. and P. McKenzie
1985 *Adnjamathanha Genealogy*, South Australian Government Printer, Adelaide.

Dix, J.K.
1978 The Aboriginal Heritage Act of 1972. In M.C. Howard (ed), *'Whitefella Business': Aborigines in Australian Politics*, Institute for the Study of Human Issues Inc, Philadelphia, 81-82.

Gumbert, M.
1981 Paradigm Lost: An Analyses of Anthropological Models and the Effects on Land Rights, *Oceania* 52(2), 103-23.
1984 *Neither Justice Nor Reason: A Legal and Anthropological Analysis of Aboriginal Land Rights*, University of Queensland Press, St Lucia.

Hiatt, L.R.
1962 Local Organisation Among the Australian Aborigines, *Oceania* 32, 267-86.
1968 Ownership and Use of Land Among the Australian Aborigines. In R.B. Lee and I. DeVore (eds), *Man the Hunter*, Aldine, Chicago, 99-102.

Howard, M.C.
1982 Australian Aboriginal Politics and the Perpetration of Inequality, *Oceania* 53(1), 82–103.

Jacobs, J.M.
1986 Understanding the Limitations and Cultural Implications of Aboriginal Tribal Boundary Maps, *The Globe* 25, 2–12.

Jones, D. and J. Hill-Burnett
1982 The Political Context of Ethnogenesis: An Australian Example. In M.C. Howard (ed), *Aboriginal Power in Australian Society*, University of Queensland Press, St Lucia, 214–46.

Langton, M.
1981 Urbanising Aborigines: The Social Scientists' Great Deception, *Social Alternatives* 2(2), 16–22.

Maddock, K.J.
1981 Warlpiri Land Tenure: A Test Case in Legal Anthropology, *Oceania* 52(2), 85–102.
1982 Aboriginal Land Rights Traditionally and in Legislation: A Case Study. In M.C. Howard (ed), *Aboriginal Power in Australian Society*, University of Queensland Press, St Lucia, 55–78.

Stanner, W.E.H.
1965 Aboriginal Territorial Organisation: Estate, Range, Domain and Regime, *Oceania* 36, 1–26.

Tatz, C.
1982 *Aborigines and Uranium and Other Essays*, Heinemann, Melbourne.

Toyne, P. and D. Vachon
1984 *Growing Up the Country: The Pitjantjatjara Struggle for their Land*, McPhee Gribble/Penguin Books, Melbourne.

Weaver, S.
1984 Struggle of the Nation-State to Define Aboriginal Ethnicity: Canada and Australia. In G.L. Gold (ed), *Minorities and Mother Country Imagery*, Social and Economic Papers 13, Institute of Social and Economic Research, Newfoundland.

4. Howard Creamer

Aboriginality in New South Wales: beyond the image of cultureless outcasts

The nature of Aboriginal identity in New South Wales is seen by many as problematic and becoming more so. To increasing numbers of white people, the proposition that there exists in this state, and elsewhere in southeastern Australia, a group of people who can claim a different identity based on Aboriginal culture, seems untenable. While there is nothing new in Aboriginal people[1] coming under attack, this present assault on their cultural integrity calls for support from anthropologists and others to assist in defining Aboriginality, especially in the closely settled parts of Australia.

It was Goodenough, who in 1964 observed that 'the anthropologist's basic task...is to describe specific cultures adequately', and that is what is needed for present day Aboriginal culture in southeastern Australia. While other chapters in this volume have drawn attention to those aspects of Aboriginality which are largely a response to the agenda set by the dominant culture (eg Beckett Chapter 12 and Jacobs Chapter 3), the emphasis in this chapter is rather on how Aboriginal identity is constructed and how it can be described. This is done by looking at the composition of knowledge in the Aboriginal community with special reference to sites, the landscape, and the current renascence of Aboriginal culture.

The task of clarifying what is meant by Aboriginality is vital, not only for the acceptance of modern Aboriginal identity by the general public, but also for the provision of services by the government, which relies on the identification of Aboriginal people as a special group. Without such recognition, it becomes increasingly difficult to justify special programs for Aboriginal people to a public that in many instances does not believe that there are any 'real' Aborigines left in southeastern Australia.

There are major theoretical problems in describing present day Aboriginal identity. As with other complex acculturation situations, the frontier of contact is no longer clearly defined but exists all around (Bohannan 1967); the group lacks clear boundaries. In short, a culture which has been more or less embedded in western society for nearly 200 years, and has undergone considerable change from its pre-European contact forms, does not readily lend itself to the structural-functionalist approach on which the anthropological method was founded. 'Trying to understand what the organisation really is and how it works', does not work as it used to when Radcliffe-Brown (1930, 426) pioneered Aboriginal anthropology in the 1920s. In keeping with other studies of the time, he attempted to reconstruct the pre-contact life of Aboriginal groups, yet even in 1929 he found difficulty describing the Dhangadi people of the Macleay River valley, in terms of traditional culture (Radcliffe-Brown 1929, 408, emphasis added): 'Unfortunately, as these tribes have *abandoned their own culture* for half a century, none except a few of the very old people know...anything about the increase rites.'

The equation of 'Aboriginal culture' mostly with that which existed prior to 1788, is a familiar theme in many early accounts and one which has since become entrenched in public perceptions of Aboriginality. For instance, Elkin (1951) talks of young people not being entrusted with 'sacred' knowledge and so losing their Dreaming. 'Thus, psychological disturbance is added to the reduction in numbers and strength—and the remnant is "lost".' Many commentators refer to 'remnants' of Aboriginal people in New South Wales, while in reality meaning remnants of traditional culture, like Calley's (1958, 208) 'remnants of the Bandjalang tribe'. There is ambivalence in these accounts though, for like Radcliffe-Brown before him, Calley found that ample knowledge of the past had survived up to the 1950s, on which to prove a distinctive Aboriginality.[2]

Yet there is no denying that Aboriginality had changed, and was changing; much knowledge that could justifiably be called 'traditional' was fast disappearing. By the 1930s there was already a major breakdown of secret knowledge and information on traditional marriage systems. Beckett (1958, 101) notes that, 'By 1930 Dutton was the only surviving *wiljaru* man in New South Wales', and Janet Mathews (1977), quoting Jimmie Barker, reports that in 1927 the last tribal doctor of the Muruwari people, known as 'Muckerawa Jack', died at Goodooga. Radcliffe-Brown (1929) is adamant that it was by then all over for the Bundjalung, 'The scanty remnant of the original virile population is now gathered into reserves and camps, where nothing of the original native life remains'. Beckett (1967, 456), writing about Aboriginal people in western New South Wales, reports that contact with whites brought about disruption to tribal life and decimation and annihilation of native populations. In another paper Beckett (1965, 7) documents the disappearance of traditions as follows, and in so doing makes a real contribution to describing the much altered state of Aboriginal culture by the 1950s:

> Although one may speak of an Aboriginal way of life, this implies little that is tribal. The old tribal groups are dispersed...no boys and girls (sic) have been initiated for 50 years or more; the old rules of kinship behaviour are not merely disregarded but forgotten; tribal languages are scarcely spoken, even at home...The eating of wild

foods such as kangaroo, is perhaps the only conscious carry-over from tribal times. Loss of their indigenous culture has not, however, made them any more ready to adopt the White 'Australian way of life'.

That Aboriginal people should adopt the 'Australian way of life', is however a major concern for many white people, who from about this time on, play an increasing part in defining Aboriginality, mainly to suit their own interests. The policy of assimilation, begun in 1940, became central to the denial of legitimate Aboriginal identity in southeastern Australia by the dominant majority. Whereas for a century and a half there had been the pretence of caring for a dying race, now it was official—Aboriginal culture as a separate way of life in Australia was to cease. Bell (1964, 61) explains:

> The policy of assimilation means that aborigines are expected eventually to attain the same manner of living as other Australians...enjoying the same rights and privileges, accepting the same responsibilities, observing the same customs and influenced by the same beliefs, hopes and loyalties as other Australians.

With external constraints such as these, there appears to be no room for a distinctive Aboriginal identity. The chances of promoting such are further threatened by the development of the sociological concept of a 'culture of poverty'. As Bell (1964, 68) sees it, 'these groups are just like groups of poor whites. The policy for them must be one of welfare.' From many accounts written in the mid-twentieth century, there emerges a picture of Aboriginal people without Aboriginality, of lost traditions with nothing to replace them. Thus begins the image of cultureless outcasts, in a kind of cultural vacuum, neither ready for, nor accepting, the assimilation offered by white society. This is the 'between two worlds' model of Aboriginal culture which contributes little to culture theory, because it says little about the actual cultural construct that has emerged; the ideas, beliefs and values of the Aboriginal people who remain; their rules for living; their symbols and their view of the world.

It is also not a helpful model when it comes to convincing the public that Aboriginality is a reality, being lived by Aboriginal people. The problem in equating Aboriginal culture with traditions which are lost, is that the conclusion is reached that Aboriginality should have disappeared too. In the absence of a more pervasive theory of culture and cultural change, the public has generally fallen back on theories of race. As Colin Tatz (1980, 356) has accurately commented, for many people, Aboriginality equates with skin colour—'Culture is seen as related to and contingent upon gradations of colour'. A recent letter to the New South Wales Ministry of Aboriginal

Affairs from a rural council asks, 'Does...the definition of Aboriginal under the (Aboriginal Land Rights) Act require any person so defined...to have Aboriginal blood?' and goes on to ask, 'If so, what % of Aboriginal blood?' and, 'why does it appear to be a fact that some people without Aboriginal blood currently receive benefits as though they were Aboriginals?' Without the advantage of an anthropological perspective, most people hold the view that culture is somehow inherited and clearly visible, rather than learned and frequently subtle in its manifestations. The lightness of the skin of many New South Wales Koori people, and the fact that their lifestyles do not correspond with the images of traditional culture most people are familiar with, leads many to the conclusion that there is no real Aboriginal culture left in the state.

For the record, Aboriginal people continue to be defined in law, though not as extensively as in the past. The current definition is contained in the 1983 Aboriginal Land Rights Act, which is legislation specifically for Aboriginal people, hence based on the proposition that Aboriginality exists in New South Wales. Yet it is almost totally economic, and therefore welfare-oriented in its direction. Section 4 (1) of the Act states that 'Aboriginal' means a person who: (a) is a member of the Aboriginal race of Australia; (b) identifies as an Aboriginal; and, (c) is accepted by the Aboriginal community as an Aboriginal.

Whereas for a long time Aboriginal people were 'defined to confine' spatially, legally and culturally, there is today far less emphasis on either racial or cultural qualifications in defining Aboriginal. In what is undoubtedly a reaction to the strict classifications of the past, it is not uncommon to hear some people say quite simply that a person is Aboriginal if he or she says so. Such apparent looseness in the criteria for membership of the Aboriginal community worries many people, who wrongly perceive a whole range of benefits being available to those who say they are Aboriginal. What is also a problem for some whites is that they realise that control over the definition of Aboriginality has passed out of their hands. There are also legitimate concerns in this for anthropologists attempting to describe the specifics of this particular culture and to foster the notion of a viable Aboriginality in southeastern Australia. Although care is needed not to base theory on the subjectivist position that a cultural group is whatever its members say it is (van den Berghe 1967, xvi), and individual claims to be Aboriginal are not enough on their own to explain Aboriginality as a cultural entity, collectively, the knowledge of a culture possessed by its individual members, provides the basis for understanding that culture.

The development of culture theory in anthropology is notable for the increasing emphasis placed on the knowledge acquired by individuals, enabling them to operate in their particular culture. This is in contrast to the more visible activities of people and their material creations, which characterise the popular view of culture. Although more sophisticated in their analysis, modern theories of culture still retain the essence of Tylor's (1891) view of culture as consisting of 'knowledge, belief, art, morals, law, custom'. In Aboriginal anthropology, many writers have drawn attention to the possession of knowledge as a vital force in the construction of Aboriginal culture, both past and present. For instance, Maddock (1972, 187–92) describes the restriction of knowledge and control of information exercised by the older males to entrench their authority over women and youths. In this volume, Morris talks of the power of knowledge. Clearly, in Aboriginal culture, knowledge is like a currency, the possession of which bestows power. The question, 'who knows what and how do they know?' thus becomes central to any attempt to better describe and understand current Aboriginality.

An appropriate theoretical basis for discussing knowledge in Aboriginal society is provided by what Schwartz (1978, 423) calls a 'distributive model of culture'.

> The distribution of a culture among the members of a society transcends the limitations of the individual in the storage, creation, and use of the cultural mass. A distributive model of culture must take into account both diversity and commonality. It is diversity that increases the cultural inventory, but it is commonality that answers a degree of communicability and coordination.

As Keesing (1981, 71) explains:

> such a view takes as fundamental the distribution of partial versions of a cultural tradition, among members of society...(and) can take into account the different perspectives on a way of life of women and men, young and old, specialists and non-specialists.

This distributive model is particularly appropriate for description and analysis of a culture undergoing rapid change, where there is considerable variation in knowledge, depending on individual experience—who people are, how old, where they have lived and so on. Each person's reality is a different one and each person possesses distinctive ideas and information; even the same information can be interpreted in different ways. And when people die without transmitting knowledge, Aboriginal culture is altered significantly. The culture changes, knowledge is accumulated and lost. Viewing cultural information as being distributed through individuals in a population affords the opportunity to conceptualise the process of change. Internal differentiation is another aspect of Aboriginality we can expect to find easier to understand using a distributive view of culture. When Lorna Dixon of Bourke says (Mathews 1985, 102), 'I'll follow my rules until the day I die', we should not be surprised if they are not the same as those of a young man, say, in Nambucca Heads, or for that matter, her own daughter. Yet all three are legitimate manifestations of an Aboriginality which sooner or later have to be studied at the level of the individual.

Much of the knowledge and information[3] possessed by individuals is based upon the past. The past is a fundamental source of cultural knowledge, even in societies in rapid change. Among Aboriginal people in southeastern Australia, limited aspects of traditional knowledge have survived, either in fact, or transformed, while the post-contact period provides people with their own direct experiences of the past. Still other people gain their knowledge from a revival of information on the past, or have introduced their own new ideas based on the past to the 'cultural mass'. Aboriginality incorporates each of these different aspects of knowledge through its adherents—the people who identify as Aboriginal. It is the composite of knowledge in Aboriginal society which collectively constitutes Aboriginal identity.

Knowledge from the pre-contact past, mainly among older people, is one element in the overall construction of current Aboriginality. The conjunction of people and places and the transmission of knowledge with continuity through the generations, has produced a strong sense of local identity among many New South Wales Kooris. This is partly based upon the survival of aspects of traditional group identification, through language maintenance and landscape information, and partly on details revived from pre-existing sources. While Tindale (1974) maps out around seventy tribes for New South Wales at the time of first contact, there is today an identification with around twenty of these, some of which undoubtedly result from the survival of traditional knowledge. As well, much pre-contact knowledge of the environment, the animals and plants, and the various places which held economic or religious significance persists, and despite major land use changes over the years, many people are not completely divorced from the landscape which once their ancestors owned. In 1974 during sites survey work in western New South Wales, this account was obtained from Elsie Jones, which typifies the environmental detail still known to some elders in New South Wales:

> There's three kinds of goannas, a big black one that's been mistaken for a crocodile, that's the *ngarnaru*. Then there's the other one, he's a river one too but doesn't grow as big, kind of black too with white stripes. That's a *barna*. And then there's another one that lives out off the river in red soil country. Well that's the *fackulu*, he's yellow and white. He's the main one for food. Our people hunt for this a lot, it's the sweetest and best to eat.

However it is true that fewer people than in the past now know of such details of plants and animals, where to find them, their cultural labels, and the words and systems used to categorise them. Much knowledge has been transformed into more general information of the major land and aquatic resources, some of which are still eaten. Reasons for the decline in environmental details include disruption to the transmission of knowledge from old people to young, and restrictions on access to traditional food resources. To remain alive as cultural knowledge, ideas (eg details of food resources) need to be continuously stimulated by complementary actions, (the tasks of hunting, fishing and gathering), involving the material aspects of culture (sites and technology). Any break in the interaction between these three components of culture produces changes in the nature of the cultural data base. There is no denying that major changes have taken place in the construction of Aboriginal cultural knowledge, brought about through the breakdown in the transmission of information from old people to the younger ones. The following remark by Gordon Williams on the decline of the initiations in far northern New South Wales is typical of many heard over the years of the sites survey:

> That was before my time, see. That law sort of faded out. If they'd have kept it up, I'd have been in it...These younger people know nothing, nobody will learn them, see. All the old hands are dying out, that knows the laws and the rules a bit, but they don't know all that much either.

But this hiatus in cultural continuity follows a pattern that began with the first contact with whites; at different times and in different places, the flow of traditional knowledge has eventually been slowed to a trickle or stopped altogether. The effects of population loss, policies of assimilation, competition from the pastoral industry, constant pressures to abandon Aboriginal beliefs, European education and employment, all combined to induce a resignation by many people to the inevitability of adopting aspects of western culture. In these circumstances, old people often feel reluctant to pass on what appears to them, and even more so to young people, information which is irrelevant to their present lifestyle. The traditional control of knowledge in Aboriginal society, and its limitation to certain people at particular stages in their lives, have also not assisted the process of information transmission in modern Koori society.

Resettlement of Aboriginal people on reserves, then later in towns, also hindered the flow of knowledge and it was the refusal of successive state administrations to allow some Aboriginal people to live where they wanted, which led to an increased vulnerability of traditional culture. How for example could an Aboriginal mother pass on the mythology of the Brothers Rocks at Tibooburra to her children, when camped in hopeless conditions 500 kilometres away on the reserve at Brewarrina after their enforced move there in 1938? Or the men organise for an initiation in completely strange, and therefore also 'dangerous' country, belonging to other Aboriginal groups whom they either feared or despised? In other areas of the state, such as the north coast, parts of the south coast and the north central area, there was a less disruptive settlement pattern, with people living on reserves located within traditional tribal ranges. With their sites in view and easily accessible, it was possible to keep the knowledge alive and transmit it to successive generations. Goanna Headland at Evans Head, Mount Anderson at Bellbrook, Mount Dromedary at Wallaga Lake and Boobera Lagoon near Boggabilla are all examples of traditional natural features enduring because they were seen regularly or visited by the people living close to them.

These are places made by Supernatural Beings like the Rainbow Serpent, Ancestral Heroes such as Biroogun or Dirrangun, and the Sky Gods, Biaime, Ulitarra and others, which explain the creation of the world, emphasised a law, or marked some event. These Beings were believed to be ancestors of living people, and through the survival of this folklore, some in detail, much more in a general sense, Kooris today consider that their rights to the land are as old as the creation of land itself. A recent report on the sites survey (Creamer 1986) indicates that twenty-nine per cent of all currently known sites of significance to the Aboriginal community fall into the traditional category, and have been recorded by using what is assumed to be surviving, pre-contact knowledge. Being part of Aboriginal religious beliefs, along with ceremonial grounds and burials, they can truly be called sacred sites, unlike stone tools, shell middens, canoe trees and other secular sites that are often put into that category by the media, the public and Aboriginal people.[4]

In some cases, while sites are still important, the knowledge held by individuals and the community collectively is not as detailed as in earlier years. Often as a result of restrictions on access to places and a changed lifestyle, the mythology of a site (or connected series of sites) survives without knowledge of the precise location of the actual sites. This has occurred in the northwest where one of the major stories of this area, that of the creation of the Narran River, is remembered and retold in a much shortened form, without site information other than the major landscape features of the Narran Lake and the river itself. A similar pattern of a reduced flow of information on sites is apparent with other sites where we are fortunate enough to have a previous written record of the mythology, which can be compared with the versions in existence today. What differs between various areas is the period when the maximum disruption to the flow of traditional knowledge took place. For the Ualayai between Walgett and Angledool it was between 1930 and 1950, or about sixty years after white settlement. It is about forty years after initiation ceremonies had ceased in that area, at the height of demands from the pastoral industry for labour and during a period of enforced closures of old missions and movements of the Aboriginal population to larger towns.

In other places, the main hiatus in transmission of traditional knowledge occurred either earlier, as in the areas around Sydney and the Hunter Valley, or for reasons already discussed, it came later, in some parts as late as the 1970s. At Woodenbong in 1973 for example, it was still possible to obtain an account of the mythology and location of some sites, which was essentially the same as that recorded by Radcliffe-Brown in 1929. The differential transmission of knowledge has resulted in differing perceptions of sites and the landscape, between those communities which are traditionally-oriented and those which have more of a contemporary connection with sites. Opinions can differ between Kooris over the same type of site. For example, carved trees on the north coast are usually considered as secret-sacred and associated with initiation grounds because of the persistence of these ceremonies there, like the carved tree at Nambucca Heads. Yet this type of site is generally open to all to view in the west of the state, as shown by the wide community interest in the Wambandry carved tree now located at the Yarramar Cooperative office at Warren. What is claimed as a sacred site by elders in one area, might be dismissed as natural marks on a rock by others. The main factors appear to be the extent and variation of the site resources in a given local area, the knowledge which people have of sites, and the degree to which people have retained traditional site associations.

The post-contact period necessarily provides the source of all direct, lived, experience for Aboriginal people, and contributes the major input of cultural knowledge constituting current Aboriginality. However in considering the period from 1788 until the present, it is necessary to distinguish between the total of available historical data, and the knowledge which results from direct experience. This is because an increasing number of statements, beliefs and ideas about the past derive from early written sources and have only recently been added to the store of cultural knowledge. These recent additions constitute a distinct input to the cultural mass. For example, soon after contact in 1788 Aboriginal people began a resistance to white conquest that is still going on. While few whites are aware of it, the historical generalities of this resistance have always been known to Kooris. What was not known are the details now becoming established as cultural knowledge. The New South Wales Aboriginal Consultative Group calls its newsletter 'Pemulwy', as explained on the front cover, 'in honour of one of the first Aboriginal people known to have resisted the invasion of Australia'. We need to be clear in what sense the knowing is taking place if we are to understand Aboriginality.[5]

While a general knowledge of massacres persists, most of the details have been lost, mainly because by definition, not many survived to tell what happened. Many of the details now becoming incorporated as cultural knowledge are the result of historical research. One recurring story attributable to knowledge passed on from direct experience however, relates how a young child escapes from a massacre to continue the local heritage. It is a powerful metaphor for the survival of the group in the post-contact period.

Other survivors of diseases and massacres were rounded up and forced to live on reserves at places like Bellbrook near Kempsey, Stuart's Island near Nambucca, at Brewarrina, and at Warrangesda near Griffith, all established in the 1880s by the newly formed Aborigines Protection Board. Many of these old reserves are recorded as sites of significance, or have sites associated with them. As already discussed, the pattern of contact is an important factor in explaining variation in the survival of pre-contact knowledge as compared with the component of direct experience, and hence the different constructions of Aboriginal identity from place to place. The larger groups on the coast and certain inland areas appear to have coped with the protection era better than certain others, although almost all adult Aboriginal people endured the same bitter experiences of institutional control on the government reserves, similar to those described by the late Herbert Charles, an elder of the Gidabal people around Woodenbong:

> Most of the managers were ready to push the Aborigines around. Anything that cropped up, they had the police there. Just for drunkedness, I remember, it was £10. We had to report to the manager before we could walk onto our own reserve. If we

were away a week, we had to report or if you didn't you'd be locked up, just for walking back into your own home. It was bad!

Aboriginal history naturally divides into distinctive eras: the various epochs of pre-contact life; the early British colonial period; the rule of the Aborigines Protection Board; assimilation policies; and the modern era, which includes the present revitalisation of Aboriginal culture. As if to recognise that much knowledge of time spent confined to reserves across the state will be around for a long time to come, the emphasis in the current renascence is chiefly on reviving traditional aspects of Aboriginal culture. While some Aboriginal people might question whether 'revival' is the right word for what is happening, maintaining that their culture has been alive and vital all these years, there is no doubt that the past decade has seen a burst of activity aimed at strengthening Aboriginal identity in southeastern Australia. Interestingly, now is not the first time that a period of increased self-awareness has produced a process of cultural renewal. AP Elkin (1975, 147 and personal communication), perceived a similar movement in the 1930s on the mid-north coast, although then it was the initiation ceremonies that were specifically the object of the revival:

> Men in that district, disturbed by the economic depression of the early 1930's, sought to 'return to the past' with its myths and rituals and its social code and so find again a firm foundation for life...the holding of Burbung, Keepara and other Initiations in the midst of culture-breakdown...was a remarkable expression of solidarity. It crossed tribal boundaries...It expressed Aboriginal identity, a sense of belonging to a community with its own past over against the white man. Initiation Rituals were a rebirth and a renewal of strength for all who played their parts in them.

The same purposes of building a strong and lasting identity based on the past, are present in today's cultural revival; in turn, the process becomes central to forming Aboriginal views of the past. From the powerlessness that characterised attitudes of earlier generations, the Kooris of today are engaged in a vigorous promotion of Aboriginality and articulation of Aboriginal values. In this they are encouraged by availability of funding, a more tolerant social and political environment and a genuine desire by many Australians to learn more about Aboriginal culture in all respects. The aim is to achieve a strengthening of group identity, greater control over decisions and a greater share of resources. On the one hand there is cultural revitalisation, on the other there is a deliberate emphasis on cultural difference in order to achieve political or economic returns. Such returns can be quite tangible, like the enactment of land rights legislation or access to jobs where Aboriginality is the main criterion for employment. The strategic uses of Aboriginality in the multicultural state are an integral dynamic in the process of constructing identity.

However, it would be wrong to suggest that all the motives for cultural revival are somehow cynical. There is undoubtedly also a strong self-actualising aspect to cultural revival—the need to find answers to the major 'life position' questions—who am I?, where have I come from? and, where am I going? The second of these inevitably involves the construction of a model of past culture with its representations of traditional society, economy, values and beliefs, which is meaningful in terms of personal identity and group solidarity. Instead of passively accepting white reconstructions of the Aboriginal past, called 'prehistory' as if black people had no history of their own, Kooris are now promoting their own images of themselves and their former way of life.

Cultural revival involves a renewal and a renascence of Aboriginal culture. In New South Wales today, it is seen as a burst of activity and expression involving Aboriginal studies, cultural performances, lectures, poetry, paintings, stories, dances and culture camps and the building of special keeping places and cultural centres. The search for the past is continually giving new meaning and significance to prehistoric sites as they become known to the Koori community, through surveys prior to development, or from site records. Art sites near Cowra and Bourke becoming 'adopted' by the local group; stone tool scatters in the Hunter Valley and in the Sydney area likewise the focus of intense, if sometimes short-lived interest; eroding burials along the River Murray and shell middens on the coast, are all examples of prehistoric sites which have been rediscovered and incorporated into the site-specific knowledge of Aboriginal people. Aboriginal culture has always involved some innovation and this is certainly true today as people search for information with which to fill the vacuum left by the loss of traditional knowledge. In rare instances, sites have been created recently. In 1980 an Aboriginal elder, originally from another area, named an impressive granite rock outcrop near Tamworth 'Wave Rock', because of its resemblance to a wave; the site was recorded at his request because he believed that in the past it must have been an increase site for rain. While providing a dramatic illustration of continuing creativity of Aboriginal people, such inventions are likely to pose philosophical questions for site managers, as well as potential practical problems for land owners.

Aboriginal sites give tangible substance to cultural revival, relating ideas to material remains, and they are now a major focus for the construction of cultural models of the past. As the sociologist Bernice Martin (1983, 28) writes in another context, 'culture is a receptacle for symbolic artifacts which, once historically created, can be and indeed inevitably are recharged over time with new permutations of symbolic meaning and relevance'. The symbolic significance of sites lies in their antiquity, meaning and distinctiveness from the landscape and culture which surrounds them. As such, they are a powerful resource enabling cultural revival to flourish and provide an important physical context for the revival to take place.

An example of this occurred in 1978 when, after many years of having to use a European graveyard, a ceremony took place at the Aboriginal cemetery at Wallaga Lake on the south coast of New South Wales, involving the reburial of previously uncovered prehistoric bones. The ceremony drew on traditional knowledge, but also involved a degree of contemporary improvisation in its structure and wording, the body painting used and even a reading from AW Howitt's 1904 ethnography. In this way the ideas of the people (their wish to revive Aboriginal culture through the reburial of ancestral remains), gave rise to specific actions (the repossession of the bones followed by the burial ceremony), to create, or more precisely, re-activate a sacred site (the material, physical aspects of culture). The combination of knowledge, organisation and place gives structure to cultural revival, making it a powerfully symbolic statement about the distinctiveness of modern Aboriginal identity. This description of the event comes from its creator, the charismatic Aboriginal elder, Guboo Ted Thomas (1978, 8):

> For the first time at Wallaga Lake we've just had a burial ceremony for one of our ancestors who was uncovered near Wallaga and taken to the School of Anatomy in Sydney without consulting us. It is the first time we have ever been able to claim an Aboriginal skeleton...It is a wonderful feeling to bury one of our ancestors in our cemetery at Wallaga Lake—that we know our people's spirit is at rest and that Darama, the Great Spirit, is working. The way is open to act now.

The essence of cultural revival is a redefinition of cultural reality. Tribal boundaries become formalised where a few years ago there were none, sites become incorporated into the collective knowledge of a local community where previously they were unknown, and contemporary beliefs and ideas gain a new clarity as ancient truths. Like the various manifestations of contact religion, this is a truly syncretic phenomenon, drawing on the past for its content, the present for its direction and future for its inspiration. Yet much of the re-invention has a traditional basis, however distantly located. For example, the danger attributed to many sites which have only recently gained renewed significance, has its origins in the countless warnings from elders, for other places at other times—'We wasn't allowed to fish here, I don't come down here fishing, I keep my mother's word' (Milli Boyd), and, 'There was one fig tree at Saltwater and he said to me, "Never sit under that tree my girl, or you'll be sick"' (Margery Maher). So when members of the Western Regional Land Council say that the Snake Cave at Mootwingee Historic Site was an initiation ground which women were not allowed to see, or the same kind of statement is made for the Devil's Rock engraving site at Maroota, they have in mind traditional laws, in this case the exclusion of women from much of the men's religious life, which they either have direct experience of, or have heard about in the context of rediscovering their cultural inheritance.

Whether or not such restrictions actually applied to these sites in pre-contact times is a question which would occur to those who would like to see an accurate reconstruction of the past. With growing frequency, sites are being vested with a significance they may only possibly have originally possessed. In just a few days, Norah Head on the central coast gained a rich mythology from one enthusiastic local elder which very nearly prevented a major public works project, until initiated men were brought in from the north coast to separate newly acquired individual knowledge from pre-existing, shared cultural beliefs and thus determine the validity of the claims. Likewise, prehistoric sites in a forest proposed as a possible site for an army base quickly became 'sacred' for nearby Kooris who had not actually seen them but who realised their potential value for the construction of a local Aboriginal identity; and Aboriginal school children taken to a rock shelter in the Sydney area during their Aboriginal studies course complained of feeling sick because they thought that, according to a traditional law they have only fleetingly glimpsed, they should not have been there.

While reconstructions of the past are based partly on traditional information handed down to young people from their elders, and therefore truly part of their cultural inheritance, they also incorporate many new ideas, acquired from outside the group, including some of the results of recent archaeological research. The date for human occupation at Lake Mungo of around 40,000 years is an example. Over the years, there is a gradual replacement of 'inherited' knowledge with 'acquired' knowledge in the process of building models of the past, as the pre-contact era becomes even more remote in the collective memory, and old people with traditional knowledge die. The information acquired during the current burst of revitalisation is destined to become incorporated into the cultural mass of Aboriginal groups and be passed on again as inherited knowledge, in the cyclical way that people have always renewed and updated their cultures. A good resource place is found or ancestral rocks revealed in a dream, and the knowledge of their whereabouts and significance is acquired by the group, subsequently to be transmitted to successive generations as inherited knowledge with all the authenticity and sanctity implied by their association with the past.

In describing the process of cultural revival, care is needed to avoid giving it the appearance of happening 'out there' with its own momentum and existence, independently from the people themselves. Rather, it is very much the product of the actions of individuals and their own perceived versions of Aboriginal culture. How people use the knowledge they have gained from experience and integrate it with other recently acquired information, and to what ends it is put, are the central issues in exploring this cultural phenomenon. It is also clear that what is now happening is more than a repetition of past renewals in Aboriginal culture. There exist today several factors, each a product of the jostling for resources and the search for identity in the affluent, pluralist, western society we live in, that are encouraging and helping to shape this renascence. But whatever the influence of factors beyond Aboriginal control, it is within Aboriginal society, in the ideas and actions of its individual members, that the main thrust for cultural revival is coming. The emphasis on individual initiative lends credence to the distributive view of culture adopted previously. It is individuals, albeit working within a particular milieu of language, beliefs and ideas, who create culture and give it form. The process of cultural revival assists many people to find a new direction by seeing Aboriginality as a cultural reality, integral and substantive with a past, a present and a future.

In examining the loss of pre-contact cultural knowledge among Aboriginal people in New South Wales, the point has been made that many individuals have been left in a sort of 'cultural vacuum', not achieving success in white society, yet without the traditional support structures, laws and access to sites and resources which their predecessors enjoyed. They feel quite rightly that they have been robbed of their own culture without being given anything in return. In these circumstances, it is left to each person to take the initiative by building a cultural revival on what survives of the traditions and history of their group, as well as through their direct experiences of being Aboriginal in New South Wales. The leadership provided by a small group of charismatic elders articulating the directions of change is both a stimulus to and an outcome of cultural revival, since in Aboriginal society, deprived as it often is of influence in mainstream politics, cultural knowledge which includes details of sites, is a way to increase individual power and influence in the community. There are some Aboriginal people who have undoubtedly strengthened their leadership roles through becoming closely associated with the control of sites, claiming to possess considerable knowledge about them and striving for their protection from threats by development.

The intention in this chapter has been to move beyond the image of Aboriginal people in New South Wales as cultureless outcasts. That current Aboriginal identity is a complex construct is not denied. However this is an attempt to demonstrate that it can be explained using an anthropological perspective which is based on the role of individual knowledge in constructing cultural systems. Such a theory accounts for differing versions of Aboriginality within the Koori community through the different compositions of individual cultural knowledge. In turn, cultural knowledge is an important factor establishing a person's position within the community. The changing composition of individual knowledge—the product of traditions, direct experience or revival, accounts for changes in the construction of Aboriginal identity. Cultural revival is seen as the main motivating force, proving to be a vital and dynamic process in constructing present reality.

In a multicultural world, Aboriginal people of New South Wales are doing no more in redefining and strengthening their identity, than many other groups—Irish Catholics, American Indians, and even white middle class Australians researching their family trees. All have a political element, an ulterior motive, yet all embody that universal need to know what our origins are, to foster that sense of belonging to our own group which we learn at a very early age. Cultural revival takes Aboriginal people beyond cultureless outcasts to being citizens in a modern multicultural society, with a distinctive identity based on a distinctive heritage.

Notes

1. In line with increasing practice, the term Koori is sometimes used here as an alternative for Aborigine. As James Miller (1985, vii) explains, 'The word Aboriginal is a Latin-derived English word which...did not give my people a separate identity (and) always has derogatory connotations'. By contrast, the word Koori is indigenous to much of southeastern Australia and is gaining increasing vernacular acceptance in this part of the country.

2. The Bundjalung are still one of the stronger Aboriginal groups in New South Wales, in terms of their identity, and have even provided

contemporary linguists with enough data on which to base a detailed study of their language (Sharpe 1985).

3. Although used here as if they mean the same thing, there is a subtle distinction between knowledge and information, expressed with typical terseness in T.S. Elliot's reflection on western society, 'where is the knowledge we have lost in information?'

4. The process of symbolising all sites as sacred is however an interesting development and illustrates another transformation, where some traditional information survives, but in a much altered state.

5. We should be clear that it is not traditional knowledge that is being used, but recent information gained from detailed historical research. Another attempt to honour a hero of early Aboriginal resistance is being made through the efforts of the Tharawal and Gandangara (themselves recently 'revived' names) Land Councils, to have Sydney's new airport named 'Caryanbal', after a local guerilla leader (ADC 1986).

References

Aboriginal Development Commission (ADC)
1986 Sydney's Next Airport Should be Named After Aboriginal Hero, *ADC News* 2(3).

Beckett, J.
1958 Marginal Men: A Study of Two Half Caste Aborigines', *Oceania* 29, 91–108.
1965 Kinship, Mobility and Community Among Part-Aborigines in Rural Australia, *International Journal of Comparative Sociology* 6(1), 7–23.
1967 Marriage, Circumcision and Avoidance Among the Maljangaba of North-West New South Wales, *Mankind* 6(10), 456–64.

Bell, J.
1964 Assimilation in New South Wales. In M. Reay (ed), *Aborigines Now: New Perspectives in the Study of Aboriginal Communities*, Angus and Robertson, Sydney.

Bohannan, P.
1967 Introduction. In P. Bohannan and F. Plog (eds), *Beyond the Frontier: Social Process and Cultural Change*, American Museum Source Books in Anthropology, New York.

Calley, M.
1958 Three Bandjalang Legends, *Mankind* 5(5), 208–13.

Creamer, H.
1986 A Gift and a Dreaming: The New South Wales Survey of Aboriginal Sacred and Significant Sites, National Parks and Wildlife Service, unpublished manuscript.

Elkin, A.P.
1951 Reaction and Interaction: A Food Gathering People and European Settlement in Australia, *American Anthropologist* 53(2), 164–96.
1975 R.H. Mathews: His Contribution to Aboriginal Studies, *Oceania* XLVI(2), 126–52.

Goodenough, W.
1964 Cultural Anthropology and Linguistics. In D. Hymes (ed), *Language in Culture and Society*, Harper and Row, New York.

Howitt, A.W.
1904 *The Native Tribes of South East Australia*, Macmillan, London.

Keesing, R.
1981 *Cultural Anthropology: A Contemporary Perspective*, Holt, Rinehart and Winston, New York.

Maddock, K.
1972 *The Australian Aborigines: A Portrait of Their Society*, Allen Lane, the Penguin Press, London.

Martin, B.
1983 *A Sociology of Contemporary Cultural Change*, Blackwell, Oxford.

Mathews, J.
1977 *The Two Worlds of Jimmie Barker*, Australian Institute of Aboriginal Studies, Canberra.
1985 Lorna Dixon. In I. White, D. Barwick and B. Meehan (eds), *Fighters and Singers: The Lives of Some Australian Aboriginal Women*, George Allen and Unwin, Sydney.

Miller, J.
1985 *Koorie: A Will to Win*, Angus and Robertson, London.

Radcliffe-Brown, A.R.
1929 Notes on Totemism in Eastern Australia, *Journal of the Royal Anthropological Institute* 59, 399–415.
1930 The Social Organization of Australian Tribes, *Oceania* 1, 34–63.

Schwartz, T.
1978 Where is the Culture? Personality as the Distributive Locus of Culture. In G. Spindler (ed), *The Making of Psychological Anthropology*, University of California Press, Berkeley.

Sharpe, M.
1985 An Introduction to the Bundjalung Language and its Dialects, Armidale College of Advanced Education, typescript.

Tatz, C.
1980 Aboriginality as Civilisation, *The Australian Quarterly* 52(3), 352–62.

Thomas, Guboo T.
1978 Darama...The Great Spirit, *Aboriginal Quarterly* 1(1).

Tindale, N.
1974 *Aboriginal Tribes of Australia*, University of California Press, Berkeley.

Tylor, E.
1891 *Primitive Culture*, John Murray, London.

van den Berghe, P.
1967 *Race and Racism*, John Wiley, New York.

5. Barry Morris

The politics of identity: from Aborigines to the first Australian

The construction of an account of the contemporary context of Aboriginal groups in Australia does not begin with the same assumptions that inform the United States and Canadian situations, where limited forms of sovereignty rights and residency rights on reserves accompany Indian status. The existence of treaties between these nation states and the respective Indian nations has long provided them with a distinctive legal status.

The Aboriginal people of Australia do not possess such a unique legal position. Nevertheless, the status of Aborigines has recently undergone some important change. The change has occurred as part of the higher profile that the Commonwealth government has taken in Aboriginal welfare policy. The Commonwealth performed only a limited and auxiliary role in welfare servicing compared with that of regional state governments in the 1970s and early 1980s. However, it did achieve a rehabilitation of the notion of an Aboriginal collectivity as expressed in terms of special services (medical, legal, arts etc) and land rights. These innovations in government policy are part of a shift from an assimilationist to a cultural pluralist program, cast in the idioms of 'self-determination'.

What I intend to address in this chapter[1] are the controls and the limitations of the policies of 'self-determination'. To understand their limitations it is first necessary to digress and outline the constitutional status of Aborigines. The current policies, I argue, represent another government attempt to deal with Aborigines who, as a dispossessed indigenous minority, remain a constitutional anomaly. The present solution to the Aboriginal 'problem' is sought through the recognition of cultural difference rather than the specificities of colonial dispossession and domination. The stress upon cultural distinctiveness is not arbitrary but emanates from the 'legal fiction' on which the constitutional sovereignty of the nation state is based—the judgement passed down by the Privy Council of Britain (1788), that at the time of colonisation Australian land was 'practically unoccupied without settled inhabitants or settled laws' (cited in Detmold 1985, 58). It is this judgement that forms the basis for the non-recognition or denial of the sovereign rights of Aborigines.[2]

Specifically, the denial of indigenous rights stems from the categorisation of Australia as a 'settled colony' rather than a 'conquered colony' where limited forms of sovereignty were granted. The demonstrable historical falsity of such a legal claim has produced, as in the case of Coe v Commonwealth (1979), a view of history which argues that legal theory takes precedent over historical evidence. As Blackburn J, the presiding judge, stated: 'once made practice or judicial decision will not be disturbed by historical research'; or again, 'what is important is the legal theory, and for this purpose historical fact may give place to legal fiction' (cited in Detmold 1985, 60). In short, the judgement affirmed the status quo, namely, that constitutionally the rights of Aborigines as an indigenous people remained unaltered. The cultural pluralist program attempts to resolve the anomaly that original inhabitants pose for the modern state, but in the absence of any acknowledgement of their sovereign status.

The purpose of this digression has been to separate, from the outset, the political rhetoric of pluralist policies from their constitutional core. I have argued elsewhere that the expanded role of the welfare system in Aboriginal affairs, primarily at regional state level (New South Wales), has led to an increase rather than a decrease in the monitoring and surveillance mechanisms of government (Morris 1985).[3] This analysis will be applied to consider Commonwealth policies. My focus will be to draw out the extremely bureaucratic approach of policy and its underlying logic. Such an approach largely concurs with a number of studies which have as their focus a process of domination sustained by relations of dependency, that is welfare colonialism (see Paine 1977; Collman 1979; Howard 1980, 1981; Beckett 1983). It is my contention, however, that the political and economic mechanisms of control do not exhaust the field where power is exercised nor how it always functions. My intention is to extend the analysis to the terrain of ideology and culture. It is to consider the hegemonic forms that power assumes, which are associated with the politics of identity. The politics of identity refers to an aspect of power whereby a subjugated group is turned into an object of knowledge. In effect, they lose the right to speak for themselves as the production of their identity is invested in experts and authorities and mediated by institutions of the state system.

The latter part of this chapter will consider the hegemonic positions that are ascribed to Aborigines within the discursive practices of multiculturalism. Particular attention will be given to their positioning as a cultural entity within the 'new nationalism' generated by multiculturalism, where Aborigines are increasingly defined as the 'first Australians' or the 'first immigrants' rather than an indigenous people. The appropriation of Aborigines as cultural/historical figures reveals clearly the contradiction that exists between these new ideological representations of Aborigines and their constitutional/legal status. The substantive material is drawn from the experiences of the Dhan-gadi people of the Macleay Valley. In my discussion of the Dhan-gadi, I will deal with some of the contradictions that develop between their own experience and understanding of the past and the production of the past by the state.

The ideology of cultural pluralism

Paine's (1977) notion of welfare colonialism has provided us with a conceptual tool for penetrating the contemporary circumstances of Fourth World peoples in liberal democracies. The process of continuing domination, he argues, is facilitated through the development of relations of dependency between indigenous minorities and welfare departments in the relatively permissive context of a partial recognition of such groups as a collectivity. The relationship, as Paine (1977, 3) characterises it, is 'solicitous rather than exploitative, liberal rather than repressive'. Such policies reflected the success of liberalism over previous racial and discriminatory practices, but also its limitations. (In the Australian context see above mentioned authors and also Beckett Chapter 12.) As Beckett (1983, 3) aptly reminds us, 'it is the colonisers who make the decisions, even if they are supposed to be for the good of the colonised'. In this connection, the critical probing into contemporary policies, initiated by Paine, has brought into focus the subtle forms of political and economic control associated with apparently 'non-demonstrative colonialism'.

The functioning of a demonstrable colonialism ceased in the 1960s with legislative changes (discussed below) which brought an end to race and racial discrimination as the central dynamic of state control of Aborigines. In New South Wales, like the other states, colonial relations have been given expression through the idiom of race and it was race that provided the morality for discriminatory practices. Under the assimilation policies of the late 1960s, the objectifications of Aborigines that emerged were those of a 'deprived social group' with special quantitative needs. They were deviations from a statistical norm, which provided the beginnings of their incorporation into the general welfare system of the state. Their admission was based on quantitative forms of specialised intervention in health, education and housing. During the 1970s, however, the multiculturalism policy resulted in some recognition of the qualitative needs of Aborigines. Under this new doctrine, it is ethnicity which provides the morality for special services to Aborigines.[4]

This new emphasis emerged with the expanded role of the Commonwealth government in Aboriginal affairs. This followed the amendments to the Australian Constitution made in the 1967 referendum, which enabled the Commonwealth government to assume the responsibilities for Aborigines previously carried out by departments in various states. Specifically, this involved changes to Section 51(26), changes which empowered the Commonwealth government to enact special laws for Aborigines. As Hanks (1984) has pointed out, the constitutional power of Section 51(26) had originally been intended to support discriminatory legislation associated with a 'white Australia policy' for immigration. Under Section 51(26), the Commonwealth government had the 'power to make laws for the peace, order and good government of the Commonwealth with respect to...the people of any race, other than the Aboriginal race in any State, from whom it is deemed necessary to make special laws' (Hanks 1984, 20). The removal of the reference to Aborigines in the referendum enabled the transfer of legislative controls to the Commonwealth Parliament.

The referendum promoted the incorporation of Aborigines into Anglo-Australian society. The view enshrined in the 'white Australia policy', which sought to preserve the homogeneity of Anglo-Australian culture, sanctioned an expanded assimilation program for Aborigines (see Morris 1985). It continued to equate homogeneity with the imperatives of 'peace, order and good government' and heterogeneity with the seeds of social divisiveness and potential conflict. The powers of Section 51(26) were not used until a new government was elected in 1972.[5] Special laws by government from this period were interpreted to include positive forms of discrimination. While the constitutional changes were ultimately to have far reaching consequences, they did not exclude the use of negative or positive forms of discrimination. The use of Section 51(26) validated the recognition of cultural differences within constitutional bounds. The changes bestowed validity in its legal sense, rather than questioning the legitimacy of the ultimate power of the Commonwealth in relation to the indigenous population.[6]

Nevertheless, government legislation in the 1970s provided the basis for the limited development of Aboriginal control and staffing of legal services, medical centres, preschools and economic enterprises, such as housing cooperatives, pastoral stations and so on.[7] In effect, the government endorsed the growth of some degree of authority within Aboriginal communities. Perhaps the most significant example of this was the granting of Aboriginal Land Rights in 1976 to groups under the jurisdiction of the Commonwealth in the Northern Territory.[8] Similarly, despite the earnest endeavours of the assimilation policy for migrants, the large numbers of immigrants of non-British origin who settled in Australia in the post World War II period changed the social composition and political character of Anglo-Australian society. Martin (1978), and Kalantis, Cope and Hughes (1984–85) have shown that there was an evolution in immigration policy, paralleling that in Aboriginal affairs. Government recognition of land rights and ethnic rights occured simultaneously in the 1970s.

The limited nature of the reform intended by cultural pluralism is apparent in the final report of the Commonwealth Committee on Community Relations (1975),

> Pluralism, as defined here, implies first and foremost mutual tolerance and respect for cultural differences by all the members and institutions of Australian society...*It is in striking a balance between the pressures and requirements of a wider range of ethnic groups and the host society that a fine line divides cultural pluralism from structural pluralism*...Separatism and segregation become characteristic of (such) a situation which allows a society to develop 'plural structural units' and enshrines the potentiality of conflict and tensions between these units. *Institutional differences will inevitably prevent common sharing and participation in a universalistic value system and sharing in key social institutions*...However, the viewpoint of 'cultural pluralism', as advocated by this Committee, does enable ethnic groups, if they so desire, to establish their own structures and institutions usually of a cultural and social nature, for example, the media, clubs and restaurants, shops and community organisations...While recognising the utility and value of ethnic structures in achieving the ends of pluralistic integration, it has to be borne in mind that an excessive emphasis on self interest programs may be harmful both to ethnic groups and the host society. *These inherent dangers of structural pluralism can be avoided if the interaction between all groups is sustained at all levels and in particular through their common participation in the shared and universalistic structures of the wider society* (cited in Martin 1978, 56, emphasis added).

The committee recommends the restructuring of community relations. Nevertheless, the report, which preceded the establishment of a Commissioner for Community Relations, sought to remove fears of any secessionary logic associated with cultural pluralism. While the 'universal value system' and 'universal structures' of the wider society were to remain unaltered, specific additional domains were to be demarcated for expressions of cultural distinctiveness.

These principles guided the implementation of new structures and services for Aboriginal communities, catering to their special needs. The processes of control in this seemingly solicitous form of government intervention are twofold. In the first place, it is the state which controls, economically and politically, the extent and scope of pluralist practices. Secondly, while the state no longer suppresses cultural and social differences it domesticates them in controlling the domains in which they can be 'legitimately' expressed. Control here is not so much political (in the narrow sense) or economic, but rather ideological. I have already suggested that to understand this social phenomenon it is necessary to understand the historical/social relations between Aborigines and the sovereign order of the state—the relations one is concerned with here are colonial relations. These, it should be stressed, are real; they are historically specific social realities. As a process of mystification, hegemonic domination is constituted in the identification and selection of particular symbolic representations of Aboriginality. In guaranteeing expressions of 'ethnic difference', both historically and culturally, the state attempts to centralise and manage the production of the representations of identity.

To begin with I will consider the auxiliary nature of the government funded projects (and hence the perpetuation of the 'universal structures' of the wider society) established for Aborigines in the Macleay Valley. Significantly, the majority of Aboriginal families were living in some form of state housing accommodation in Kempsey, the major town in the valley in 1980–81 (see Morris 1986). The establishment of an Aboriginal housing cooperative in 1978 had little impact upon the housing needs of Aborigines in Kempsey. The shortcomings in terms of community needs were expressed to me as 'too little to help the people, band-aid treatment: six houses a year when you need twenty. All it does is get the community fighting.' At one level, this reflected the nature of external control associated with the allocation of funding; that is, the number of houses that could be built and the number of people employed. Such structural forms of dependency conformed to external controls associated with welfare colonialism.

However, control did not restrict itself to this external form. It also penetrated the internal workings of the cooperative. The cooperative had to conform to the rational and codified rules and regulations associated with bureaucratic organisation. For example, monies allocated for housing were to be strictly used for such purposes. In one year, the houses were completed within the allocation and the surplus was spent by the cooperative on acquiring better machinery and a truck. Such expenditures were regarded as being outside the allocation and had to be returned to departmental revenue. Furthermore, to increase funding for housing and employment, the cooperative applied for monies from another Commonwealth scheme. The application was granted but subject to direct supervision. The building team, which had been working together since 1978, was placed under the supervision of a 'whitefella' who was required to be 'on the job for eight hours a day'.

Thus, the universal application of rules and regulations took precedence over internal structures of authority defined in terms of self-determination. Above all, the cooperative had to reproduce the same organisational model that applied to welfare programs in general.

The recognition of Aborigines as a collectivity by the Commonwealth government is limited both in the scope of autonomy associated with self-determination and the overall allocations of resources provided for communities. Where the particularity of Aboriginal concerns in the Macleay Valley have been acknowledged, it is in a manner unlikely to threaten overall policy. Similarly, in education, the vast majority of Aboriginal children of school age in 1980–81 were incorporated into the local state school system. At the secondary school level, there were 106 Aboriginal children in a school population of 1,150 pupils.

In general, government policy has facilitated the incorporation of Aboriginal children into the local school system rather than exclude them which had previously been the policy. The Commission of Inquiry into Poverty (1977) found that 42.5 per cent of Aborigines over fifteen years in 1967 had not been educated beyond primary school level (Altman and Nieuwenhuysen 1979, 121) which reflected the level of education that had been attainable in state-controlled segregated schools on reserves in the past. Rowley's studies of country towns in New South Wales reveal a marked improvement in the formal attainments of Aborigines within the state school system. In 1965, only 13.4 per cent of Aborigines over fifteen years remained at school, while in 1980 the figure had reached 35 per cent (cited in Young 1982, 16). Such government practices were politically motivated to achieve equality of opportunity and sought a more equitable distribution of Aborigines throughout the social hierarchy of the dominant society.

In the contemporary context, government policy has predominantly addressed the individual needs of children. In Kempsey, Aboriginal teacher aides are employed to ease the problems of those who find difficulty in fitting into an overwhelmingly European context. Similarly, special grants are provided to improve the educational performance and credentials of individual Aborigines by encouraging them to remain at school. (The Aborigines Secondary Grants Scheme provided students attending high schools with a text book and uniform allowance of $2.50 a week in 1980.) Such policies have sought to redress the significant quantitative differences between Aborigines and Europeans. (The corresponding figure for non-Aboriginal children remaining at secondary high school is 56 per cent, see Young 1982, 16.)

For example, a government spokesman in Kempsey had this to say (talkback radio, Kempsey, 1980):

> The reason why we have special measures for Aboriginal children is that for over the past 100 years or so they have fallen so far behind the white community in general. If you ever look at the statistics, I think one Aborigine became a lawyer, none ever became a doctor, none became a dentist, engineer, few became teachers and so on. That's a situation a modern country like Australia cannot continue to have...The governments, both state and federal, have decided to try and give some opportunities, not handouts or favours, to Aboriginal kids.

Such policies gain their importance as an atonement for past policies rather than necessarily enhancing self-determination. The concern expressed here is with the quantitative differences between Aborigines and non-Aborigines.

What needs to be stressed is that the individualising logic of bureaucratic intervention that is fostered also takes the form of voluntaristic solutions to an 'Aboriginal problem'. The solution sought in improved education or better job training is to increase individuals' bargaining power in the job market through improved educational credentials and/or job skills. Education is understood in terms of an instrumental or means/end logic—its transformative potentials translated as an individual acquisition. The determination of such individualistic and voluntaristic remedies is not only contained in the content of such knowledge and skills but also in the structures of the pedagogic practices which impart knowledge as an individual rather than collective acquisition. For it is the performance of each individual which is evaluated and ranked according to individual abilities to conform to a set of normative standards. The pedagogic procedures focus upon the individual attainment of formal qualifications which may benefit individual Aborigines in gaining employment.

By contrast, the only government program which provided local Aboriginal groups with autonomy from the state school system, was the funding of a mini-bus to take young boys to bush locations to educate them in the knowledge of traditional bush skills. (This will be discussed more fully later.) While a cultural and educational program was also established, it was as part of the state school system. During the short term of its funding (two years), the program produced spin-offs for the community through the participation it generated. Nevertheless, the principle was to collect information about 'traditional culture' for inclusion into the local primary school curriculum. In short then, the overwhelming involvement of Aborigines in the Macleay

Valley was in the universal structures of the dominant society. Qualitative differences had been given a partial recognition and a subordinate role in overall policy.

The economic and political dimensions of welfare colonialism reveal only a limited recognition of Aborigines as a collectivity. At an ideological level, the same is also the case. In general terms, through multiculturalism, the state attempts to create the institutional and social spaces in which divergent cultural forms can be given complementary expression within the state. The emphasis on cultural differences signals that we are dealing with deviations from the dominant Anglo-Australian core culture. As Neuwirth (1969) has pointed out in the North American context, such labelling discloses that members of the core culture continue to monopolise certain kinds of political and economic power and their ethnic values constitute the norm. The dominant cultural forms are valorised as universal rather than historically and culturally relative. In this respect, the concessions implicit in the ideological structuring of such relations legitimates the existing order and perpetuates its dominance.

In the absence of any relativising of the dominant culture, fictional notions of equivalence mask inequality. Cultural pluralism represents culture as a reified form which exists outside power relations. It is, as Bauman (1985, 13) suggests, a vision of a multiplicity of equivalent cultures after the pattern of the market place. This relativising of values does reflect an ideological break from assimilation models, which upheld the privileged and absolute values of the dominant society and its educative (civilising) role. The valorisation of the institutional forms of the dominant society as universal structures reveals the partial recognition that notions of cultural equivalence mask. Earlier discussion of the individualising and voluntaristic solutions provided for Aborigines in education policies highlights the fact that they are cultural rather than simple political solutions to the 'Aboriginal problem'. In addition, it draws attention to the role of such institutions in reproducing the cultural norms of the dominant society. The individualising strategies of pedagogic practices and the constructions of knowledge in terms of a means/end logic manifested in credentialism both conform to central cultural values of the dominant society.

The definition of culture used here refers to a general process of externalisation or objectification of all human activity into cultural forms. In this, cultural forms, are understood, not only in terms of concepts and beliefs, but also of their objectification in practices, institutions and forms of speech, gesture and behaviour. By contrast, the representation of Aboriginal culture in the culture and education program and elsewhere reproduces it in a fetishised form—culture presented as an aspect of the past separated out from everyday existence. The accent on 'traditional' culture suspends contemporary cultural forms, privileging those of the past. To push the point further, such separation aestheticises Aboriginal culture into an essentialist form.

As it aestheticises 'deviant' cultures, cultural pluralism dehistoricises. The particularity of Aboriginal social and historical experience, conquest, domination and loss of sovereignty, is reduced to a recognition of a reified and restricted notion of cultural particularity. This decontextualised Aboriginality is removed from the contemporary experience of Aborigines in New South Wales—a contemporary experience which includes an interpretation of the recent past. Nevertheless, such an aestheticisation constructs a form of Aboriginal particularity which is compatible with the new nationalism of multiculturalism.[9] That is, the state appropriates it as a unique aspect of the 'ancient history' of the national heritage which separates Australia from other nations.

The cultural pluralist production of the past by the state provides for the ideological incorporation of Aborigines. The conflation of culture as history or history as culture mystifies the historical relations of domination by replacing them with cultural representations of Aborigines in an essentialist form which exists outside of time and space. In effect, the legislative guarantees of cultural pluralism provide for expressions of 'ethnic difference' at the same time as they enable the state to control and centralise the constructions of these symbolic representations. It is not so much access to knowledge but rather the production of knowledge itself that constitutes this hegemonic form of power. In the following, I will consider some of the contradictions that emerge in the application of such policies.

The politics of identity

For the Dhan-gadi, an understanding of the past and its uses is derived not only from the immediate contingencies of government policies but also from the meanings and values generated by their own forms of knowledge and experience. The oppositional forms that expressions of collective identity assume can be made apparent if we consider the meanings attributed by Dhan-gadi people to notions of a separate heritage. This is not simply expressed in terms of cultural equivalence, but in opposition to it. The stress in the political rhetoric of cultural pluralism upon equivalence reduces the particularity of Aboriginal culture to one among a multiplicity of cultures recognised by the state. For the Dhan-gadi, the meaning of a separate heritage was one which differentiates them from all other members of society because it pre-existed European occupation. The focus on being the original inhabitants provides a form of resistance to the globalising aspects of cultural pluralism.[10] This was made apparent to me at a meeting discussing Aboriginal education held in Kempsey, where a hapless education officer was praising the more enlightened attitude to ethnic groups in the school system. He was immediately challenged by a woman who stated that Aborigines were not an ethnic group but the original inhabitants. The dangers inherent in the recognition of ethnic groups by the state is that such cultural equivalence threatens to subsume the historical particularities of Aboriginal existence. For Aborigines in the Macleay Valley, cultural pluralism has generated a process of ethnogenesis. This process has been defined by Diamond (1974, 23) as 'the generating of new forms of social life—dialectically related to the spirit, but not duplicating the letter of the past'. Cultural pluralism has provided the basic conditions for Aborigines to articulate a more sharply defined cultural identity through their dealings with state apparatuses, such as legal, medical or housing systems. At the same time this is heightened by the political necessity of differentiating themselves from other ethnic groups. Elements of the past are drawn upon to assert this distinctiveness. For example, as a locally produced Aboriginal magazine (*Bread and Wine* 1981) states, '*The Aboriginal people have retained the spiritual values of our Dreamtime; togetherness and sharing is still a natural part of our lives; but we no longer share our campfires, only our micro-wave ovens!!!*' Continuity with the past is stressed here as the unifying source of identity. Social identity is preserved in the perpetuation of inner values, untouched by a material world largely shaped and dominated by a European presence. In this context, the symbolism of the Dreaming evokes an identification with values that pre-existed and survived the impositions of the new sovereign order.

At the same time, the importance of maintaining a distinctive social identity is expressed in terms of regaining what has been lost and a need to get back to earlier and superior forms of social life. For a number of people this was to be achieved by what was spoken of as a 'cultural renascence' through the revival of the initiation ceremonies. During the period of my research, the surviving initiated men were placed under increasing pressure to put the young men 'through the rule'. In effect, the demand was for a more conspicuous and institutionalised expression of cultural distinctiveness which characterises the assertiveness now attached to public aspects of collective identity. For young men, a return to the integrity of Dhan-gadi identity is to be achieved through the revival of such ceremonies.[11]

Another expression of this was the purchasing of the mini-bus, through government funding, to transport young boys to bush sites. Ostensibly, the excursions were to facilitate the transfer of skills and knowledge related to bush foods, in a formal context, from older men to young boys. The meaning of such a practice was conceived to extend beyond the mere transfer of technically usable knowledge. Indeed, the learning of bush skills was simultaneously equated with the acquiring of men's esoteric knowledge. The absence of women from such excursions, particularly in a social domain where they would normally have been included, emphasised that the transfer of knowledge involved both secular and esoteric forms of knowledge restricted to men. This involved the young boys in learning what was called 'men's dancing' which included public performances but also the acquisition of 'inside knowledge'.

The 'revival' of the past was not unproblematic. Such a revival was not universally approved of within the community. For some, it was felt better to 'leave it alone'. However, this concern was not so much determined by a desire to forget or turn away from the past, but a recognition that one is dealing with dangerous mystical forces.[12] The past in this context, is not a lifeless ensemble of habits, beliefs and artefacts. The transfer of knowledge 'not for women's eyes' involves an engagement with mystical forces which is potentially dangerous for those participating. In this respect, the capacity and the expertise of those in authority was a major point of discussion—that is, their capacity and expertise to manipulate and constrain such forces for the safety of those involved and perhaps the community in general.

The significance is that the excursions reflected organisational principles and engaged forms of knowledge different from the pedagogic practices of the state. These principles were premised on differential, rather than universal, access to knowledge. In addition, the participation of those in the mini-bus excursions reflected differential selection based upon the mobilisation of kinship and other social affiliations. The same was also the case for those seeking the revival of the initiation ceremonies. By contrast, the state practices are associated with universal access to knowledge embedded within a cultural logic which assumes the equivalence of individuals as independent units. Concomitantly, such knowledges realise their full potential in one's ability to mobilise them in a strategising manner or, more generally, as technically usable knowledge.[13] The efficacy of knowledge is constituted as a resource and chiefly conceived within a cultural logic associated with instrumental or purposive rationalism. Social differentiation is linked to a model based upon the strategising individual. The constitution of knowledge, as referred to above for the Dhan-gadi, realises its full potential in the ability to differentiate between the 'illusory' and 'truth', which is determined by the possession of secret knowledges.[14] The perpetuation of the possession of exclusive understandings determines the organisation of knowledge and provides a significant basis for social differentiation.

These social activities are marginal in terms of overall government policy. Their importance is that they reveal difference in a context where the Dhan-gadi themselves exercise a large degree of control. In them, we are dealing with cultural differences objectified in a relatively unmediated context. There is an objectification of internal differentiation that reveals a structure of shared assumptions. It is difference rather than opposition to the organisational forms of the state that is expressed here. Yet, the distinction between difference and opposition is never complete. That such practices occur in the breach rather than as the rule directs attention to the hegemonic nature of cultural pluralism.

Conversely, the oppositional practices of the process of ethnogenesis are produced within this structural relationship which draws attention to an essential feature of ethnogenesis—the regaining of control over the production of knowledge of one's own cultural and political identity. By definition, this requires the establishment of some form of social closure (see Neuwirth 1969, Dolgin and Magdoff 1977). Commonality is established through the identification of a special relationship between specific social practices and values and a collective notion of self. The concepts of group and person are metonymised.

In this context, bush tucker has gained a greater significance. Previously, the effects of domination had rendered problematical what Europeans called 'dirty blackfella food'. Even today, this legacy is revealed in the ambiguous way people will delight in describing the eating of different bush foods while reassuring me (a European) as to how clean such cooking is. Nevertheless, despite these problematical vestiges, bush tucker is one of the sources for the demarcation of a distinctive identity. Thus, the community bus was purchased to teach young boys, among other things, knowledge and skills related to bush foods. Ideologically, what is reaffirmed through such practices is a special relationship expressed in terms of access to, and control and understanding of, a body of knowledge and skills not available to others. In effect, those capable of participating and understanding such a relationship are also differentiated. The reintroduction of young boys, in a formal context, to such practices gains new significance as an important aspect of the reclamation of identity.

This is often extended further in assertions that 'whitefella food' is a big problem affecting Dhan-gadi people. It is said that Dhan-gadi men, for example, were bigger and stronger in the past because they were healthier through bush foods. As one man put it, 'You only gotta look at the mens in them days, women (too) all big. I tell em today they're not worth looking at, they're skinny. Since they got on the white man's food, they went to pieces.' The body is used here as a metonym of the social condition of the Dhan-gadi.[15] Central to such ideological statements is the relationship between food and a collective notion of self. The relationship asserted here is between culturally specific items of food and the images of the Dhan-gadi themselves.

The ethnogenesis of the Dhan-gadi is indicative of a major shift in the politics of opposition. For the major part of this century, expressions of Aboriginality have been a distinct social and political disadvantage. Previously, the political opposition of Aborigines has been constructed in terms of the political idioms of the dominant society, that is appeals to egalitarianism based on equal rights or human rights. Such a political response sought to expose the hypocrisy of the dominant society by challenging it in the context of its own ideology. The distinguishing feature of opposition in the contemporary context is contained within the overt expressions of a collective identity drawn from a common past and associated with a distinctive social identity. The increasing awareness and increasing articulation of separate origins signifies a determination to gain control over their own cultural and social identity.

The legitimacy of their right to speak and articulate their own experiences underpins an increasing awareness of the politics of identity. The metonymic connection of Dhan-gadi identity with a specialised body of knowledge in effect denies Europeans the capacity to gain authentic access to, and understanding of, matters Aboriginal. The oppositional aspect of the politics of identity is directly linked to the politics of representation itself. Such a cultural politics moves away from the redistributive politics of equal rights and egalitarianism to the politics of difference. The emergence of the politics of culture is linked to what Jameson (1984) has called the struggle of the 'inner colonised'—indigenous minorities, ethnic groups, deviants, other marginals and in a different sense women. I would argue, following Foucault (1980), it is precisely those groups and individuals who have been subjected intensely to the gaze of experts and authorities and, hence, to modes of objectification outside their control. Domination constituted, not necessarily through restrictions of access to knowledge, but control of the production of knowledge itself; that is, through the establishment of a hierarchy which denies the legitimacy of such groups to speak for themselves except through some mediated form.

Fundamentally, the assertions of a distinctive identity provide a challenge to those forms of hegemonic power. The rejection of the validity of constructions of identity by others is not simply a question of understanding, but, more specifically, a rejection of the forms of control that such objectifications sustain. As Aborigines in Kempsey pointed out, they did not want to be studied 'like animals' or 'like plants in a green house' or, stated more directly, 'you are here to steal our secrets'. These statements refer to the relations of power associated with being turned into an object of knowledge. An explicit connection is seen to be made between Aborigines and lesser forms of life, for example like animals and plants. Perhaps, more importantly, what is identified is a relationship in which they lose control of their own identity. Thus, the politics of identity is an expression of resistance to attempts to make Aborigines experience themselves in the terms defined by the dominant society.

The politics of cultural pluralism have generated two conflicting processes. At the same time as the state attempts to encourage expressions of cultural distinctiveness, it also attempts to centralise and control them by demarcating particular institutional sites for their expression. Nevertheless, they provide a focus for notions of separate identity which exist beyond those constructed by the state.

This is evident in the development of the major issue of the late 1970s for Aboriginal groups—land rights. Land rights legislation opened up new sites for the development of major political concerns. In 1977, for example, an Aboriginal Land Council was formed in New South Wales to struggle for the recognition of land rights there (see Wilkie 1985). It was an independent body organised and controlled by Aborigines and open to all Aboriginal communities. Its formation followed closely the granting of land rights to groups in the Northern Territory, in the previous year.

Between 1977 and 1981, the Land Council received ten land claims from regional groups to submit to the New South Wales government (see Aboriginal Land Council in New South Wales 1981). Furthermore, the claims for land rights were outside the ambit of the Commonwealth legislation which required demonstrable evidence of comprehensive religious links with the land as the sole criterion (see Maddock 1983). The report of the New South Wales Parliamentary Committee on Aboriginal Land Rights (1980, 62) recommended four bases for claims to land: 'needs (spiritual, social and economic); compensation (both monetary and land); long association; and traditional rights'. The boundaries established for land rights under Commonwealth legislation were redefined and expanded within these recommendations. Therefore the cultural pluralist environment has also led to the empowerment of the political practices of Aboriginal groups and facilitated the process of ethnogenesis.

The state, through its attempts to control the construction of Aboriginality, has also provided an arena in which such ideological constructions can be contested. As stated earlier, the ideological aspect of cultural pluralism is found in the mystification of historical relations between Aborigines and the dominant society. In the 'plagiarised' expressions of Aboriginal culture, they are 'assimilated' as 'cultural/historical' figures who symbolically represent the 'ancient heritage' of the modern Australian nation. Aborigines are given a unique place in the new nationalism associated with multicultural Australia.

In the final section of this chapter, I will turn to some of the processes that facilitate the production of Aborigines in this symbolic form and a series of contradictions which emerged in relation to their application to Aboriginal communities. The complexities of this interplay can be seen in the relations that developed between the Aborigines and the National Parks and Wildlife Service (NPWS) in the early 1980s. Under the National Parks and Wildlife Act (1974), this agency was empowered to administer the Act and identify, record and protect Aboriginal places of significance and relics. The control, protection and acquisition (if deemed necessary) remained in the hands of the Director of National Parks and Wildlife (Act No 80, 57). Such relics were 'deemed to be the property of the crown' and the Director was empowered to take legal action against those who disturbed or removed them (Act No 80, 75–79). In effect, the intention of the state was to record, protect and preserve those remaining features of an Aboriginal heritage as an aspect of the state's history. An important aspect of this, based on an initiative of the NPWS is the identification of sacred sites primarily as artefacts or relics of an Aboriginal heritage. The polity implemented was to fence off such sites and to erect public signs to explain their significance for Aborigines, as well as the penalties that would be incurred for interference, destruction or removal (Act No 80, 78).

I should stress that the Act provided the only legislation for the protection of such sites and artefacts of significance identified by Aborigines in New South Wales (see Haigh nd). Perhaps the most widely known success of the NPWS was the protection of sites at Mumbler Mountain in southern New South Wales which were under threat from the encroachments of an international wood chipping operation (see Egloff 1979). The NPWS was a significant force in the protection of important Aboriginal sites. As an institution, NPWS was equally important in the role it performed in the active recruitment of Aborigines to participate in this work. Through its policies of protection and participation it provided both a focus and a stimulus to a developing sense of identity among many Aboriginal communities. However, what I am concerned with here are the ideological frames in which the legislation operates. The terms for the protection and preservation of the Aboriginal heritage are couched in the cultural logic of the dominant society. In the first place, the sites, as well as other relics, are conceived in the legislation to be worthy of control so that they might survive to be appreciated by all members of the state and succeeding generations.[16] Underpinning this understanding of the sites is a particular secular/temporal understanding which reduces them to historical artefacts. This same importance and meaning is seen to be commensurate with those held by Aborigines in New South Wales as is implicit in the notion of heritage, the legislation operates in terms of dealing with things of the past.

For initiated men, both Dhan-gadi and Gumbaingirr, the control and access to such sites posed a major dilemma. As one man put it,

> In the old days we looked after our sacred sites ourselves without letting white people, white men and white women taking care of them. We know what to do and that's why I always say they should never interfere with our sacred things. If there were a lot of things that weren't sacred that's alright for them to go and see. Kiddies of ours, even young men, we wouldn't let them go past our sacred sites, trees even, that was anywhere in the bush or sacred site rocks. We wouldn't let em go because they wasn't men. They had to be initiated before they could go to these things and they are sacred to us, very sacred things. We don't say nothing to anybody because we look after these things ourselves. That's why we don't like white women or white men coming to ask different things about our things or they should do this or that...That's our sacred places. Our young people, young men, they should never be there either because it's not right. It's not right at all. They should be all initiated before they get the job on the Parks and Wildlife to do these jobs.

In effect, the dilemma arose out of conceptions of access markedly different from those framed in the legislation. Different access to the sites was counterposed to egalitarian access in the legislation. Indeed, the practices of the NPWS in fencing off and signposting such sites are constituted in notions of public, egalitarian access. For these Aboriginal men, however, the principle is one of restricted and differential access as such sites are part of a body of secret-sacred knowledge. They distinguish between members within the Aboriginal community as well as white men and women.

Authority and care of such sites is conditional on control of a particular body of knowledge gained through initiation ceremonies. Such sacred sites are not invested simply with a secular historical significance but are associated with mystical sanctions and mystical powers. They do not symbolically represent a past heritage but are sites where mystical power resides in a concretised form. As one man put it, 'you can't act the goat with our law, it'll kill you'. This statement was made in the course of discussing a transgression of ritual in an earlier period, when, it was asserted, a young initiated had violated eating taboos. In this, he had eaten a wild turkey in defiance of ritual sanctions—in the result 'feathers and bones came out his knees'. The ritual sanction is conceptualised here in terms of an analogical transfer of properties attributed to the agency of mystical force. Such analogical thought reflected the retention of a more anthropomorphic view of the world in which all elements 'are bound up in a world of efficacy' (Cassirer 1955, 157).

The influence of this mystical connection, where analogical thought and action are evident, is apparent in the case of an Aboriginal man who developed cancer while recording sites for the NPWS. It was said that this was due to his work on sacred sites which were too powerful for him. The logic of the construction of the illness was connected with an analogical transfer through direct contact with such sites. What emerges here are forms of knowledge and understanding of the social world that differ significantly from those that prevail.

It is not contended that this apprehension of reality in itself provides an independent and homogeneous world view which sustains a clear cut distinction between the Dhan-gadi and the wider society. The causal relationship between mystical agency and illness and death is no longer held as a totalising world view. Indeed, the effectivity of mystical agency is seen to be active largely upon those participating in the now specialised and restricted domain of religious activities. Generally, illness in everyday life is considered to be a pathological condition of the body as it is in the wider society; but, as in the specific case above, it can still be considered to be causally related to an independent object associated with a mystical agency which may enter and damage the body. The perception of social relations and the classification of social experience retain distinctive differences which form the basis of an essential contradiction. Such a perception of the world stands in direct contrast to the secular and historical view which underpins the state's appropriation of Dhan-gadi sacred sites.

These cultural forms condition opposition to the hegemonic appropriations of Aboriginal history and heritage. The processes of cultural incorporation serve to heighten an Aboriginal sense of identity which challenges rather than utilises the conventional political idioms of the state. The conscious articulation of a collective social and cultural history stresses the uniqueness and particularity of Aboriginal identity which had pre-existed European occupation. As one man stated to me,

> before the white people came over here from pommie land or England...to come and take over our country, they (Aborigines) carried on as before they (Europeans)

ever came across here. They (Aborigines) carried out business in their own way. They did it properly...It all belong the Aborigines of Australia. You fellas, the white fellas, have come here and tell us what to do, do it this way and do it that way.

What is stressed is the contradiction that their dispossession, domination and loss of sovereignty provided the foundation for the development of the modern state. By locating the 'otherness' of Aborigines within its own institutional sites, the state has attempted to contain and control the possible sites and expressions of otherness. They have also provided new areas of struggle in the construction of identity which resist such hegemonic relations of power.

Notes

1. I wish to acknowledge my debt to a number of Dhan-gadi and Gumbaingirr people for their patience and guidance: J.D. Quinlan, E.M. Davis, C. Campbell, R. Campbell, J. Kelly, R. Kelly and L. de Silva.
2. I am endebted to Chris Charles for drawing my attention to Detmold's excellent discussion of the constitutional aspects of the status of Aborigines.
3. This is especially the case between 1945 and 1978 when the number of employees in the New South Wales Public Service changed from 30,315 (including teachers) to 77,000 (excluding teachers): an average increase of 4.33 per cent per year (Regional Development and Employment Prospects, Part II, 1978, 269). See also Encel who provides employment figures for the 'administrative revolution' of both Commonwealth and state bureaucracies between 1939 and 1959 (1962, 219-20).
4. As Brown (1984) has pointed out, there is a distinct analogy between racist ideologies with their emphasis on inherent biological factors and interpretations of 'ethnicity' associated with inherent cultural forms. The moral underpinning that ethnicity provides in Aboriginal policy may be seen in the functioning of the Land Rights Act (Northern Territory) 1976. Access to land is regulated by (1) a demonstrable traditional link to the land; and (2) its being unoccupied crown land (land not utilised by Europeans). The legislation enshrines a static view of culture which at the same time, dehistoricises the colonial context rather than a relational and processual one.
5. The government remained firmly committed to the assimilation policy. As the Minister for Immigration stated, 'We must have a single culture. If migration implies multicultural activities within Australian society, then it was not the type Australia wanted. I am quite determined we should have a monoculture with everyone living in the same way, understanding each other and sharing the same aspirations. We do not want pluralism' (cited in Kalantis, Cope and Hughes 1984-85, 195).
6. The terms are drawn from Detmold. As he points out, 'legitimacy is not the same thing as validity. To say a law is valid implies that it is authorised by a higher law. Legitimacy

relates to the highest law, the point where no question of validity can arise: the ultimate power of the Commonwealth is not valid but legitimate...Lawyers, quite at home with questions of validity, are often uneasy when questions of legitimacy are canvassed. *Such questions are political in the strictest sense; that is, they are concerned with the power of apolis (or Commonwealth, to use our word)*' (1985, 49, emphasis added). The issues that have received the most anthropological interest, not unnaturally, have been questions which concern Aboriginal local organisation or land tenure. They have followed largely from the impact upon anthropology of the *Gove Land Case* (1971) and the Land Rights Act (1976) (see among many others Gumbert 1981, Maddock 1983, Keen 1984 and more recently Williams 1986). The questions that are primarily raised are those of recognition in terms of validity within the existing legal system. By contrast, the same attention to the political implications of the *Coe v Commonwealth* case (1979), which deals directly with the question of legitimacy, as yet has not occurred.

7. The significant legislation passed in the 1970s included the Aboriginal Loans Commission Act (1974) which enabled a statutory commission to advance loans for Aboriginal business enterprises; the Aboriginal Land Fund Act which allowed corporations and Aboriginal land trusts to acquire land; the Aboriginal Councils and Associations Act (1976) which provided for Aboriginal community councils and Aboriginal associations (non-profit or business enterprises), see Hanks 1984, 25. The other significant legislation was the Aboriginal Land Rights (Northern Territory) Act (1976).

8. Several authors have written on the development and the consequences of the land rights movement (see especially Maddock, 1983).

9. The most explicit expression of this 'new nationalism' was made by the Prime Minister in 1982. As he stated, 'We cannot demand of people that they renounce the heritage they value, and yet expect them to feel welcome as full members of our society ...Multiculturalism...sees diversity as a quality to be actively embraced, a source of social wealth and dynamism...The (Galbally) report (has) identified multiculturalism as a key concept in formulating government policies and recognized that Australia is at a critical stage in the development as a multicultural nation' (cited in Kalantis, Cope and Hughes 1984–85, 195–96).

10. This opposition to the globalising aspects of multiculturalism is also reflected at a state-wide level in the non-participation of Aboriginal groups in the annual folkloric festival. The festival is held in Sydney and symbolically expresses the ethnic diversity of Australian culture. It is celebrated in a parade that winds its way through the streets of Sydney where different national/cultural origins are displayed through music, dance and dress.

11. No initiation ceremonies were held during the period of my fieldwork. However, in late 1985, after a fifty year break, such a ceremony was held.

12. Another example of this was expressed to me in an anecdotal story about a man living in the community whose father had been a 'cleva fella'. When his father had died his 'dilly' bag' containing dangerous substances used in sorcery had been hung over his grave. His son had never ventured near it fearing the harm it would do him.

13. This is commonly reflected in discussions about the desirability of education for

Aborigines to increase their bargaining power in the job market or to improve their job skills. Lippmann's (1981, 148) discussion of the transformative potential of education is an example of this logic. As she states, 'The number of years of formal education does not necessarily equip one with "success" from an individual's standpoint, but a lack of adequate schooling takes away the choice of life-style to which all Australians should be entitled. Knowledge is political and adds to the power of those who hold it: the insights which it brings can be translated, where desired, into action.'

14. I draw this point from a communication by Andrew Lattas to me. He is currently engaged in research in New Guinea in which he is concerned with the constitution of knowledge principally in the area of gender relations. The issue he raises is in terms of forms of knowledge which are constituted in a processual hierarchy, differentiating between those who possess an understanding and control of the 'truth' as opposed to lesser and hence more illusory forms of knowledge. It seems pertinent to me and to Aboriginal studies as well. It needs a more extensive elaboration than has been possible here.

15. See Carter (1983) for a more comprehensive development of the use of the body as a metaphor of Aboriginal identity in another New South Wales community.

16. It should be noted that the Head of the Aboriginal and Historical Resources Unit of the NPWS has recently made a similar point. As she stated, 'We consider that we should remove the word "relic" from the Act. It denotes culture no longer exists and belies the fact of Aboriginal culture today' (cited in Wilkie 1985, 103).

References

Aboriginal Land Council
1981 *Land Claims in New South Wales*, New South Wales Aboriginal Land Council, Sydney.

Altman, J. and J. Nieuwenhuysen
1979 *The Economic Status of Australian Aborigines*, Cambridge University Press, Cambridge.

Bauman, Z.
1985 On the Origins of Civilization: A Historical Note, *Theory, Culture and Society* 2(3), 7–14.

Beckett, J.
1983 Internal Colonialism in a Welfare State, Paper Presented at American Anthropological Association, Chicago.

Brown, K.
1984 A Bad Year for Avocados: Blainey and Immigration, *Arena* 67, 70–77.

Carter, J.
1983 The Body: Source of Mediation in Aboriginal Identity, Paper Presented at AAS Conference, Adelaide.

Cassirer, E.
1955 *The Philosophy of Symbolic Forms, Mythical Thought*, Volume 2, Yale University Press, London.

Collmann, J.
1979 Fringe Camps and the Development of Aboriginal Administration in Central Australia, *Social Analysis* 2, 38–57.

Department of Decentralisation and Development
1978 *Regional Development and Employment Prospects*, Part II, New South Wales North Coast

Region, New South Wales Government Printer, Sydney.

Detmold, M.
1985 *The Australian Commonwealth*, The Law Book Company, Sydney.

Diamond, S.
1974 *In Search of the Primitive*, Transactional Books, New Brunswick.

Dolgin, J. and J. Magdoff
1977 The Invisible Event. In J. Dolgin, D. Kemnitzer and D. Schneider (eds), *Symbolic Anthropology*, Columbia University Press, New York.

Egloff, B.
1979 *Mumbulla Mountain: An Anthropological and Archaeological Investigation*, New South Wales Government Printer, Sydney.

Encel, S.
1962 Power. In P. Coleman (ed), *Australian Civilization*, F.W. Cheshire, Sydney.

Foucault, M.
1977 The Political Function of the Intellectual, *Radical Philosophy* 17, 12–14.
1980 Intellectuals and Power. In D. Bouchard (ed), *Language, Countermemory, Practice: Selected Essays and Interviews*, Cornell University Press, Ithaca.

Gumbert, M.
1981 Paradigm Lost: An Analysis of Anthropological Models and Their Effect on Aboriginal Land Rights, *Oceania* 52(2), 103–23.

Haigh, C.
nd Some Special Aboriginal Sites. In NPWS (ed), *The Aborigines of New South Wales*, National Parks and Wildlife Service, Sydney.

Hanks, P.
1984 Aborigines and Government: The Developing Framework. In P. Hanks, and B. Keon-Cohen, *Aborigines and the Law*, Allen and Unwin, Sydney.

Howard, M.
1980 Aboriginal Land Rights: The Selling of Australia, *ARC Newsletter* 4(4), 1.
1981 *Aboriginal Politics in South Western Australia*, University of Western Australia Press, Nedlands.
1982 Aboriginal Brokerage and Political Development. In M. Howard (ed), *Aboriginal Power in Australian Society*, University of Queensland Press, St Lucia.

Jameson, F.
1984 Periodising the 60's. In S. Sayres, A. Stephanson, S. Aronwitz and F. Jameson (eds), *The 60's Without Apology*, University of Minnesota Press, Minneapolis.

Kalantis, M., B. Cope and C. Hughes
1984–85 Pluralism and Social Reform: A Review of Multi-culturalism in Australian Education, *Thesis Eleven* 10/11, 195–215.

Keen, I.
1984 A Question of Interpretation: The Definition of 'Traditional Aboriginal Owners' in the Aboriginal Land Rights (NT) Act. In L. Hiatt (ed), *Aboriginal Landowners*, Oceania Monograph 27, 24-25.

Lippman, L.
1981 *Generations of Resistance: The Aboriginal Struggle for Justice*, Longman Cheshire, Melbourne.

Maddock, K.J.
1983 *Your Land in Our Land*, Penguin, Harmondsworth.

Martin, J.
1978 *The Migrant Presence*, George Allen and Unwin, Sydney.

Morris, B.
1985 *The Deregulation of a Colonial Being:*

Aborigines as 'Universal Man', Sydney Association for Studies in Society and Culture Conference, University of Sydney.
1986 The Dhan-gadi and the Protection of the State, PhD thesis, University of Sydney.

Neuwirth, G.
1969 A Weberian Outline of a Theory of Community: Its Application to 'Dark Ghetto', *British Journal of Sociology* XX(2), 148–63.

Paine, R.
1977 *The White Arctic*, Newfoundland Social and Economic Papers No 7, University of Toronto Press, Newfoundland.

Parliament of New South Wales
1980 *Aboriginal Land Rights and Sacred Sites*, First Report from the Select Committee of the Legislative Assembly upon Aborigines, New South Wales Government Printer, Sydney.

Peterson, N.
1982 Aboriginal Land Rights in the Northern Territory of Australia. In E. Leacock and R. Lee (eds), *Politics and History in Band Societies*, Cambridge University Press, Cambridge.

Wilkie, M.
1985 *Aboriginal Land Rights in New South Wales*, APCOL, Chippendale.

Williams, N.
1986 *The Yolngu and Their Land*, Australian Institute of Aboriginal Studies, Canberra.

Young, E.
1982 Aboriginal Town Dwellers in New South Wales. In E. Young and E. Fisk (eds), *Town Populations*, Australian National University Press, Canberra.

6. Gillian K Cowlishaw — The materials for identity construction

In those parts of Australia which were colonised early, Aboriginal cultural identity has been forged historically in rural communities on the fringes of country towns.[1] Further, it is in these communities that most Aboriginal political leaders have been nurtured. An Aboriginal representative's legitimacy depends to some extent on the relationship with such communities. However, the 'grass roots' people are hidden from the public eye and excluded from the dominant discourse on Aboriginal issues by a wealth of political verbiage and media comment. It is important therefore to distinguish these Aboriginal communities from the dominant images of so called 'traditional' Aborigines and also from the white society in which they are embedded. Here we find Aboriginal traditions which were developed during this century in response to remarkable social conditions, out of sight of all except their immediate neighbours and the Aborigines Protection Board. Since about 1970 marked changes in their conditions have created a new strategic problem for Aborigines concerning their cultural identity.

First, I want to describe something of the kind of traditions being discussed. Rather than an ethnography of an Aboriginal community in New South Wales, I shall sketch what I believe to be the material conditions under which such communities have constructed their identity. Thus presenting a way of understanding cultural dynamics which can be used at least for rescuing such communities from the popular misconception that they have lost their culture.

Aborigines have been conceptualised in very different ways at different periods in Australia's history. For many years the dominant images were of savages, noble or ignoble. Later, when anthropologists took over the defining, Aborigines became people with kinship and ceremonies or tribal remnants who had lost their culture (cf Elkin 1935). Recent political changes have meant that Aboriginal voices now challenge all such characterisations. These challenges are based on the principle that Aboriginal identity can only be determined and promulgated by Aborigines, and that it must encompass all Aborigines throughout Australia. The 'grass roots' communities are remote from these challenges.

The conscious and explicit presentation of an identity in the public arena, which seems to be a necessary part of political unity, poses serious problems. Aborigines have drawn on a number of themes from their past, but ignored others. Forty thousand years of history and spiritual links with the land gain a more sympathetic hearing than accusations of past injustices and displaying of old wounds received in the struggle for equality. The traditions of 'fringe dwellers' lack the prestige associated with the more distant past. But it is my view that in underplaying the more recent cultural history as a basis for identity, a major source of political energy is being denied.

Dominant public images are complex and changing, particularly in the political arena (as shown by Jacobs and Beckett in Chapters 3 and 12), but some themes and conflicts may be better understood if they are linked to the rural background. The example of a town in western New South Wales illustrates processes which have occurred in similar ways elsewhere.[2] The history of relations between the state's Aborigines and the wider society are not well known even to many Aborigines,[3] yet it is this past that has been a crucial factor determining the focus of Aboriginal culture in New South Wales.

Eric Wolf (1982, 18) has taken anthropologists to task for ignoring the history of those people they want to create as 'pristine replicas of the precapitalist, preindustrial past in the sinks and margins of the capitalist industrial world'. He is not simply asking that we include history as a quantitative addition to studies of Aboriginal peoples. Rather he is proposing a different, dynamic account of culture (1982, 387):

> In the rough and tumble of social interaction, groups are known to exploit the ambiguities of inherited forms, to impart new evaluations or valences to them, to borrow forms more expressive of their interests, or to create wholly new forms to answer to changed circumstances. Furthermore if we think of such interaction not as causative on its own terms but as responsive to larger economic and political forces, the explanation of cultural forms must take account of that larger context, that wider field of force. 'A culture' is thus better seen as a series of processes that construct, reconstruct and dismantle cultural determinants.

Genovese (1975, 72) also argues that groups are not passive carriers of culture. He stresses the political implications of an oppressed people's culture:

> culture is ever changing. In one of its decisive aspects it serves oppressed people as a strategy for survival through the organisation of daily life. As such it is profoundly political, for it provides the essential context, both material and spiritual, from which a people forges its politics, strictly defined.

Talal Asad (1979, 619) accuses anthropologists of ignoring 'the question of how different forms of discourse come to be materially produced and maintained as authoritative systems'. He asks us to seek 'the specific political economic conditions which make certain rhetorical forms objectively possible and *authoritative*' (1979, 616).

In treating culture as ideology encapsulated in discourse, Asad forces us to pay attention to the source of the discourse. Until recently the authoritative voices on the identity of Aborigines have been those of the anthropologists, and it is the traditional culture which was the mark of that identity (Cowlishaw 1986a). That is, the dominant image and understanding of Aborigines depended on one popular usage of the term culture—that referring to the exotic practices of other societies. Thus discussion of Aboriginal culture has been largely limited to those forms which were forged in pre-colonial times, especially those related to religion and kinship and which only remain visible in the remoter parts of the continent.

Aborigines in New South Wales have nothing that the whites, or many anthropologists, will call culture. The legitimacy of Aboriginal 'fringe dwellers' as a race, as a culture and even as a category has continually been questioned by their fellow residents of country towns. Since 1970 that questioning has taken place at the same time that Aborigines as a category have been targets of government policies and public discussion. The social drama generated by this situation has attracted little analysis, though much research is still conducted with more remote Aborigines.

If we identify culture in the wider sense recommended by Wolf, Asad and Genovese, as a creative response to the conditions of existence experienced by a group, then every social grouping, including all Aborigines, have as much a culture as any other. The analysis of cultural groups then depends more on the nature of the boundaries and relations between cultural groups than on their defining characteristics. Genovese (1974, xvii), in his study of 'the world the slaves made' asserts,

> An understanding of the slaves requires some understanding of the masters and of others who helped shape a complex slave society. Masters and slaves shaped each other and cannot be discussed or analysed in isolation.

Likewise Aborigines and whites in Australian country towns cannot be seen in isolation from each other however much they want to define themselves independently. One example to set the stage is the way local historical societies present their towns' histories. They commonly celebrate the invasion of pastoralists and show great interest in old families of early settlers. No attention is paid to the history of living Aborigines, and the dusty collections of stone tools in the local museums are often accompanied by a patronising quotation from an early settler about the local tribe which once inhabited the area. In this case the denial that Aborigines are part of a town's historical development, even where they may constitute a third of the population, illustrates the hegemonic process.

The arguments presented here can be divided into three parts all of which take issue with the usual ways of talking about culture in general, and Aboriginal culture in particular. First, culture is shown to be a domain of political struggle. The narrow and controlled political economy of Aboriginal communities is the ground on which their culture has been and is still being formed. Second, I argue that Aborigines' distinctive pattern of life is, perforce, in opposition to that which dominates the wider society. The very notion of what Aborigines are has constantly been intruded upon by white authorities. The meagre material from which an Aboriginal identity could be constructed, such as a niche in the pastoral economy, has been regularly snatched away at the point where it appeared to be a solid foundation for building (cf Morris 1985, Anderson 1983, Castles and Hagan 1978). Land rights appears to be rapidly going the same way. The third part of this argument is that the oppositional culture is faced with severe challenges in the contemporary political climate where benign policies toward Aborigines are based on apparently enlightened views.

The New South Wales past

Accounts of the lives of Aborigines in rural New South Wales are so rare that the popular notions of 'dispirited remnants' and 'detribalised blacks' are entrenched. They call forth a picture of dirt and misery which has little room for real and varied groups of people living their lives out, sometimes with an intense awareness of their historical situation.

The popular metaphors of lost culture and destroyed society are misleading, stressing as they do only one part of the process of change. It is necessary to explore the active relationship between immigrants and indigenous groups, the blurring of the boundaries and the manipulation of meanings, those processes that Wolf (1982, 387) says 'construct, reconstruct and dismantle cultural determinants'. Even though Aborigines' power to manipulate meanings (status markers, evaluations etc) in an authoritative manner was severely limited, it is important to see Aboriginal reaction as a positive force, both in the creation of their own identity and as something that employers and government authorities as well as the rest of the local groups had to deal with.

The New South Wales Aborigines Protection Board was established in 1883 and from 1909 administered the Aboriginal Protection Act 1909–1963 with its various amendments (Rowley 1972, 77). The Board, reconstituted in 1940 as the Aboriginal Welfare Board, had the responsibility of solving the 'problem' of the Aborigines. Large Aboriginal communities remained in many parts of the state although the land had been mostly alienated, the population decimated and European ancestry became increasingly common. These communities were seen as nuisances and in need of control (Rowley 1972, 268). The Protection Board's 'solution' entailed interference with all aspects of the lives of those defined as Aborigines which until 1918 referred only to those defined as 'full bloods' and after that date to all with 'an admixture of Aboriginal blood'. Reserves, sometimes called missions were created and attempts were made to have all Aborigines live on them under the control of a manager. Aborigines had little freedom under the Act. If there was no staffed reserve the local police and other officials could administer the Act. The invigilation continued until the Protection Act was amended in 1963, and even then the Board retained special controls over children and reserves until 1969 (Rowley 1972, 406).

Aborigines in the state gradually ceased many cultural practices which previously had been central to their lives. Rather than this being some automatic consequence of European interference or attempt at suppression, such transformations were partly at least the subject of decisions and disagreements within the Aboriginal community. Traditional sentiments, ideas and practices were the focus of conflicts about strategic wisdom in an embattled situation. Evidence of this comes from the few anthropologists who worked in New South Wales in the 1940s and 1950s.

In some situations the old people refused to teach the younger ones either the specific esoteric knowledge of ritual and religion or the kinship rules and language. In some cases the younger people refused to learn them. The complexity of Aboriginal evaluation of tradition is captured in Beckett's (1958a, 37) comment that the old dance steps were facetiously called the 'blackfellers' Charleston' and that while 'Men...can still sing the old songs...the younger generation don't like to hear these songs. They giggle and say it makes them feel "shamed". "We're like white folks, now" they say.'

In the 1940s Reay (1949, 111) found conflicting attitudes to the performance of 'corroborees' in Moree. These sometimes caused deep rifts in the community, particularly between those who were 'not ashamed of being a blackfeller' and those for whom it meant that the participants were still ignorant 'old timers'. Song cycles were performed 'only in the presence of a few old men for whom the songs have not lost their meaning. Younger mixed bloods scoff at these songs, which have many obscene elements, mimic them in their drinking parties, and treat them as an obscene jest' (Reay 1949, 96).

Judgements about whether to teach or use the language, about whether to perform the rituals or tell the stories were to some extent conscious rational judgements made under extremely oppressive social conditions. One factor influencing such judgements was the status of the overt and more external expressions of culture, such as language and rituals, in the eyes of those who dominated Aboriginal social life. Prohibitions on language use or wailing at funerals (Reay 1949, 91, 105; Fink 1957, 110) and experiences of ridicule, might confirm a belief that such forms of knowledge were inappropriate under the new conditions. Aborigines in remote regions today also experience considerable conflict about practices which are overtly despised by Europeans (cf Cowlishaw 1983, 67). A measure of ambivalence is not surprising in the relationships of the young to old people, to the ritual life and to the kinship and marriage systems. Thus the processes Wolf refers to as constructing, reconstructing and dismantling cultural determinants are also the subject of internal conflict.

Because such practices represented the different meaning the world held for Aborigines they were also the focus of a continuing struggle to retain such meanings and to defy the new order (cf Morris 1985). Reay's account shows that in 1944 there was a struggle within the Aboriginal community concerning the traditional marriage rules with some people fighting to retain their validity while others claimed ignorance of them (Reay 1945, 311). Thus there has been no single simple rejection or retention of tradition, but a complex history of changes in the context of a political struggle for survival in which different and contradictory strategies were being adopted.

There were other more subtle and pervasive understandings of the world that continued to flourish in the new conditions. That most widely recognised is the interdependence of kin. Reay (1949, 114) observed that the European way of life, involving 'making a home' and 'getting on in the world' conflicts with the system of sharing and borrowing which operates among people 'of their own colour'. Other examples of interpersonal relations such as the way children are socialised, are more difficult to specify and they have received little descriptive or analytical attention.

For some, acceptance of the new regime necessitated the rejection of the old. The account of a police tracker's life by his elderly daughter indicates one strategy. 'He would not talk about the past or teach the kids the language. He said we had to learn to live the white way. Perhaps it was because of the killings' (personal communication). This aquiescence can be contrasted with the resentment of a man of about thirty-five whose family nurses a bitterness and stubborn determination to survive. He says:

> Mum came from Tibooburra and before that from Coopers Creek. When gold was found there the Aboriginal people were got out and our family was moved in a truck. Mum was 7 or 8. She dont talk about it often but when she do you know it wasnt a pretty sight to see Aboriginal people shoved in trucks and moved onto reserves all over NSW and the people didnt take care of who they grabbed and families were split up (personal communication).

For this family these events are a major point of reference in their lives.

Exclusion

Ambivalence and conflict about Aboriginal traditions was a consequence of lack of power, not only due to the Protection Act but also the local hegemonic processes. The citizens of outback towns complemented the work of the Board by excluding their dark neighbours sometimes formally and sometimes informally, from the churches, swimming baths, hotels and schools. Aborigines were of course aware of the way their camps and their habits were seen by whites. The Protection Act and the Protection Board far from protecting Aborigines from such discrimination exacerbated it.

Given the conditions of the invasion of their territory and under the Protection Act it is not surprising that prejudice against Aborigines was reinforced by the conditions which had been imposed. '(Whites) consider "the abos" an unregenerately delinquent group on whom government assistance paid out of the taxpayer's pocket is simply wasted' (Beckett 1964, 36).

Aborigines who might have been eligible for 'citizen's rights' or who could have 'passed' as whites often chose not to do so for it would entail identifying with those who despised one's kin. Those who did aim for higher status earned the resentment of others (Reay and Sitlington 1948). Individuals had to reject anything concerning their dark relatives if they were to join the whites (Fink 1957, 101).

The relationship between black and white populations is often treated as if it were a consequence of the cultural difference between them. But that relationship has been one basis out of which the differing values and priorities have been created. The relationship between the two groups, based as it was on the power of one over the other in virtually every realm, has been crucially important in the creation of contemporary Aboriginal culture. The rebellious display of disreputable behaviour is one distinctive response to oppressive conditions. Fink (1957, 103) observed an aggressive assertion of low status. Reay (1945, 300–01) found drunkenness conferred prestige. Her account of two Aborigines boasting competitively about having the most convictions for drunkenness indicate their contempt for an unjust law and the lack of shame associated with imprisonment.

Little is known of any systematic ideological response by Aborigines to the multifarious and involuntary adaptations that were taking place. Eliza Kennedy's reactions to the learning of white ways shows an awareness of loss and gain, and of a certain reversal of status markers (Kennedy and Donaldson 1982, 11). Reay (1949, 98) discusses the 'minority group tradition' in which 'social inequality is an *idee fixee*'. Beckett's (1958a, 37) description of the music Aborigines developed in western New South Wales is perhaps the nearest we come to the unique qualities of Aboriginal ideology in the protection era.

> They would make up a song about anything—rainmaking, catching porcupine, a lost child. When the white man appeared they made up songs about him. When the white station manager sent his aboriginal workers off to a distant paddock, while he returned to fornicate with their women, there was a song about it. There was a song about the government man who, coming to inspect rabbit infested stations, was taken into the parlour and plied with whiskey.

Many songs concerned the practice of drinking. The taste for strong drink and the bouts of drunkenness which Beckett says are common to the old time bushman and Aborigines may be linked to common conditions of living; harsh and despised. But it was the fact that alcohol was illegal for Aborigines that gave their drinking practices their most distinctive features. Aborigines were denied entry to that shrine of mateship, the pub, except as mendicants at the back door or begging from a workmate, someone with 'citizen's rights' or a relation whose pallor allowed them entry.[4] Even the possession of liquor placed them outside the law. Surveillance of camps and harassment was a constant experience. The police felt themselves obliged to attempt to enforce the law, probably under pressure from the townspeople. The ludicrousness of the situation is evident in Beckett's story of one man 'In flight from the police, who drained his bottle of port as he ran; when he had emptied it he stopped and, throwing the bottle aside, said "Alright, now you can take me!"' (Beckett 1958a, 39).

Beckett (1958a, 46) went so far as to assert that drinking activities 'provided a core around which a new a consciously distinctive aboriginal folklore is developing'. The songs recorded in Wilcannia in 1957 give a unique insight into the realities of Aboriginal life and into the spirit of their response which is at once cynical and defiant. The pleasures of drinking, even of drinking metho are described, as is the release from pain which comes from having a spree, or cutting a rug.

> The people in town just run us down.
> They say we live on wine and beer,
> But if they'd stop and think, if we didn't drink,
> There'd be no fun around here.

The awareness of the disapproval of the whites is accompanied by a defiant refusal to comply with their judgements or to even pay lip service to their standards. One man indicated his preference for a syrup tin to drink from as a statement of loyalty to Aboriginal standards (Beckett 1965, 40).[5]

Miscegenation and identity

The term 'miscegenation' is a product of scientific racism[6] but the outcome is not. Scientific racism might predict that mixing of gene pools would destroy racial boundaries, but the logic of theories about race did not dominate the social process of differentiation. Two racial groups continued to exist albeit one being designated as 'mixed bloods' or 'half-castes'.[7]

There have been various summary statements about the attitudes of one or another group toward liaisons between whites and Aborigines or to 'half-castes'. Some white policy makers advocated miscegenation as a method of assimilation, following the logic of scientific racism (McGrath 1984), but few actually offered to participate in the scheme. Those white men who did participate by forming long term or marital relations with Aboriginal women seem to have merited universal disapproval or horror among their local white fellow citizens.

It seems that Aboriginal views of miscegenation were not fraught with the kind of moral disapprobation and status meanings which abounded in the dominant society. Responses reported by white observers range from acceptance to extreme disapproval (Kelly 1944, 147; Eyre 1845, 324). We have virtually no first-hand evidence from those involved concerning miscegenation. I simply want to point out that such silence is indicative of the potency and complexity of the issue (cf McGrath 1984).

The contrast between Fink's (1957, 104) finding that a group of 'Upper' part Aborigines try to marry whites, and Kelly's (1944, 147) finding that light-coloured people want to resolve their identity by marrying dark-skinned people is not as contradictory as it appears. While both authors present somewhat oversimplified motives for marriage, the stated preferences of their informants reflect different strategies in a situation where skin colour seems to determine one's social place.

With a large proportion of the contemporary Aboriginal population in New South Wales country towns having some white ancestry and thus being party to such mixing of gene pools, miscegenation could hardly be a subject for shame. Among Aborigines today who recognise the status meanings of such liaisons among whites, and are aware of the sexual and social dynamics involved, miscegenation is at times a subject for humour and cynical comment. Both the advantages and disadvantages for a woman of taking a white lover or husband are widely understood in the black community.

While European genetic heritage is common, any financial inheritance from the same source is extremely rare. Stories of intended legacies abound. George Dutton's father was a nomadic white stockman who 'drifted away up into Queensland soon after, where he died. He left the boy a legacy but George says he was never able to lay his hands on the money' (Beckett 1958b, 97; cf Hardy 1979, 5). The legacy of names also gives a clue to the social process which kept the races apart while they were getting together in the most intimate fashion. In one valley 'there live to-day descendents of earlier Australians, both black and white...men distinguish one family from another by speaking of the white or black Smiths, Joneses or Hogans' (Ward 1966, 201).

In one case the offspring of a Scottish land owner and his Aboriginal wife helped their father with the station work until he died and his brother took over the property. The brother's white descendants now own the land and pronounce their name with a stress on the second syllable. Their black kin stress the first, thus cooperating with the differentiation which dispossessed them a second time. In such ways the process of miscegenation was countered by another process which continued to divide into racial categories those who were descendants of people from different 'races'. This division is not reproduced as a consequence of scientific racism or any other ideological formulation, nor as a result of any biological distinctiveness. Rather racial categories are extended and pressed into service to give a particular meaning to the ubiquitous forces of social differentiation (Cowlishaw 1986b).

I want to pursue briefly the usefulness of depicting Aboriginal society in New South Wales as having developed an 'oppositional culture' before showing the problems that such opposition poses in the current era which I call, with intentional irony, the enlightenment.

Oppositional culture

If it is true that 'Dignity is as compelling a human need as food and sex' (Sennett and Cobb 1973, 191), then one strategy for powerless groups is to create their own arena of dignity. The necessary conditions for a dignified bearing can be redefined. I believe that such a process is evident in the earlier period discussed above, as it is evident today.

Dignity need not for instance depend on wearing shoes in the street or on neat attire. Being apprehended by the police does not preclude a sense of dignity when one's father and aunt have had the same experience. Sitting on the ground playing Bingo is not undignified for Aborigines in New South Wales country towns. Members of a group can gain their sense of honour from the group's integrity rather than from those who dominate the economic and political arena. From this viewpoint, rather than the culture of Aborigines being a barrier to acceptance, it is their defiant reaction to rejection and their haven from the indignities meted out to them. I use the term 'oppositional culture' to specify the active creation and protection of this arena of social meaning in an embattled situation (Willis and Corrigan 1983). Not all or even most Aborigines take an active part in this creation. Many are passive and some oppose the opposition.

Aborigines are of course a varied group in lifestyles, aspirations and loyalties. In discussing their oppositional culture, I have mainly in mind the large groupings which resides at the Aboriginal end of towns in western New South Wales or on the reserves, which are closely interwoven through ties of kinship and marriage, and a shared past on the reserves. Most have little interaction with, and little knowledge of whites—some try to limit their involvement with the group and remain on the periphery. Leaders and spokespersons who are well known to whites from their involvement in organisations, may none the less be a part of this oppositional culture. For most there is not a self-conscious identification with a particular cultural group but simply an acceptance of the identity conferred on them by growing up in the Aboriginal community. Thus, this community which has an oppositional culture is as complex and contradictory as any community. It is for instance, bound together by its meaningful conflicts as much as by a notion of common purpose.

Whites dislike, disdain or pity Aboriginal practices in rural New South Wales rather than according them dignity. Had Aborigines been passive and silent in the face of such judgements there would be little need for the vilification to continue. Rather than responding with shame, oppositional culture acts as both a challenge to those who would despise Aborigines, as well as a defence against them. The fact that certain of its features are an immediate trigger to white hostility confirms and reactivates the oppositional nature of Aboriginal culture.

In a rural community the pressure to conform to standards of propriety are strong, but notions of propriety among whites conflict with Aboriginal loyalties. For instance, white reactions to Aboriginal drunks on the street varies from disgust or fear to disapproval and embarrassment whereas Aborigines deal with the familiar 'bottle men' without having to humiliate them. The logic of defiant reactions such as the drunken swearing at those who evince disgust are understood and treated with amusement by other Aborigines. Such amused reactions seem to implicate all in the threat posed by defiance of proper standards and respect for property.

While most Aborigines of course do not take part in acts of defiance, resistance or public drunkenness the significance of such acts is well understood. Satisfaction is gained from the story of the Aboriginal woman who threw her clothes off and repeatedly shrieked for help when the police tried to put her in the paddy wagon in the street. The police did not persist, but climbed into their van and departed. The street that is covered with broken glass is jokingly called 'crystal city'. Young blacks gain amusement from the obvious discomfort and disapproval by whites of swearing and drunkenness.

Money is not necessary for a sense of honour in Aboriginal communities, though sharing is. Those who acquire a car or a washing machine will expect, though not always happily, that it will be used by a wide network of kin.[8] This process is recognised by whites to be in conflict with individual ownership which is essential to the sort of competitive striving for jobs and goods fundamental to our society. When a public servant explained that 'money is the tool. If they don't want money you can't do anything to help them', he is clearly aware of the cruicial role of oppositional culture in defying dominant priorities.

Even in relation to cultural practices that are usually seen as legitimate, Aborigines are forced into opposition. For instance while it might be expected that funerals would be generally respected, in country towns it depends on whose they are. A businessman asserted that blacks have the attitude that 'If Uncle Fred dies in Wilcannia we will all go to the funeral and that is no good to an employer' (personal communication). It is implied not only that this is part of a careless attitude to work which explains Aborigines being unemployed, but also that there is something wrong with going to a relative's funeral—or perhaps that Aborigines have too many 'uncles'. This judgement about the significance of kinship and funerals is made without consideration of the extent of grief, or of what religious or social function mourning practices have. Aborigines faced with such disapproval can only reject the basis on which it is made.

Aboriginal reactions to white cultural practices are also a part of Aboriginal culture. When young Aborigines stole turkeys and chickens one Christmas Eve most were retrieved by the police. The fact that none could be sold or even given away was seen by the Aborigines to make the retrieval pointless and punitive and an example of dog-in-a-manger attitudes by whites. The outrage and fury of the owners of the store and those who lost their Christmas dinner was a source of amusement rather than shame in the Aboriginal community.

The hypocrisy of white people loudly bemoaning Aboriginal drinking is apparent. Drunken white men are often enough visible in public, sometimes indeed at their places of work, making it clear to all that alcohol addiction is not a monopoly of Aborigines. The fact that European drinking is mostly done behind closed doors seems to confirm that white people are ashamed of their habits. Aborigines have a wealth of humorous and ironic comments on such white practices.

In rejecting the humiliation involved in, for instance, being gaoled, Aborigines are taking an active role in the reproduction of racial separation. They have not conformed and surrendered to white hegemony. Thus it is in opposition that the ongoing recreation of a distinct cultural heritage occurs. This culture has its distinctive vocabulary, family form, pattern of interpersonal interaction and even its own economy. The lack of power that has forced Aborigines into opposition has also precluded their being able to present a discourse of dissent as a legitimate cultural response to their historical situation. This lack of legitimacy in turn leads to assumptions which underlie what I call the enlightenment in Aboriginal affairs.

Opposition in an enlightened era

A new source of conflict in this community has developed in recent years as Aborigines respond to benign government policies. These policies are a form of what Paine (1977) has called welfare colonialism which operates in ways that appear 'as solicitous rather than exploitative, as liberal rather than repressive'. In this situation oppositional culture can make Aborigines appear to be biting the hand that not only feeds them, but demands nothing in return except that they become self-managing. I want to conclude by suggesting that the oppositional nature of Aboriginal culture is in direct conflict with the underlying assumptions of the enlightenment.

From a past which consisted of confinement on reserves and subjection to intrusive laws, the new federal legislation enacted in the late 1960s and 1970s seemed to promise an era of liberty and equality for the Aborigines of Australia. Almost twenty years on it has been increasingly recognised that the legislative and funding changes have not solved the medical, legal, educational and economic disadvantages of Aborigines (cf Gale and Wundersitz 1982).

Changes came about in the 1960s normalising the legal status of Aborigines. In New South Wales no laws discriminating against Aborigines remained after 1967, but thereafter other kinds of laws that appealed to racial categories began to be implemented. These are the policies ostensibly designed to normalise Aborigines still further by removing informal barriers to equality of opportunity with white Australians. Special access to resources could only be arranged by targeting Aborigines for particular benefits. Thus education, housing, health and welfare policies were developed for Aborigines. These were to be implemented under the rubric of local decision making by Aborigines or self-management as the policy came to be known.

The federal government's Council (later Department) of Aboriginal Affairs (DAA) developed policies which were designed to equalise standards. Rural Aborigines were not involved in formulating and implementing these schemes. Rather they came from 'progressive thinking by the individuals in the Council' (Cooper 1976, 35). As time went by, needs and wishes were expressed by the Aborigines who became spokespersons. However the bureaucracy retained control even when rural Aboriginal groups began to formulate their views. Housing was requested by Aborigines but not the particular housing scheme devised by the Council and certainly no one requested the confusing red tape that accompanied the funding procedures. Further, Cooper has estimated that of $61.4m spent in 1973 on Aboriginal affairs no more than $3m was spent on organisations which could be considered Aboriginal (Cooper 1976, 36, 43).

A major area of difficulty was Aboriginal representation and organisation at a local level. Few individuals besides activists with urban experience had any knowledge or skills relevant to the formation of committees and cooperatives. The only whites most people had dealt with were police. Those elected as representatives were usually the few who had taken part in the basically white run 'advancement associations'. These were not representative of oppositional culture.

However, more fundamental misunderstandings bedevilled the enlightened initiatives. First some poorly thought out notion of self-determination or independence underlay the new policy. There was no clear consideration of the limits which existed to self-determination in the wider society. Aborigines were going to 'make their own decisions' just as white people did. It was never clear which white people and which decisions were alluded to. The limits of self-determination are fairly clear for people who are unemployed or rely on pensions and reside in public housing. The intentions of the policy were further confused by notions of community. It seems to have been assumed that Aborigines formed natural homogeneous and harmonious communities which could be given resources to determine their own future. Thus each community, or the Aboriginal community would make its own decisions. One might wonder what community provided the model for such a policy.

The claim that Aboriginal groups were to ask for and get what they wanted disguised the obvious fact that only certain things could be requested. It was not within the power of the bureaucrats to deliver a diminution of white hostility for instance, or a reduction of alcoholism, or any number of dreams of freedom that members of an Aboriginal community might have. But the limits on what the bureaucracy could provide were not spelled out.

Further, despite protestations of support for Aboriginal self-management, many of the white personnel involved in implementing the new Aboriginal policies have not been sympathetic toward those black viewpoints which are radically at odds with dominant cultural practices or political and economic structures. This is not so much to do with personal limits of tolerance or lack of imagination, but rather with the belief that only realistic aspirations can be achieved. Few radical alternatives have been given expression, let alone discussed and those that have been mooted by Aborigines often seem trivial or divisive to the bureaucrats involved in dispensing large sums of money.

For instance in discussing ways to combat vandalism, Aborigines have suggested they might teach the young people to use the land either for hunting or pastoral activities. But few have access to land. Provision to allow and enable Aborigines to fish and hunt wild game freely could have significant consequences—at the least its significance to some of the local Aborigines is far greater than to the bureaucrats.

The call for land rights has not been applauded by the bureaucracy. Other less tangible desires are also outside the bureaucratic arena.

Another barrier to the new policies is the sharp contrast between the enlightened bureaucrats and older white residents of country towns. The former are often so conscious of their own and Aboriginal conflicts with the more outspoken 'racist whites' that they fail to notice that the Aborigines are really at odds with the enlightenment. The government officials try to show the black groups how to formulate 'realistic goals' but in some cases they seem unaware of the social reality with which they are dealing.

As mentioned earlier, rural Aborigines were not initially demanding the housing and educational benefits that the enlightenment brought them. People who have lived their lives in dirt-floored shacks or humpies, cooking on an open fire do not necessarily long for a suburban bungalow for which they have to pay rent. The presentation of educational achievement as the key to all good things may also not convince those with no familiarity with books and schooling. There has been little serious consideration in the bureaucracy of how government initiatives fitted with the aspirations and the political aims of those being encouraged to higher education.

It transpired that the policy makers did not recognise the social dynamics among those to whom they were ministering. For instance the kin-based groupings which soon began to dominate the local housing cooperatives and legal service committees conflicted with the official DAA view of democratic, rationalistic, community-wide organisations, in which all would be interested and involved.

Another example of misunderstanding concerns payment of rent and electricity bills which made Aboriginal tenants poorer by increasing their financial responsibilities. These new demands were sometimes not understood as concomitant with gaining a house. I am not arguing that better housing was not desired. Indeed housing became the focus of desire in a situation where few material desires were ever satisfied.

This leads to a consideration of the indirect effects of the new policies on the aspirations and political direction of rural Aborigines. Self-determination seems to mask what is really a realignment of Aborigines toward a new form of inequality characterised by dependence on, and therefore direction by, government departments.

The affirmation of an Aboriginal identity is the price asked for gaining one of the jobs as an Aboriginal liaison or advisory officer. Of course there are not many such jobs and those individuals perceived as most likely to succeed are usually the least representative of the oppositional culture.[9] This does not mean they do not want to 'help their people'. But that help is often seen in terms of abandoning those values and behaviours that are in opposition to the dominant whites. Thus the affirmation of oneself as Aboriginal is occurring at the same time that many are being enticed with the opportunity to cease being Aboriginal in the ways of the past, to desert the kinship networks as well as depressed circumstances and, of course, to desist from opposition.

Taking advantage of government largesse appears to involve abandoning opposition in direct ways. Aboriginal organisations have had to become involved in meetings with white bureaucrats, learning about representation, formal decision making, accounting for money and allocating resources on objective criteria. A system of patronage has developed between Aboriginal organisations and the bureaucracies that nurture them.

In a country town the Aboriginal community does not have a unified view of the matter of Aboriginal identity much less of cultural differences. Some want not to emphasise differences. Those who had recognised that being black did not bring any rewards and obediently had tried to assimilate, are now being rewarded if they will identify as Aboriginal. These people are most likely to succeed in the secure and respectable jobs such as Aboriginal health worker, school liaison officer or welfare trainee. Such jobs have been created largely to service other Aborigines. The whole uplifting exercise is destined to regroup the black population into those co-opted to minister to those who are welfare dependent.

However, just as whites try to promote adherence to orthodox views,[10] there are attempts by Aborigines to command loyalty to the oppositional culture. For instance those who learn the techniques of being responsible for community money, such as by collecting rents, come into conflict with others who do not consider the paying of rent from meagre incomes to have top priority. The rent collector can then be accused of pretending to be white. Active members of a housing cooperative may be held responsible for allocating houses unfairly, and there is no fair way of allocating insufficient houses. Those who appear to favour the white world in any one of a number of ways may be accused of disloyalty, or derided as coconuts—black on the outside but white on the inside. Culture has thus become a sphere of overt political struggle. This is not necessarily a self-conscious decision to keep others in line, but a process stemming from intense consciousness of the meaning of behaviour which is threatening to the hegemony of whites.

However, besides opportunities for employment, there are areas of social life where young people especially are tempted to cease opposition. The attractions of joining the whites in sporting and social events are evident, and the opportunity is there, albeit conditional on conforming in certain ways and affirming certain values. Those who would attempt to make the definition of Aboriginal include aspects of the culture that are in opposition to the dominant world of the whites and to define these differences in a positive way, are in conflict with those who do not want to be oppositional. Unashamed opportunists, the latter group consider it foolish to reject opportunities.

It is clear then that Aborigines in towns do not have one self with one mind. The affirmation of Aboriginal identity does not by any means refer to all aspects of Aboriginal experience. One does not affirm one's identity by recalling the police officer who came to the reserve in 1968 and woke one's parents up, arresting them if they were believed to be drunk. Nor do the more distant family stories of being trucked from one's home reserve because it was being closed, to another where the population had declined, count as the basis for identity. Even less can one celebrate Aboriginality via the traditions of opposition to police, the school and the establishment of the town. Such negative experiences must be sloughed off.[11] Far less tension is generated by the assertion of Aboriginality through the 40,000 years of history. While the local establishment will not willingly accept these claims either, their power to control the generation of images is being bypassed by more powerful national forces including government bureaucracies. It is these forces which are dominating the new images of Aboriginal identity.

Notes

1. I am generalising about processes that need more detailed treatment for particular areas. The field research on which this paper is based has been conducted mostly in western New South Wales.

2. Based on preliminary research in Northern Territory towns, I would assert that similar processes are played out there.

3. Most Aboriginal families of course have direct experience of living under 'protective' legislation, but there is a lack of knowledge of the widespread and systematic nature of the protection era.

4. The definition of who was to be denied liquor depended on 'racial' identification made by publicans and police largely on the basis of skin colour.

5. Beckett (1965, 38) wrote of his difficulties in trying to 'describe a situation which my Aboriginal friends took for granted but which my white readers would find shocking, while I hung uncertainly between the two'. This dilemma faces many liberal minded when they confront poverty, depression and destructive drinking (cf Shepherd 1976). For Aborigines the dilemma is more painful. Kevin

Gilbert (1977) has 'Grandfather Koori' challenging Aborigines with their destructiveness and lack of self-esteem.

6. The term is said to have originated as a hoax to exacerbate the issue of race in an election in the United States in 1864 (Bloch 1958). It could only gain currency on the basis of the theory of race.

7. One common misunderstanding is that the miscegenation which occurred in the early years created a 'mixed race' community which then ceased to marry outside itself. The situation in New South Wales today suggests that mating and marriages continue to cross the barriers of race as they seem to have always done. The fact that children of such matings are nearly always raised in the Aboriginal community means that their social world is defined accordingly.

8. The slogan 'caring and sharing' has gained a certain currency among Aborigines as an affirmation of distinctive social values but there is a negative side to such edicts. Few can afford to be generous and the inequality generated when a minority gained well paid jobs has created a new source of tension.

9. A powerful support for oppositional culture stems from the fact that there are really very few Aborigines who could achieve the material basis for being accorded dignity by the dominant whites. Those who try can easily attract derision from both white and black community members.

10. A good deal of effort by the more powerful whites (Councillors, Chamber of Commerce) goes into keeping sympathy and understanding of the blacks from interfering with their vilification. While the vilification seems to emphasise the differences between blacks and whites, any positive emphasis on this difference is treated with scorn.

11. Again this is a contentious matter. Some want to assert a shared oppression as the basis of identity. Such matters have been powerful in the 'politics of embarrassment'. But for many the sanitised symbols of identity are favoured.

References

Anderson, C.
1983 Aborigines and Tin Mining in North Queensland, *Mankind* 13(6), 473-98.

Asad, T.
1979 Anthropology and the Analysis of Ideology, *Man* 14(NS), 607-27.

Beckett, J.
1958a Aborigines Make Music, *Quadrant* 2(4), 32-46.
1958b Marginal Men: A Study of Two Half-caste Aborigines, *Oceania* 24, 91-108.
1964 Aborigines, Alcohol and Assimilation. In M. Reay (ed), *Aborigines Now: New Perspectives in the Study of Aboriginal Communities*, Angus and Robertson, Sydney.
1965 The Land Where the Crow Flies Backwards, *Quadrant* 9(4), 38-43.

Bloch, J.M.
1958 *Miscegenation, Melalukation and Mr Lincoln's Dog*, Schaum Publishing Co, New York.

Castles, R. and J.P. Hagan
1978 Dependence and Independence. In A. Curthoys and A. Markus (eds), *Who are our Enemies*, Hale and Iremonger, Melbourne.

Collmann, J.
1979 Fringe-camps and the Development of Aboriginal Administration in Central Australia, *Social Analysis* 2, 38–57.

Cooper, J.
1976 The Politics of Consultation with Aborigines 1968–75, MA thesis, University of Sydney.

Cowlishaw, G.K.
1983 Blackfella Boss: A Study of a Northern Territory Cattle Station, *Social Analysis* 13, 54–69.
1986a Anthropologists and Aborigines, *Australian Aboriginal Studies* 1, 2–12.
1986b Race for Exclusion, *Australian and New Zealand Journal of Sociology* 22(1), 3–24.

Elkin, A.P.
1935 Civilized Aborigines and Native Culture, *Oceania* 6(2), 117–47.

Eyre, E.J.
1845 *Journals of Expeditions of Discovery 1840–1*, Boone, London.

Fink, R.
1957 The Caste Barrier—An Obstacle to the Assimilation of Part-Aborigines in North-West New South Wales, *Oceania* 28(1), 100–12.

Gale, F. and J. Wundersitz
1982 *Adelaide Aborigines: A Case Study of Urban Life 1966–1981*, Development Studies Centre, Australian National University.

Genovese, E.
1974 *Roll, Jordan, Roll The World the Slaves Made*, Pantheon Books, New York.
1975 Class, Culture and Historical Process, *Dialectical Anthropology* 1, 71–79.

Gilbert, K.
1977 *Living Black: Blacks Talk to Kevin Gilbert*, Allen Lane, Melbourne.

Hardy, B.
1979 *The World Owes Me Nothing*, Rigby, Sydney.

Kelly, C.
1944 Some Aspects of Culture Contact in Eastern Australia, *Oceania* 15, 142–53.

Kennedy, E. and T. Donaldson
1982 Coming Up Out of the Nhaalya: Reminiscences of the Life of Eliza Kennedy, *Aboriginal History* 6, 5–27.

McGrath, A.
1984 'Black Velvet': Aboriginal Women and Their Relations with White Men in the Northern Territory, 1910–40. In K. Daniels (ed), *So Much Hard Work: Women and Prostitution in Australian History*, Fontana/Collins, Sydney.

Mathews, J.
1977 *The Two Worlds of Jimmie Barker*, Australian Institute of Aboriginal Studies, Canberra.

Morris, B.
1983 From Underemployment to Unemployment, *Mankind* 13(6), 499–516.
1985 Cultural Domination and Domestic Dependence: The Dhan-Gadi of New South Wales and the Protection of the State, *Canberra Anthropology* 8, 1–2.

Paine, R.
1977 *The White Arctic*, Newfoundland Social and Economic Papers No 7, University of Toronto Press, Newfoundland.

Reay, M.
1945 A Half-Caste Aboriginal Community in North-Western New South Wales, *Oceania* 15, 296–323.
1949 Native Thought in Rural New South Wales, *Oceania* 20, 89–118.

Reay, M. and G. Sitlington
1948 Class and Status in a Mixed-Blood Community, *Oceania* 18, 179–207.

Roth, W.E.
1908 Marriage Ceremonies and Infant Life, *Ethnography Bulletin* 10, Australian Museum Records 7.

Rowley, C.D.
1972 *Outcasts in White Australia*, Penguin, Melbourne.

Sennett, R. and J. Cobb
1973 *The Hidden Injuries of Class*, Vintage Books, New York.

Shepherd, T.
1976 *Children of Blindness*, Ure Smith, Sydney.

Ward, R.
1966 *The Australian Legend*, Oxford University Press, Oxford.

Willis, P. and P. Corrigan
1983 Orders of Experiences: Working Class Cultural Forms, *Social Text* 7, 8–103.

Wolf, E.
1982 *Europe and the People Without History*, University of California Press, Berkeley.

7. Deirdre F Jordan

Aboriginal identity: uses of the past, problems for the future?

One site which is crucial for the construction of Aboriginal identity now, and for the structuring of an Aboriginal 'world of meaning' for the future, is education. To illustrate this assertion I shall discuss the construction of 'worlds' by Aboriginal people in three different locations and the particular identities and worlds offered to Aborigines by non-Aborigines in educational institutions in these same locations.

Conceptual framework

From a sociological perspective, identity may be defined in terms of social interaction. Berger and Luckmann (1966, 194), for example, suggest: 'Identity is formed by social processes. Once crystallized, it is maintained, modified, or even reshaped by social relations.'

Individuals are born into a particular world of meaning where, 'world' is taken to mean 'the comprehensive organisations of reality within which individual experience can be meaningfully interpreted' (Berger 1971, 96). Worlds of meaning provide models that are objectivated by theorising or explanatory schemes contained in society's general knowledge about the world—'what everyone knows'.

Individuals construct their identity by locating themselves within a particular model which is made credible or real, within this framework of theorising. Theorising that produces a world of meaning may be found occurring at different levels. The conversation of everyday life contains incipient theorising. The very language used by any group in society acts to legitimate and perpetuate meanings through this form of theorising. The use of derogatory names, for example, such as 'Abo', 'boong', or the use of depersonalising names (Jackie, Mary) are examples of incipient theorising. Each of these names conjures up a cluster of associated typifications and expected behavioural patterns. Rudimentary theorising offers pragmatic explanations of the reality around us. Schutz (1973, 72ff) talks about 'recipe' knowledge, everyday accounts of how the world works. Statements that explain the identity of Aboriginal people, their particular location in society, are part of this recipe knowledge or rudimentary theorising of the non-Aboriginal world. Such statements as 'It's no good trying to teach them, they can't learn', are examples of this low level form of theorising. Explicit theories characterise a higher level of theorising. Such theories are found in the construction of a symbolic universe, defined as 'bodies of theoretical tradition that integrate different provinces of meaning and encompass the institutional order in a symbolic totality' (Berger and Luckmann 1966, 113). An example of a symbolic universe is Aboriginal Law, which both explains reality in a coherent fashion and ordains appropriate behaviour.

For individuals, the possibility of forming a stable identity is dependent upon their ability to objectivate such a symbolic universe by theorising, and then to locate themselves within this universe in a manner that is plausible to them and others. That is, they must be able to recognise their self-sameness and continuity in this world and be conscious that others also affirm this location of the self.

Theorising about a world of meaning once objectivated is perceived as a given—a 'facticity' standing over and against individuals, and having power to act on them. That is, once a particular 'Aboriginal identity' is formulated, the very formulation acts to produce a reality within which individuals may find identity and which calls forth certain behaviour. (The world of tradition-oriented people, for example, is different from that of urban people, and results in different responses.) At the same time that the world is thus objectivated as a 'reality' for actors themselves, it is also presented as a coherent whole to others.

It is precisely in this process of theorising that uses of the past to objectivate characteristics that are specifically Aboriginal assume immense importance. The memories of old people, anthropological writing, archaeological remains, documentary records are elements which become the subject of theorising, that is, they are used to legitimate particular worlds of meaning. It must be pointed out, however, that within any particular Aboriginal world there may be a number of differing constructions of reality, depending upon which period of the past is used as a source for selecting 'identials' (that is, objective attributes by which individuals are able to locate themselves and are located by others, within a particular world of meaning).

Furthermore, while the processes described above apply to the establishment of identity in general, an additional factor is introduced in the case of Aboriginal identity. Since Aboriginal people are a minority ethnic group, they interact not only with structures within their own society, but also with the structures of the dominant society. There are 'competing constructions' of worlds, the result not only of Aboriginal but also of non-Aboriginal theorising. One of the problems for Aboriginal people is that they move in two worlds—Aboriginal and non-Aboriginal. The identity read back to them in one world may not be read back in the same way in the other world. Thus, the identity given by the white world of efficient worker, may be read back as 'coconut—brown on the outside, white on the inside' by a particular Aboriginal world.

A further problem is that the identity offered by white society has not been predictable or stable. The dominant group, at different periods, has offered different identities to Aboriginal people. For example, the latter were encouraged by government bodies in the 1950s and 1960s to become assimilated into white society, acquiring a status having certain cultural and behavioural expectations. In the 1970s and 1980s, the theorising of governments concerning self-determination and self-management for Aboriginal people, pushed the latter back to an 'identification with their own people' (King cited in Stone 1974), requiring them to construct quite different attributes by which they could be identified as Aboriginal.

In order, then, to investigate the way in which the past is used for the construction of identity, Aboriginal worlds and Aboriginal identity must be studied as they are conceptualised by both Aboriginal people and mainstream Australian society. If Aboriginal people are to locate themselves in an Aboriginal world, then at all levels of theorising this world must be plausible not only to them but also to others. It must offer the possibility of location in a world of meaning that has characteristics specifically Aboriginal and which provide a particular reality with which individuals can interact to establish a stable, credible Aboriginal identity.

The past as category

It is important for individuals from white society (whether they be members of government or those involved in education or research), to keep reminding themselves that Aboriginal people do not form a monolithic group and the past is not homogeneous.

Different worlds exist for Aborigines today because, in the past, the articulation by mainstream society of different policies (that of segregation, for example, as opposed to assimilation or of integration as opposed to assimilation) offered different identities to Aboriginal people. Early policies of *laissez-faire*, permitted Aboriginal people to maintain and adapt traditional culture, to preserve the vernacular, to continue initiation ceremonies and the socialisation of youth. Some missionaries (cf Jordan 1986b), deliberately chose a path of destroying Aboriginal culture, in order to Christianise, 'civilise' and socialise the people. This policy was taken up by governments in the 1960s, and categorised as assimilation.

> The policy of assimilation means that all Aborigines and part Aborigines *will attain the same manner of living as other Australians* and live as members of a single Australian community enjoying the same rights and privileges, accepting the same responsibilities, *observing the same customs and influenced by the same beliefs, hopes and loyalties as other Australians* (Commonwealth Parliamentary Papers 1963, emphasis added).

The different categories used in successive censuses demonstrated (Jordan 1985a) differing policies toward Aborigines, and accorded a different status to them. Each change in census categories reflected a change in the way Aborigines were located by mainstream society in the latter's world of meaning. Legislation also controlled the options for identity offered to Aboriginal people. The Aborigines Acts of 1911, 1917 and 1919 which remained in force until the 1960s, permitted the exemption of certain people from categorisation as Aborigines. The 1939 Act of South Australia, for example, defined all people of Aboriginal descent as Aboriginal, unless, 'in the light of their character and standard of intelligence and development', they had been exempted. Those having 'positive' characteristics, could be classified as non-Aboriginal. Aboriginal people were to be typified negatively.

Just as census categories allocated Aboriginal people different statuses at different times, so different phases of the past were characterised by different policies, legislation, and practices on the part of mainstream society. These located Aboriginal people in different worlds of meaning and therefore offered different identities— Aboriginal, part-Aboriginal and white—each with positive or negative characteristics. So also in contemporary society, depending upon which phase of the past is emphasised, there will be quite different implications for the construction of Aboriginal identity. In order to examine this assertion, history is segmented into three periods: the *recent past* of the post-referendum and post-war era; the *past-of-the-middle-range* of colonialism; and the *remote past* of early white contact.

I argue that the remote past incorporates positive Aboriginal identials, that the past-of-the-middle-range is characterised by oppression on the part of mainstream society, and by the creation of negative identity and negative stereotypes found today in sedimented knowledge[1] (ie, 'what everyone knows about Aborigines'), and that the recent past is identified by theorising about self-determination, self-management ('we will do it ourselves'), and the construction by Aboriginal people of a positive

Aboriginal identity. The category labelled the recent past requires detailed explication because of its integration with the present.

A watershed in the location of Aboriginal people in society may be seen in the referendum of 1967, in which the people of Australia voted overwhelmingly for the Commonwealth to assume powers for the welfare of Aborigines. The effects of the referendum were seen in the early 1970s when a Labor government came into power and a new era for Aborigines was ushered in. The Labor government projected policies of self-determination, setting out theorising about the rights of Aboriginal people to control their own lives and their own future.

As a corollary of Labor's policies of self-determination, there was a change in the locus of the power to name. The naming of Aborigines, their location in a particular world was to be through a process of self-identification. A movement was initiated, inchoate in its beginnings, toward the development of a separate Aboriginal identity. It is this post-war, post-referendum period which I designate as the recent past. Aboriginal people began to theorise, in an incipient and rudimentary form, about the possibility of socialisation into a positive Aboriginal identity—a theorising which had already been fostered in South Australia by the legislation of the Dunstan government in the late 1960s.

Following the 1967 referendum, South Australia was the first state to bring forward legislation setting Aboriginal affairs on an entirely new path. Rowley (1971, 409) saw this as the most daring and positive innovation of any Australian government. Len King, then Minister for Aboriginal Affairs, proposed an abandonment of the policy of assimilation of Aborigines. In its place, he supported a policy of integration, aimed at making it possible for Aborigines to 'identify with their own people', but yet remain within white society. King (cited in Stone 1974) defined the policy of integration as: 'the right of the Aboriginal people to live in our community on fully equal terms but retaining, if they so desire, a separate and identifiable Aboriginal heritage and culture'.

King (cited in Stone 1974) advocated the politicisation of Aborigines through an active encouragement of a 'sophisticated and articulate aboriginal public opinion'. He looked to the development of autonomous government on reserves, and to the participation of Aborigines in the political community. The policy of integration put forward by King neither treated the Aboriginal world of meaning as worthless, nor attempted to assimilate it, but rather provided for the choice of an identity which, while being characterised by Aboriginal identials, was, at the same time, located within mainstream society.

For the first time there was positive, official theorising which Aborigines were quick to appropriate. For the first time since the country was colonised, the indigenous people of Australia had the possibility of interacting with positive typifications emanating from the dominant group, offering the possibility of a positive identity.

The Australian Labor Party (ALP), at the national level, reflected and interacted with the policies of the South Australian government. In particular, South Australian legislation anticipated the policy of self-determination that was to be put forward at the federal level when a Labor government came into power.

The ALP policy of 1973 with regard to Aboriginal education was that:

> Every Australian child be taught the history and culture of Aboriginal and Island Australians as an integral part of the history of Australia. Adult education is to be provided as broadly as possible. [To this was added in 1975:] The Australian Government to provide funds to expand the general availability of courses of study at Teachers Colleges and/or Colleges of Advanced Education in race relations and Aboriginal society so as to enable the teaching thereof as a compulsory subject in all schools, and Aboriginal Studies generally.

The stage was set for the construction of a positive Aboriginal identity. However, so great was the confusion engendered by earlier policy and practice that, in the contemporary social climate where it is acceptable to identify and be identified as Aboriginal, before such identification can be accomplished, fundamental questions have to be asked by Aboriginal people seeking Aboriginal identity.

For Aborigines who have been treated as minors, as perpetual adolescents by law, the crisis of identity usually thought of as a developmental phase, existed not only, through their adolescence but their adult life as well.

> we can see the start of some slight search for 'Aboriginality'. But what is Aboriginality? Is it being tribal? Who is an Aboriginal? Is he or she someone who feels that other Aboriginals are somehow dirty, lazy, drunken, bludgers? Is an Aboriginal anyone who has some degree of Aboriginal blood in his or her veins and who has been demonstrably disadvantaged by that? Or is an Aboriginal someone who has had the reserve experience? Is Aboriginality institutionalized gutlessness, an acceptance of the label 'the most powerless people on earth?' Or is Aboriginality when all the definitions have been exhausted a yearning for a different way of being, a wholeness that was presumed to have existed before 1776? (Watson 1977, 184)

It is this confusion which impels people to seek identials from the past. The question to be asked is: Which era of the past will provide elements for constructing a plausible, positive Aboriginal world of meaning?

The past as currency: the construction of worlds

In the analysis of selection from the past that follows (drawing on data from earlier research by Jordan 1983), three Aboriginal worlds will be examined. The first is that of a tradition-oriented group in the Pilbara area of Western Australia; the second that of rural-urban people in Port August, a town at a geographical and cultural crossroad. The third world is the city of Adelaide. Manifestly, these are 'types'. There are vast numbers of Aboriginal worlds, each differing from the other according to their past history.

The Mob: the remote past as personal experience

While it may appear to be a contradiction in terms to refer to personal experience of the remote past, there are still some Aboriginal people who conceptualise their contact with the remote past as one of personal experience, although the memories of this experience and the ability to recall it may have been submerged under the experiences of white contact. In the case of tradition-oriented groups, such as the Mob, where there is a movement back to a traditional way of life, there is no conscious question of selection—the past, insofar as it can be established, is embraced as a totality. The Mob has moved culturally to revive the Law in all those aspects which can be recalled. The recall may be at first hesitant, then growing in detail and confidence. The use of the past in constructing an identity highlights the issue, not so much of a selection from the past *qua* past, as a delving into memory and a resurrection of the past. The real problem of selection becomes, paradoxically, one of selecting from the recent past of white contact, a process of particular importance in the area of education.

The socialisation of young people into Aboriginal society traditionally finds its place within the Law. The model for the education of young people is thus found in tradition. At the same time, the need for numeracy and the need to be literate in English and in the vernacular are given high priority. White schooling must also be accommodated within the traditional world of meaning. Adaptations of practice are needed, and must be made in the light of the spirit of the Law; that is, theorising must be objectivated to legitimate and integrate these new accretions derived from the past activities of governments and of churches. There is a rejection of white values, theorising, and practices, though not of individual white people. At the same time, drawing on the contact of Aboriginal people with the white world in the past, there is a selecting out of those elements which make their continuation as a group viable.

The Mob's solution is to employ white people to teach white people's knowledge, particularly numeracy and literacy. The structures of white schooling are adopted and adapted by the Mob for their own purposes. From the recent past of contact with the white world, knowledge is selected about what a school should look like and how it should operate. Committee structures have been adapted from the white world to run the school—an Aboriginal board with elected members, including women, is responsible for school policy. Clearly, structures not found in the Aboriginal world have been selected from the white world and incorporated into the Aboriginal way of life.

It must be noted that, while the content of the Mob's theorising leads back to the remote past of tradition-oriented structures, the framework for the articulation of the theorising is the recent past constructed by government theorising. Their point of reference is that of self-determination. 'We will do it ourselves', 'The *marrngu* are the boss', 'It's our turn now', are slogans functioning to make plausible their model of a world of meaning.

The theorising of these tradition-oriented people is strong, clear and coherent because it is situated within an overarching, symbolic universe, provided by the Law. This is not necessarily the case with urban people who may be geographically and culturally separated from each other, even within the one urban complex, and where different worlds of meaning may overlap. The latter phenomenon is particularly evident at Port Augusta.

Port Augusta: the pasts intertwined

The location of Port August at the intersection of the north–south, east–west travel routes results in the fact that, even today, bush people are coming into the town and into the schools. The primary school frequently enrols Aboriginal children who speak only their native language, an indication of the closeness of some of these people to traditional life, and a witness to their contemporary experience of the remote past. Many recently urbanised people (Aborigines have been permitted to live in Port Augusta proper since 1968), know their bush relations and go and stay with them. Others have frequent contact in the town with people (including initiated men) who have traditional backgrounds.

For some who were taken away from their parents at an early age, there is a profound desire to go back and find their people and their origins. For most, however, there is a deliberate turning away from a tradition-oriented way of life. The choice before them is seen not as one of selecting knowledge from the past, but of whether or not to experience the past as present, as tradition-oriented people are choosing to do. The decision expressed by the people of Port Augusta is that 'it would be a step backwards', 'it would be taking on a half a culture'. Young men express fear that the 'red men' from the north will take them back for initiation into traditional life (Jordan 1983).

The tradition-oriented world is plausible to the people of Port Augusta as a world within which Aboriginal identity may be found. They do not, however, accept this world for themselves. Rather, they conceptualise an Aboriginal society that has historical origins firmly rooted in the tradition-oriented world, but which contemporaneously, is different both from that world and the world of white society. In this evolving world, knowledge about the tradition-oriented world is given high status. The people select from the past, to be taught in school, the language, the history, the customs and culture of their tradition-oriented kin. In interviews at Port Augusta (Jordan 1983), all the people contacted supported the inclusion of Aboriginal studies in the schools, but they supported them for all students, not just Aboriginal students. That is, there was a clear wish to objectivate an Aboriginal world, and to present it to others.

As was the case with the Mob, the people had interacted with theorising about self-determination. Because, however, they had less coherence as a group, self-determination as a concept was individualised, and construed in personal terms as being able to control one's future, or having control over one's life. Some Aboriginal people had set up an adult education centre at the Davenport Reserve, on the outskirts of the town, to give people the skills they needed to work in Aboriginal agencies. For those working in these agencies, however, the notion of self-management was often categorised as delusory. As long as white people controlled the distribution of funds, they were seen to control also, to a large extent, the areas to which funds could be applied and hence to control the formulation and articulation of policy.

It is not possible within the framework of the world of meaning being constructed at Port Augusta to talk of selection from the past in a reified way, as if the remote past were dead. The remote past and the present are entwined. Similarly, in a different location (Adelaide), the recent past and the present are entwined.

Adelaide: the past mediated by white society
In the case of the Aboriginal people of Adelaide, the trickle of migration to the city began in the comparatively recent past of the post-war period. Adult Aboriginal

people in this group firmly situate themselves in the past-of-the-middle-range. The past they know from experience is contexted in a white construct, namely the missions/reserves of Point McLeay and Point Pearce. For this group, the mission is home; it is their world; a given into which they were born. For them, knowledge of the remote past has to be mediated by others. Even the language is preserved only in the writings of an early missionary.

For non-Aboriginal people, and for most urban Aboriginal people, the remote past of this group is mediated through the writings of anthropologists. Manifestly, there is a problem in that the issues researched are selected by non-Aboriginal people on the basis of the latter's interest, or self-interest. The researcher operates out of a different world of meaning; issues are seen through European eyes, subjected to European methodologies, organised within European paradigms; thereby slanting the world of meaning within which identity is constructed. For most Aboriginal people, however, the writings of anthropologists have little immediate impact. Rather, it is enough to adhere to a somewhat vague, unspecific knowledge of the remote past that is a form of sedimentation of knowledge passed on from generation to generation. Thus the older urban Aborigines may refer to 'secrets' that they possess (though they do not possess the language). They may stand in awe of tradition-oriented people and, in an inchoate way, they may appreciate the coherence of the culture of that group. Nevertheless, the tradition-oriented culture does not provide for urban dwellers a model with which they can readily identify in their daily life, although they ally themselves with causes (such as land rights) which pertain to tradition-oriented people.

Urban people too, seek self-determination and see education as an area of vital importance in this regard. Their construction of state and federal Aboriginal education committees has been designed both to promote their control over curriculum and to increase the participation of Aboriginal people in education.

The questions to be asked are: What are the identities offered to Aboriginal people in educational institutions; and in what way do educators perceive and interact with the uses of the past made by Aboriginal people?

Identities offered to Aboriginal people in educational institutions

Higher education
Encouraged by the Labor Party policy of the 1970s, colleges of advanced education in all states developed Aboriginal studies courses. The content of this segment of the

curricula was constituted, by and large, from selections touching on the Aboriginal experience of colonialism, mostly from within the disciplines of history and political science and occasionally from sociology. The issues selected for study, for example race relations, were often structured from the point of view of Europeans intending to champion Aboriginal causes or to demonstrate to non-Aborigines the oppression suffered by Aborigines in the past-of-the-middle-range, and subsequent disadvantages perpetuated.

At the same time that these courses were introduced, the colleges developed special entry programs for adult Aborigines. For many of these adult Aboriginal students, their first organised approach to their history and to an understanding at a cognitive level of the issues involved, was through participation in Aboriginal studies. This introduction to Aboriginal issues and history presented an Aboriginal identity that was mediated by the white world. For Aboriginal people, the selection from their experience and cultural heritage became a second order selection. First-hand knowledge of the experience of 'me Mum', 'me Dad', 'Auntie Glad' or 'Auntie Olga', communicated personally by these people, was reconceptualised by scholars to fit within a particular framework.

Adult Aboriginal students complain that this reconceptualisation, by concentrating on white oppression, constructs a world of meaning for Aborigines which seems designed to call forth in them responses of hostility and racism and which, they believe causes a crisis of identity. My own investigations (Jordan 1985b, 14–15) showed that:

> students thought that Aboriginal Studies was an important topic, to be studied by both Aboriginal and non-Aboriginal people. However, where this topic was presented in a way that emphasised only the bad, indeed the horrifying aspects of Aboriginal and non-Aboriginal interaction, there were cases where a crisis of identity was provoked, with students feeling that they were being forced into a particular form of racism which required them to reject non-Aboriginal people, perhaps even those they had looked on as parents. They also felt that the same forces impelled them into certain forms of Aboriginal identity which they would not have freely chosen. [I drew the following conclusion.] It is important that non-Aboriginal staff recognise the traumatic nature of a crisis of identity provoked by exposure to Aboriginal Studies when this course is presented in a way that expects students to identify with, and internalise all the negative aspects of the horrendous treatment Aboriginal people have suffered, with the result that a positive attitude to the present is set at risk.

Interviews with older Aboriginal people who have experienced in their own lives the events of the past-of-the-middle-range (Jordan 1983) have led me to conclude that their response to oppression differs from that of Europeans in the crucial sense that, for Aboriginal people, rudimentary theorising about past events is personalised and particularised. Judgements made are also particularised—X was a good boss, or Y was racist because these individuals, as individuals, acted in certain ways. In the case of Aborigines, it is not usual for such knowledge to be generalised. Europeans, in general, are not seen as racist, for example. Rather, people coming into the Aboriginal world are watched and judged on their personal merits. The generalisation of whites as racists comes from knowledge cast within white frameworks. The tendency to particularise rather than generalise constitutes a major difference between knowledge as mediated by Aboriginal agents and European scholars, and in turn, creates problems when Europeans select knowledge about Aborigines and communicate it in an organised fashion within the framework of Aboriginal studies.

It is interesting in this respect to contrast the viewpoints of young guest speakers at a university in Tatz's (1975) book, and those of people interviewed by Gilbert (1977). In Tatz's book, the young people see the past almost exclusively in negative terms of humiliation, degradation, reflecting the selections from the past made by the academics of the white world. In Gilbert's (1977) book, where older Aboriginal people speak for themselves, there is, it seems to me, greater tolerance of past injustice, a more perceptive analysis of the contemporary situation, and a constructive view regarding escape from degrading situations by building identity. This view is encapsulated by Gilbert (1977, 304–05) in theorising attributed to 'Grandfather Koori':

> Aboriginality, eh?
> I don't care how hard it is. You *build* Aboriginality, boy, or you got nothing. There's no other choice to it. If our Aboriginal people cannot change how it is among themselves, then the Aboriginal people will never climb back out of hell.

In sum, those constructing Aboriginal studies programs, in selecting from the writings of historians, sociologists and political scientists, have often focused unduly on the racism and oppression of the past-of-the-middle-range. The responses of hate, frustration, anger and bitterness that are precipitated as an unintended consequence by these studies is a source of unease to students (Jordan 1985b) and is not widely reflected in personal contact with an older generation (Jordan 1983), who have suffered deeply, absorbed the suffering and indeed have often become ennobled by it. This is not to excuse in any sense the source of suffering, but to point out the selectivity of white academics and its implications.

Certainly, many Aboriginal people believe that, if Australian history is to be rewritten, it should dwell not only upon the facts of the oppression of Aboriginal people, but also on the strengths the people showed under oppression, and on the positive contributions made by Aboriginal people in Australia's history. It is only recently that account is being taken of the positive attributes of Aboriginal society in the face of oppression, and of Aboriginal resistance to the oppression. An analysis of the courses offered in higher education institutions would be a fruitful exercise for Aboriginal educational groups as they move to reassert their ownership of knowledge in this area.

A second strand of government policy in the 1970s which promoted the notion of self-determination/self-management was seized by Aboriginal people and integrated into their theorising. The push by Aborigines for the Aboriginalisation of services, including the management of support services in higher education, must be located within this particular framework of theorising.[2] It is likely that one of the clearest characteristics identifying urban Aboriginal people to others in a positive way will be the leadership given within Aboriginal organisations and within Aboriginal sectors of other organisations. Such positions give them high visibility in situations that have positive feedback.

A further point should be made with regard to higher education institutions. It is not only from the past that academics select knowledge for the construction of Aboriginal identity, but also from the present. I found, for example (Jordan 1985b, 14) that:

> problems arose from efforts made by staff to promote a positive sense of Aboriginal identity by bringing Aboriginal speakers to the campus. This move was much appreciated by most students and seen as a powerful means of reinforcing a positive sense of identity. Some students, however, who were not 'politically' oriented, felt that activities aimed at what they termed consciousness-raising (even the mere presence of these Aboriginal leaders on campus) put psychological pressure on them to get involved in Aboriginal issues whether they wished to, or not. There were instances of students claiming that differences of opinion emerged amongst them over the lack of commitment on the part of some to a spirit of activism. This causes dissension within the group.

Certain groups (Aboriginal and non-Aboriginal) select from among competing constructs a perception consonant with their own theorising of Aboriginal identity; this is then held to be universal, and to be imposed on others. There are real Aboriginal people; there are middle-class professionals; there are those who have always identified themselves as Aboriginal; there are those whose mothers denied their

Aboriginal origins 'in case the welfare came and took the children away'; there are those who believe that all Aboriginal people should be activists and those whose inclinations do not impel them in this direction—a situation also reflected, of course in non-Aboriginal society.

Identity and selection from the past in the school situation

Staff In the case of tradition-oriented people, selection from the past for the purposes of schooling is controlled by the people themselves, not white teachers. It is the people who decide what the curriculum will contain. There is a symmetry between the theorising about Aboriginal identity for the group and for individuals, since no allowance is made for competing constructs. Young people are socialised into a world of meaning which is projected as the only one possible. This is not usually the case in the urban situation. As with other ethnic groups, Aboriginal children of school age interact with and accept or reject the Aboriginal identity offered by their parents or the Aboriginal identity offered by reality definers in schools. The principals and staff of schools project particular forms of theorising about Aboriginal identity which may or may not be symmetrical with that offered by parents. Similarly, Aboriginal students will interact with the theorising of non-Aboriginal students.

In a research project carried out to investigate the construction of Aboriginal identity in the school (Jordan 1984), an examination of curriculum (taken to refer not only to subject content and teaching methodologies, but the general policy and practice of the school), showed that, while the theorising of parents about Aboriginal identity differed from one site to another, there was symmetry in each location between the theorising of parents and the theorising of the school. In both cases, the theorising was related to governmental policies of the recent past. That is, parents and staff highlighted the processes of self-determination, both focused on the construction of a positive Aboriginal identity. At Port Augusta, the explicit theorising of school staff supported the theorising of Aboriginal people. The teaching of Aboriginal language and history and culture was formalised in Aboriginal studies programs. School personnel, in constructing and presenting the curriculum, recognised the status of men educated into traditional ways. School staff made considerable effort to check their presentations of Aboriginal studies with those Aboriginal people who asserted their rights as custodians of knowledge, and who decided not only which knowledge was authentic, but also which knowledge might be revealed, and to whom. Elders were invited to visit the school, within the Aboriginal studies program, to communicate their knowledge.[3]

At the same time, it was evident that the theorising of the white world of schooling interacted to a large extent with the knowledge sedimented from the writings of anthropologists. Understandably, in the past-of-the-middle-range, anthropologists (mostly males), had access only to knowledge owned by male Aborigines and, by and large, selected out the male Aboriginal world for analysis. Although a balance is now being brought to this perspective, sedimented knowledge about Aboriginal worlds leads people in schools to invite Aboriginal men into the school to communicate knowledge. The worlds of Aboriginal women are ignored. When the world of meaning is controlled by Aboriginal people, however, women take part. They participate, for example, in the deliberations of school boards. Similarly, Aboriginal elders from Indulkana, with the status of senior lecturers in ethnomusicology at the University of Adelaide do not teach only men's music. They bring women with them when it is a question of communicating women's knowledge. There is the possibility then, that certain aspects of the process of selection from the past taking place in schools, itself creates mythologies for the construction of gender within Aboriginal identity.

In the city situation, where there is less contact with tradition-oriented people, different processes operate. There, as in Port Augusta, staff of schools made every effort to discern the direction of theorising of Aboriginal parents about Aboriginal identity. Aboriginal studies courses were not constructed as separate entities, but integrated wherever possible into the normal subjects found in the curriculum. Topics included were designed to highlight those aspects of Aboriginal history and culture that would engender feelings of pride in Aboriginal students and positive attitudes in non-Aboriginal students. Clearly non-Aborigines also play a part in the construction of identity through their interaction with Aboriginal students. They also define reality by their selections from the past.

Non-Aboriginal students In the case of non-Aboriginal students at the schools studied, it was found that students made use both of the recent past and the past-of-the-middle-range in the theorising that they objectivated about Aborigines. When students were asked to typify Aborigines, the typifications were negative on all the characteristics offered (Jordan 1984, 287). On the other hand, when students were offered statements containing rudimentary theorising about the location of Aborigines in society, their responses were positive (Jordan 1986a).

A plausible explanation for these findings is that selection is occurring from two different periods of the past and that this is taking place at two different levels. That is, incipient theorising (typifications) on the part of students is drawn from the past-of-the-middle-range as sedimented knowledge acquired in the process of socialisation, whereas rudimentary theorising is consonant with the positive theorising of governments from the recent past and school personnel from the present.

Support for the explanation is given by examples such as that provided by Turnbull (1972, 233) who related the following anecdote:

> People selling buttons in Melbourne streets for an Aborigine cause not long ago were astounded by the savagery of the answers given by some of those asked to buy—'I'd rub the lot out', 'Give 'em bait'.

The incipient theorising contained in the responses is that Aborigines are 'less than human', and therefore they can be 'rubbed out'. They can be treated like animals. In Turnbull's judgement, these people 'had probably never seen an Aborigines'. Their theorising could be explained as stemming, not from first-hand knowledge, but from knowledge sedimented from the past-of-the-middle-range, when such actions against Aborigines were permitted by white society and indeed seen as providing a solution to the 'Aboriginal problem'. A missionary gives the following account of events in Port Augusta in the late thirties (Cantle 1978):

> The Aboriginal children were neglected and not welcome at the Pt. Augusta School but public opinion was stirred and in 1937 a portable classroom was erected in the vicinity of the camp and a subsidised teacher was appointed...one councillor stood up and gave his opinion that the best thing to do was to turn a machine gun on the whole camp and wipe it right out, people and all.

Similarly non-Aboriginal students at school possess sedimented knowledge about Aborigines not gained from the theorising of the school as it is available in policy or practice. This knowledge is acquired at an early age from primary socialisation. Palmer (1986, 81) reports the incipient theorising of pre-school children at Port Augusta: 'Can some little Aboriginal boys or girls come to your Kindy sometime?' 'No, cause I kill em, all of 'em.' Thirty-two preschool children were asked to analyse stories read to them. Palmer's findings (1986, 77, 79) were that:

> Twenty-nine showed a definite tendency to associate positive terms with the white characters and negative terms and feelings with Aboriginal characters. Some of the negative feelings expressed were dislike, hatred, contempt and fear accompanied by a sense of danger. Many subjects stated quite simply...'I don't like black people'. However, other children's feelings were much stronger:
> Why don't you like Aborigines?

> Cause they're black and I hate black people.
>
> Then, in a later session:
>
> Would you like to have an Aboriginal friend?
>
> Na.
>
> Why not?
>
> Cause (pause) I reckon they're horrible. Aborigines.

Thus before students even meet Aboriginal children, their attitudes have begun to form. The child from the Port Augusta preschool who expressed the intent to kill, reflects the attitudes contained in the statement of the Port Augusta councillor. The negative rudimentary theorising of the preschool children is coherent with their incipient theorising: 'Ya gotta like white people and not Aboriginals'. The rudimentary theorising is couched in language that is derogatory:

> Which one's a dirty boy?
>
> (Child points to Aboriginal child in the illustration.)
>
> Why is he dirty?
>
> Because he's a black boong.

Clearly the attitudes of white children are being formed in the family situation by a process of selection on the part of parents from white views of the past-of-the-middle-range. This selection from the past provides a way to locate Aboriginal children in contemporary society. The destruction of Aboriginal culture in the past, the incidence of theorising about extermination, pseudo-Darwinian theories about Aborigines as the missing link between apes and men, the enforcement of segregation—all these factors acted to permit the categorisation of the Aborigines as 'not quite human' and therefore able to be killed or at least as inferior to white society and therefore to be excluded.

Citizenship was not granted to Aborigines until after the 1967 referendum. For the preschool child for whom knowledge continues to be sedimented from the past, Aborigines continue to be non-citizens, non-Australian. Palmer (1986, 72) documents the following conversation:

> Child: I only like Australian.
>
> Researcher: Aren't Aborigines Australians?
>
> Child: They live in Australia, but they're not Australians.

The theorising projected in the family is, in many cases counteracted in the schools. As children proceed through school, they are exposed to the theorising of the teachers which, on the whole, is positive. Aboriginal history is rewritten as the past is reconceptualised. In many cases, children learn about Aborigines either within an Aboriginal studies program or in a component of subjects such as social studies, history, geography, art or English literature. It becomes possible then, for white students as well as Aboriginal students to interact with positive theorising, and at this level to respond positively to theorising statements locating students in a multicultural Australia. This is what I found in my research. Non-Aboriginal students at the level of incipient theorising continue to adhere to negative stereotypes; at the level of rudimentary theorising, they agree to positive statements about Aborigines in contemporary society (Jordan 1986a).

Conclusion

It may be hypothesised that selection from the past functions to stablise a situation of identity diffusion. The latter arises from the fact that the dominant group in Australian society has continually changed the identity offered to Aborigines. Moreover, while theorising at one level about assimilation, it has acted to exclude Aborigines on the level of day-to-day interaction.

For Aboriginal people, different worlds of meaning within which they may find identity are in the process of being constructed. In the case of urban people, there are a number of worlds, each competing with the other. The elements from which these worlds are constructed are drawn from various pasts—the remote past, the past-of-the-middle-range and recent past of the Aboriginal world, as well as, in the case of tradition-oriented people, the recent past of the white world.

Much of the knowledge from which urban Aboriginal people make their selections is knowledge mediated by white people through European frameworks. The matrix into which these elements are set, however, is the present—a present of positive theorising at the overt level on the part of both Aborigines and non-Aborigines, typifications arising from sedimented rather than selected knowledge from the past.

The process of selection has acted in two different ways—on the one hand, the selection from the past results in 'lived' life. Tradition-oriented people (re)incorporate the past into their current social structures. Urban people, on the other hand select from the past to establish identials, characteristics that mark them off as Aboriginal. The problem then becomes one of how to integrate these elements into a model of 'lived' life. A point of comparison may be found in the Sami movement in Scandinavian countries. In their case, the issue is not one of the revival of a culture, but the insertion of their 'lived' culture into the modern world. Their solution is highlighted by the fact that a huge research project was begun in 1985 to adapt the language to technological developments. Crucial to their endeavour is the Sami Institut'ta, a research institute where Sami people research what they see as vital issues for education, their history, their language, their culture and their economy.

If we compare these two modes of selection from the past, emanating from in-group research in the case of Sami, and out-group research and dissemination of knowledge in the case of Aboriginal people, the construction of indigenous identity would seem to result in quite different outcomes. In the case of the Sami, the past is seen as a prior stage in the continuous evolution into the modern world. Their problem is to maintain their separate status through language, costume and customs. For Aborigines, separate status is thrust upon them and must be legitimated by selection from the past. Once Aboriginal identity is stablised in a positive mode where pride is taken in Aboriginality, then the past becomes reified—a learning about the Aboriginal way of life rather than the incorporation of elements of the past into the present.

Returning to the brief constructed to focus our attention on the uses of the past as currency, the following implications may be identified. The emphasis by European academics on the past as currency for the construction of identity pushes urban people into a mythologising about the past. The remote past is a part of their world of meaning as history. It cannot be built into their world of meaning as part of a construction of contemporary identity that inserts itself into the present. An emphasis on the remote past acts to obscure the fundamental differences between the worlds of tradition-oriented Aboriginal people and urban Aboriginal people.

Selection by non-Aborigines from the past-of-the-middle-range appear to lead to the construction of an (Aboriginal) racist identity, a political base for 'aggro' activities. It is the remote past and the recent past that offer a positive identity without the degree of ambivalence found in the past-of-the-middle-range. Nevertheless, there again, because less emphasis is given to the recent past (which leads into a positive present and future) by European conceptualisations, there is a narrowing of the options of Aboriginal people for constructing a positive identity.

An exclusive emphasis on the past in the construction of Aboriginal identity ignores the present, and the contributions of Aboriginal people to white society; it ignores the possibility of a dialectic between white society and Aboriginal society as both evolve. Les Murray (1986), in choosing poems for *The New Oxford Book of Australian Verse*, has recognised the work of traditional Aboriginal writers, and let the authors of the past speak for themselves. At the same time, in his book *Persistence in Folly* (1984), Murray has attempted not just to write about the Aboriginal genre of writing but to engage in a dialectic with it. Similar movements encouraging a dialogue between Aboriginal and European artists and musicians have taken place in universities. This sort of interchange, enriching both cultures and building a new future, runs the risk of being unrecognised when there is too great a concentration on the past as currency in the construction of identity.

The conceptualisation of uses of the past under discussion results in an absence of dialogue with regard to a further important alternative in the construction of identity, namely the possibility of biculturalism. In tradition-oriented situations, there has been an evolving policy of biculturalism in schools. I believe that newly found multicultural bodies (wittingly or unwittingly) exclude Aborigines from the framework of a multicultural society by conceptualisations that fuse ethnicity with migrant status.[4] In this world of meaning, Aborigines are pushed to find a separate Aboriginal status. Yet the practicality of the situation is that urban people most often bear European names and are oriented in work and lifestyle to white society. Their problem is to construct a credible, positive identity and yet be able to move in and out of white society—in other words, they too, are asked to be bicultural.[5]

Academics must take responsibility for their part in the construction of Aboriginal worlds and for the directions in which their writings and their deliberations unwittingly contribute to Aboriginal identity by the very way in which research topics are conceptualised. It is of the utmost importance that we do not inherit in a transformed manner the will to 'do good' found in early missionaries with such disastrous effect. Rather, our construction of reality must be now concerned not with closing options, but opening up possibilities where Aboriginal people do have the real possibility of self-determination, above all in constructing identity.

Self-determination is real, though fragile, in the case of tradition-oriented people with their movement back to the Law. Self-determination for urban people will continue to be elusive while their history and their culture is mediated by others, and the evolution of Aboriginal identity takes place, not in an autonomous fashion, but as a response to the construction of knowledge by members of white society.

Notes

1. 'Intersubjective sedimentation takes place when several individuals share a common biography, experiences of which become incorporated in a common stock of knowledge' (Berger and Luckman 1966, 85).
2. For a discussion of problems inherent in a policy of Aboriginalisation of support services see Jordan 1985b; 1986c.
3. One school reported the extraordinary awe in which an initiated man was held when he occupied a position at the school of home-school liaison officer. He relinquished the position because he was horrified at the 'bad' behaviour of the children, which he categorised as not showing respect for elders, and not showing respect for themselves.
4. The intelligentsia leading the movement to conceptualise Australia as having a multicultural identity are confronted with the same problem. The definitions of Australian multicultural identity in the early 1970s, acted to exclude Aborigines since the conceptual framework used referred to migrants and ethnic groups. Aborigines did not fit this framework—they were 'unique'. It could be argued that it is precisely the fact that they are the indigenous people of Australia that makes them uniquely Australian.
5. It is interesting (and revealing, as an example of sedimentation of knowledge) to note (in the policy referred to in Note 4 put forward by King in South Australia), that despite King's enlightened attitude, he still thought of Aborigines as identifying with 'their own people'. The Aborigines to whom he referred were part-Aborigines, and therefore also part-European. It is a commentary on the perceptions of white society that contemporary theorisers, even the most enlightened, assume that Aborigines should identify with the race of their black parent rather than their white parent, and that the identity offered by mainstream society is one of exclusion from claims to European ancestry.

References

Berger, P.
1971 Identity As a Problem in the Sociology of Knowledge. In B.R. Cosin, I.R. Dale, G.M. Esland and D.F. Swift (eds), *School and Society*, Routledge and Kegan Paul, London.

Berger, P. and T. Luckmann
1966 *The Social Construction of Reality*, Allen Lane, London.

Cantle, M.
1978 The Umeewarra Story, unpublished manuscript, Port Augusta.

Commonwealth of Australian Parliamentary Debates
1963 *Aboriginal Welfare*, Report of Conference of Commonwealth and State Ministers, July, Darwin.
1986 House of Representatives, Vol H of R 60, E.G. Whitlam, debate, Canberra.

Gilbert, K.
1977 *Living Black: Blacks Talk to Kevin Gilbert*, Allen Lane, Melbourne.

Jordan, D.F.
1983 Identity as a Problem in the Sociology of Knowledge, PhD thesis, London University.
1984 The Social Construction of Identity, *Australian Journal of Education* 28(3), 274–90.
1985a Census Categories, Enumeration of Aboriginal People or Construction of Identity?, *Australian Aboriginal Studies* 1, 28–36.
1985b *Support Systems for Aboriginal Students in Higher Education Institutions: Report to the Commonwealth Tertiary Education Commission and the National Aboriginal Education Committee*, Tertiary Education Association of South Australia, Adelaide.
1986a Aborigines in a Multi-Cultural Society: A Sharing of Dreams?, *Journal of Inter-cultural Studies* 7(2), 5–29.
1986b Rights and Claims of Indigenous People—Education and the Re-Claiming of Identity, the Case of Canadian Natives, the Sami and Australian Aborigines. In J. Rick (ed), *Arduous Journey, Canadian Natives and Decolonization*, Ponting, Toronto.
1986c Demographic and Social Changes and their Implications for the Role of Women, with Special Reference to Australian Aborigines, Paper Presented at the World Congress of Sociology, Delhi, August.

Mitchell, G.D. (ed)
1979 *A New Dictionary of Sociology*, Routledge and Kegan Paul, London.

Murray, L.A.
1984 *Persistence in Folly*, Sirius Books, Melbourne.

1986 *The New Oxford Book of Australian Verse*, Oxford University Press, Melbourne.

Palmer, G.
1986 Determining Pre-School Children's Racial Attitudes from their Response to Books, PhD thesis, Flinders University, Adelaide.

Rowley, C.D.
1971 *Outcasts in White Australia, Aboriginal Policy and Practice*, Australian National University Press, Canberra.

Schutz, A.
1973 *Collected Papers I*, Martinus Nijhoff, The Hague.

Stone, S.
1974 *Aborigines in White Australia: A Documentary History of the Attitudes Affecting Official Policy and the Australian Aborigines, 1967–1973*, Heinemann, Melbourne.

Tatz, C.M. (ed)
1975 *Black Viewpoints: The Aboriginal Experience*, Australia and New Zealand Book Company, Sydney.

Turnbull, C.
1972 Tasmania: The Ultimate Solution. In F.S. Stevens (ed), *Racism: The Australian Experience*, Volume 2, Australia and New Zealand Book Company, Sydney.

Watson, R.
1977 Ross Watson. In K. Gilbert (ed), *Living Black: Blacks Talk to Kevin Gilbert*, Allen Lane, Melbourne.

8. Robert Ariss   Writing black: the construction of an Aboriginal discourse

It is generally acknowledged that the modern nation state is the major locus of power in the contemporary world, and that all power relations which come into operation within the nation state are ultimately circumscribed by this dominant stage of power. As the final voice of authority the state establishes the conditions of possibility within which all power relations, all resistances, may operate. Beckett (1986,3), in discussing the relations of power between Australian Aborigines and the white colonial state, identifies the final locus of control in the latter.

> The state has not only controlled most of the information and expertise, as well as the means for its propogation; but has had the power to bring Aborigines some way toward external conformity with its constructions. When Aboriginal people have participated in the process it has been largely through government funded—and in the final analysis controlled—agencies.

Recognising this, how are we to better understand the position of Aborigines in contemporary Australia? The above analysis is only a beginning. Foucault has attempted to demonstrate that power relations must be seen, not as static situations, but as processes, relations of strategy, and sometimes of confrontation. Nor is it useful to visualise power as congealed into a single source. It is, rather, a dynamic system resulting from the interplay of multiple sites of power. There is a necessary reciprocity involved in any relation of power (cited in Rabinow 1984, 63-64):

> If one describes phenomena of power as dependant on the state apparatus, this means grasping them as essentially repressive...(but) relations of power, and hence the analysis that must be made of them, necessarily extend beyond the limits of the state. In two senses: first of all because the state, for all the omnipotence of its apparatuses, is far from being able to occupy the whole field of actual power relations, and further because the state can only operate on the basis of other, already existing power relations.

The issue pursued in this chapter is the place of Aboriginal literature, as a discursive field, within the relationship of power prevailing between the Aboriginal community and the dominant Euro-Australian community. I wish to show Aboriginal discourse, not simply as an image of state constructions, but also as a creative force which contributes to public constructions of Aboriginality. By focusing on the Aboriginal side of the power equation it becomes possible to see the relationship between blacks and whites in Australia not simply as one of domination and subordination, of oppressor and oppressed, but as a power relation in Foucault's sense—a relation where transformations are possible, if not necessary, in social life.

Certainly Aboriginal discourse is constrained by the dominant symbolic forms it is forced to adopt when moving into the public domain, yet this structured limitation does not exclude the possibility of a counterdiscourse having a coercive and innovative potential, a potential to effect changes in the symbolic field within which Aboriginality is discussed. The position of Aborigines is changing in Australia and I do not think this is attributable to an evolving state benevolence in itself. The intervention of Aborigines has been an essential force behind these innovations. It is they who are establishing progressively greater control over the constructions of Aboriginality. It is this intervention I wish to discuss.

Ways of seeing, styles of discourse, are a reflection of the power relationships within which they are embedded. Aboriginal discourse itself asserts an essential Aboriginality that is absent from white authored constructions. It is apparent in the analysis that this position is itself more a reflection of, and an assumed ideological weapon against, prevailing power relations between Aboriginal and European cultures, rather than having any readily identifiable reality in symbolic constructions. But it is not so much the uniqueness of its symbolic forms that is significant, as the political meanings with which such black authored constructions are imbued. This counterdiscourse is undergoing a constructive process in the attempt to locate that precise Aboriginality. The apparent essence of the discourse is a pervasive and shared sense of experience. It is the existential experience of being Aboriginal that lies at the base of Aboriginal constructions. Although the discourse is itself fragmented, an emerging (dominant) Aboriginality asserts the impossibility of the complete merging of black and white understandings. It is anti-anthropological in the sense that it defies crosscultural emic communication which lies at the theoretical root of the anthropological enterprise. It is only through the adoption of this separatist ideology, an Aboriginality of concrete otherness, that the dominant strains of black discourse seek to actualise a future offered by the dominant European culture—self-determination. Because black discourse seeks to detach Aboriginality from any form of intrusion from the dominant culture, it professes an ideology of self-determination which is qualitatively different, truer, than that sustained by the dominant culture embodied in official government policy. It is the appropriation of the loci of control of Aboriginal life, including symbolic constructions, which is seen as the only feasible means of approaching true self-determination. Superficially this is a logic identical to that of government policy, yet black discourse seeks to demystify, to expose the hypocrisy and unreality of government policy, and to reassert a more realistic ideology of self-determination.

This position of otherness raises problems of a semiotic nature. It is the problem of interpretation arising when two cultures attempt to redefine the channels through which each communicates to the other, one seeking to actualise its uniqueness in stressing its insurmountable cultural differences, while simultaneously adapting the discursive practices of the culture it is seeking to distance itself from. This raises the problem of interpretability for any non-Aboriginal reader and places a non- Aboriginal commentator in a particularly difficult position.

Cultural cohesion and political power is enhanced for the subordinate culture by entering the public discursive realm. In so doing it must to some extent adopt and work with the symbolic forms of the dominant culture. The discourse is forced, thereby, to assert its otherness without appearing to mimic cultural forms alien to it, for such a situation undermines its very authenticity. Considering this it is something of a surprise that contemporary Aboriginal cultural expressions defy cliched expressions of traditionality by espousing an adaptability and eclecticism. It is in fact popular European folk models which cling to more conservative constructions—the corroborree, the boomerang, the naked savage eking out an existence in the harsh desert environment. Such romantic images reflect (or are remnants of) an ideal power relationship. A counterconstruction which stresses cultural dynamism is seeking to negate the cultural hegemony implicit in such conservative constructions. A further difficulty arises for black discourse in the task of redefining Aboriginality in this way. There is conflict in an immutable Aboriginality which is simultaneously capable of adaptation and cultural eclecticism, an eclecticism which must not threaten a cohesive and politically efficacious construction of Aboriginality.

There are a number of distinct but interrelated loci of production of discourse within the Aboriginal domain. One is the government established, supervised and financed political and social organisations whose *raison d'etre* is (theoretically) the advancement of Aboriginal interests—for example the National Aboriginal Conference (NAC), Aboriginal medical and legal service organisations, individual parliamentarians and advisors. Another area is represented by those individuals and organisations who articulate through the media of the arts. I will focus here on the media of literature. Their presence is sustained in the public domain, through the

English language, by predominantly white controlled publishing organisations. Literature in this case is a broader range of discourse than that traditionally associated with European literature. It encompasses critical essay, interview and autobiography, myth and legend transcription and interpretation, as well as the more familiar forms like prose, poetry and dramatic text. 'I think we need to take Literature in its broader aspect, and any expression of that Aboriginal culture is Literature, black literature' (McGuiness and Walker 1985, 50).

The writers I will mainly concern myself with include Gilbert, Sykes, Johnson, Mary Coe, Bropho and Roughsey. These authors seek to give a representative voice to the differentiated mass of the Aboriginal population through the process of literary fixation. The base of their approach is personal experience, the particularistic, articulated through its identification with a community, often genealogical, which is localised but suggestive of a broader social context. This could be characterised as a pan-Aboriginality; one which transcends specific kinship ties to encompass all those who identify as Aboriginal. The process of literary fixation lifts the private into the public domain by entering, via the written word, the mainstream Australian literary tradition. These writers seek to unify diverse experience under a single rubric of Aboriginality. Aboriginal authorship is the simplest common source of identification. Locating Aboriginality separate from but simultaneously within the dominant European society, this discourse is implicitly and sometimes explicitly conscious of its Fourth World political status, as an entity subordinate to and in opposition to the dominant culture. It is by nature a political construction grounded in a post-contact history. Its second feature, integral with the first, is its identification of Aboriginality through concepts of 'tradition'. The overriding concern of this discourse is to construct a continuity of Aboriginality through the linking of the traditional and the contemporary via the common suffering of all Aborigines at the hands of the European intrusion, and through that to project a course for the future. The survival and/or reworking of particular traditional cultural forms in the face of this potentially genocidal force into the present is a recurring theme. These central tensions shape the discursive form—the tensions between the traditional–contemporary and the particular–universal.

Aboriginal discourse firstly locates its identity in its historicity. Its discursive task is to deconstruct European representations and to re-present Australian history as Aboriginal history, history from the perspective of the oppressed, the indigine, rather than the colonialist. In placing Aborigines in history as victims it seeks simultaneously to project the image of Aborigines, not as passive social 'agents' as in many dominant representations, but as active resisters, first against colonial intrusion, then as active repossessors of a fragmented culture. The activation of Aborigines in history is latent in the perspective of the first person. The discourse is primarily actor-oriented, first person, experiential. As the central characters in the historical drama, Aborigines are interpretable, not simply as acted upon, but as responding to external forces and themselves constitutive of historical events. Contrast, for example, the following two perspectives, the first white, then black (Rowley 1970, 149; Coe 1986, 30):

> we cannot, I think, fairly write a guerilla *war* waged *by* Aborigines...The lack of effective leadership was a handicap not only for physical resistance but for treaty and discussion.

> the warriors led by Windradyne, started out on their campaign for justice...the warriors divided into smaller groups which carried out guerilla-style warfare against the white man.

A further example, this time a contemporary political analysis from Bobby Sykes (1986, 16–17):

> no black community initiated and controlled organization known to me...has had an easy birth. All have been obliged to deal with negativism and opposition from government in their formative stages, and engage in a constant struggle for control of their organizations if and when federal funding was eventually extended to them...The active role of the Blacks must be minimized and passivity maximized so that the government can be viewed as both supportive and benevolent.

In this passage, Sykes identifies the prevailing passive construction of Aboriginality as an explicitly political ideology sustained for the benefit of the state. The Aboriginal response is to demystify this construction by portraying black culture, past and present, as dynamic, adaptable and the product of struggle.

The patterns of change are attributed to an immutable Aboriginality—the continuation of indigenous cultural forms, or the production of new forms under the constraints of this traditionality. The constraining and creative forces behind this construction of Aboriginality are as much located within Aboriginal culture as in the dominating culture of the white man.

This identification of cultural traits is fraught with difficulties, however. Because of the absence of written records before the European invasion, and the fragmentation of Aboriginal societies, and consequently of Aboriginal knowledge of such times, the precise nature of pre-contact culture is lost. Blacks are as aware of this as are whites. This forces black discourse to use frequent reference to European constructions to discover and sustain its own identity.

> No one can recall any such history of the third or fourth generation...that's the limit to our race of people...just lucky you have some Europeans who are interested in black peoples way of living from the past (Roughsey 1984, 120, 98).

> I am thrilled at the knowledge that has come through archaeologists and scientists about the Aborigines. To me, it is as though the ancients are trying to relay a message not only to the Aboriginal race, but to the human race (Tucker 1977, 149).

Likewise, the concept of a pan-Aboriginality is quite foreign to traditional (pre-contact) Aboriginal consciousness. It is only in juxtaposition with a foreign presence that an Aboriginal otherness becomes meaningful. Pan-Aboriginality is a politically necessary concept for Aborigines to present a united, and therefore more efficacious front to a government reluctant to recognise their demands. The recourse to traditionality is perhaps as much politically induced as a felt reality in the minds of Aborigines. In emphasising traditional culture, its otherness, Aboriginal discourse establishes itself firmly in opposition to the dominant culture. It is only from this position that Aboriginal people can resist the seduction of assimilation and confidently work at rebuilding a unique identity. The use of non-Aboriginal sources becomes a task of reinterpretation. Its origin outside the Aboriginal community does not negate its validity as an indicator of Aboriginal culture, nor of its political efficaciousness. The essential point is that when it is reinterpreted and articulated from within the political community it becomes valid, accountable. I return to Mary Coe's historical reconstruction to demonstrate this process.

Coe's book is a re-presentation of a localised Aboriginal history told through the life history of an Aboriginal culture hero, Windradyne. Interestingly, two distinct Aboriginal histories are presented in the text, the first is pre-contact, a history undifferentiated: life is in balance; cataclysmic events are absent from the Aboriginal experience; people and nature are in harmony, almost undifferentiated themselves: 'They were so close to nature that they were in it. The land owned them as much as they owned the land' (Coe 1986,7). It is instructive to compare Coe's characterisation of pre-contact culture with one of her European sources to reveal just how directly this discourse is appropriated. Compare, for example, the following two texts, white and black (see Merritt 1978; Coe 1986, 5, 7):

> A more significant proof of their integration into the environment was their effective conservation of its resources, for they lived in harmony with the environment, animal, bird and plant life...they did, however, set light to the country at times to foster fresh grass regrowth, thus making ideal browsing conditions for kangaroo and emu.

> Many large treeless areas were kept clear by controlled burning to encourage the growth of grass which kangaroos came to graze on...their culture was based on co-operation and conservation. They never needlessly killed or injured any living being.

In Coe's text history only becomes dynamic and directional with the arrival of the European. Aboriginal history becomes a history of resistance, of war. 'The white man's law did not protect Kooris from their guns so Kooris must apply their own law to the whites—for the white men were lawless' (Coe 1986, 23). Today resistance continues in different political guises but the ideology of political practice is the same. The final images in the text are of a land rights demonstration and the Aboriginal flag emblazoning the back cover—'we have survived as a nation' (Coe 1986, 62). The construction at work here is that of an immutable Aboriginal Law in operation, ensuring the continuation of Aboriginal existence in the face of the hypocritical and inimical law of the European: 'the invaders preached Christianity but few practised it' (Coe 1986, 22).

Note the shift from past to present tense, in speaking of this Aboriginal political action in the quote from page 23. This seems to reinforce the sense of the immutability, the timelessness of the Aboriginal Law. Characteristically, land and Law are one and the same: Aboriginal is land is Law. Hence this history is one of the threat to Aboriginal culture through the appropriation of land, and the continued resistance and struggle to reclaim it. Land is appropriated but identity is sustained through the operation of its ideological metaphor—the Law:

> unlike our Law, the white man's law, for good or ill, could be changed, or 'amended' with the stroke of a pen...there was nothing sacred or constant in that law...Justice and honour and national integrity had no bearing on such matters (Gilbert 1985, 37).

It is through the idiom of Law that the traditional land owning Aborigine is linked to the contemporary alienated Aborigine. Aboriginal history becomes a history integral with the fight for social justice.

The fact that the material Coe uses to construct a text is recognisably historical in the European tradition, does not detract from the text's Aboriginality. What is important is the orientation of the author and to whom the text is ultimately accountable. Langton, writing in *Identity*, stated that any discourse about Aborigines must also be written for Aborigines, that is, accountable. It is only when discourse is generated outside that community that it is questionable, non-representative, myth-generating and inevitably coloured by the power dimensions which are, because outside, inimical to that community (Langton 1981, 11). If this is correct then the source of information used is irrelevant to the overall presentation of the Aboriginal perspective. The orientation of the author is sufficient. Coe, writing from within the Aboriginal community, is creating a counterdiscourse using material from the very discursive arena that she is attempting to negate. Interestingly this method enhances her success in the eyes of the reader. The material from the public, white stage speaks against itself when placed in the context of the black viewpoint, black authorship. Coe's work demonstrates that with careful construction and the aid of the perspective of the oppressed, public, dominant discourse can be turned against itself. Black discourse does not need to create afresh new material, it need only expose the hypocrisy of the dominant modes of expression. The problem raised by this faith in black authorship is that it attributes a homogeneity to Aboriginal opinion and disregards the fact of diversity within the Aboriginal community for the sake of sustaining an image of a pan-Aboriginality—a mythical reality in itself. I will return to this problem later but first I wish to discuss further literary styles in Aboriginal discourse.

Another method by which Aboriginal discourse seeks to reconstruct its historicity, one which does not rely on the direct appropriation of European historical records, is a discursive form which asserts oral history as characteristically Aboriginal. The fascinating complexity at work here is the attempt by these writers to sustain oral traditions through written language. Two forces are at work. First, the felt need by many writers to cultivate literary forms that are identifiably Aboriginal in a traditional sense, and second, the political drive for a construction of a pan-Aboriginality which demands a crosscommunity communication and identification. 'The problem...is getting blacks just to know about each other, in such a vast country as this' (see Gilbert 1977, 115).

Aboriginal writers are conscious of the contradictions and difficulties associated with experimentation in written media. The tension between the old and the new is again a concern. As I have noted, it is the political status of Aborigines within a dominating culture that necessitates their taking up the discursive practices of that culture in order to assert its separate identity while simultaneously building communication with that culture. What each example of this particular genre attempts to do is transform instances of an oral tradition into written discourse yet simultaneously attempting to retain or even recreate its oracy. It pretends to overcome the semiotic transformation which occurs in the act of writing—the fixation of the personal and experiential into an independent, context free, open-ended text capable of generating a multiplicity of meanings. The potential interpretive problems are made more complex when one considers that this discourse is seeking to distance itself, in terms of cultural uniqueness, from the audience it is creating.

Non-Aboriginal critiques of such texts point to these interpretive difficulties. Readers familiar with their own traditional literary forms express difficulties when experiencing texts which seek deliberately to violate comfortable norms. Tess de Araugo (see Barwick 1981, 79) complains of a 'rambling, conversational and sometimes confusing style'; Ryan (1986) that the photographs tend to be 'more revealing than the text'; Corns (see Barwick 1981) of a 'thinness of information' and a 'rambling anecdotal character'. The problem here appears to be that the absence of familiar narrative structures, grammatical indicators (eg tense), or a reader's lack of culture-specific knowledge impairs a fluid reading of the text. Contrast this with a reading by an Aboriginal person and the interpretive problem seems to disappear. Kath Walker (1975, 38) of Bropho's *Fringedweller* reports that the monotony and lack of system in the unedited narrative makes 'the book not easy to read', however it bears a positive effect for her—'bound in the repetitiveness are the voices of people calling to the...government to lift them out of their misery and degradation...I became aware of a culture of poverty...I can understand the author'.

It is rather hazardous to imply that this variation of interpretation is solely due to the cultural identity of the individual reader. The diversity of the reader's experiences and expectations, black or white is an important influence in the response. It may be argued that the penchant for experimentation in European literature is well suited to accommodating challenging new styles and indeed readers should not be too surprised to be challenged themselves. Ryan (1986, 50) has likened Aboriginal oral histories to the broken narrative, 'flow of consciousness' styles of Joyce and Proust. Indeed it is precisely through breaking with conventional styles that European literature has continually sought to recreate its audience—to challenge its perceptions and to win allies. With this in mind, I would argue that it is through entering written discourse that the social and political objectives of Aborigines take on exciting new possibilities in terms of self-definition and the reorientation of white perceptions to increase receptivity to the Aboriginal presence.

Whatever the precise nature of traditional oral literature, it is certain that it undergoes a number of transformations in the process of fixation into writing. Such changes must give the literature a qualitatively different form and potential meaning. Berndt, in an introduction to the 1983 Aboriginal writers' conference, characterised traditional oral literature as encompassing a plurality of aesthetic media. The spoken word is supported by dramatic and musical accompaniment as well as the more linguistic elements of imagery, symbolism and metaphor. It is this discourse which is familiar to Aboriginal culture as the media of information and socialisation—the constitution of subjectivity (Berndt 1985, 8). In the written form, this plurality of media is reduced to the written word, with the possible support of photographic images (this is a particularly common feature). In this context the word carries a greater responsibility in conveying meaning. Also the context of illicitation has changed. Instead of being directed to a specific, culturally homogeneous and visible audience, the written discourse is generated for an invisible, culturally diverse audience of unknown size. Colin Johnson (see Davis and Hodge 1985, 88), in searching for compatible written forms finds poetry and short story 'closer' to traditional Aboriginal forms because of their greater 'immediacy', they 'come from the heart' rather than the more deliberately worked forms of prose that come 'from the head', the audience can 'hear the sounds of the words rather than the content'. Emotional immediacy seems to be a critical element in the conveyance of meaning to Johnson, much as one would suspect from a tradition which did not rely so fully on the word. In terms of content, Johnson (see Davis and Hodge 1985, 87) characterises the present literature as 'protest' literature and in that sense not 'traditional'. It is only after the political struggle that Aboriginal expression can begin to approach a truer Aboriginality—'we can go back to our roots, to our culture, and develop a much more vital Australian poetry'.

For Johnson, then, present Aboriginal expression is very much a product of its political status; it is as much a product of struggle as it is for Coe or Sykes or Gilbert. But its present form is still a perversion, an Aboriginality forced into an unfamiliar mode—the protest mode, even the written literary form itself, it is made unnatural perhaps, by the very corruption of traditional Aboriginal culture. There is an Aboriginality, yet still elusive. He glimpses its roots in the past, and anticipates it in the future. In this future Johnson sees a necessary depoliticisation of Aboriginal culture, a move I imagine the prevailing powers would condone.

This present political dimension in the production of discourse is a determinant force shaping Aboriginal writing. The fact of the necessary interaction between blacks and whites gives the discourse a political status. To be specific, it has emerged over the last few decades or so that the issue of control of production is crucial to the construction of a truer Aboriginality. There has been a gradual appropriation of control of the production of discourse. In this we can see an emergence of more fully controlled texts, though not necessarily an identifiable, coherent and singular Aboriginality, least of all anything suggestive of Johnson's apolitical traditionality. Since the white authored texts of the 1960s which narrated biographies of particular Aborigines known to whites, Aboriginal writers have gained increasing control over black input, editing and publishing. (The establishment of Black Books as an independent publishing organisation is the latest event in this history of repossession.)

The enhancement of political control over discursive production is seen within the Aboriginal community to be determinant in the emergence of a move toward, a truer Aboriginality purged of white interference.

> We maintain that unless Aboriginal people control the funding...the content, the publishing, and the ultimate presentation of the article, then it is *not* Aboriginal; then it ceases to be Aboriginal when it is interfered with when it is tampered with by non-Aboriginal people who exist outside of the spectrum of Aboriginal life (McGuiness and Walker 1985, 44).

> White Anthropologists, lawyers, and historians have a great deal of difficulty in translating Aboriginal concepts into white terminology. They simply cannot do it well. They cannot readily understand what we are doing, why we are here and who we are (Langton 1981, 11).

The issue of control and therefore of interpretation remains an operative concept in black writing.

A truer Aboriginality recognises itself less in notions of pristine traditionality than in terms of its accountability. Authorship and political motivation are more important in the definition of Aboriginality than cultural indicators such as narrative shape. This Aboriginality emerges after political control is secured. Aboriginal discourse is too concerned with the presentation of a realism of contemporary Aboriginal existence—an existence which is only thrown into relief when articulated in terms of its relationship with the dominating European society—to speak of traditionality as more than a point of reference, a symbolic counterculture. Certainly, traditional concerns have a reality in Aboriginal discourse, particularly the concerns of kinship and geographical identity, yet these are secondary, or perhaps contained within, the overriding political concerns.

Robert Bropho's *Fringedweller* has been described by Johnson as the first 'true autobiography' of an Aboriginal untainted by white interference. Having been 'more or less directly translated from the tape', it speaks more directly to the reader than would have been possible with the interference of a white editor (Johnson 1985, 25). Yet its Aboriginality is not articulated in terms of traditionality, but rather the political and social reality of the narrator. For Bropho, the issue of control over the text becomes a metaphor for his central theme—Aboriginal control over their own lives. Targeted specifically to a white audience, communication is his primary objective and he is most matter of fact in his task. There is little possibility for misinterpretations: 'You are masters of your own destiny, that's you the white man. Let us, the fringedwellers be masters of ours (Bropho 1983, 31).

Johnson (1985, 25) anticipates this form of writing to be a 'forerunner of a new Aboriginal literature'. The fact that it is the control over production rather than any inherent discursive style that is indicative of Aboriginality is evident in his description of other autobiographies. The oracy of Bropho is missing in the work of Sykes and Smith (*Mum Shirl*), the text is polished and 'articulate' yet it still 'feels' Aboriginal (Johnson 1985, 25). The problem with this vagueness of Aboriginality, an Aboriginality capable of eclecticism, quirky individualism or educated articulateness, is that its degree of Aboriginality cannot be located in the text itself. It must be sought in an extra-discursive realm, in a commentary or introduction (often supplied by a non-Aboriginal).

This pre-occupation with the purity of Aboriginality found in literature has become manifest by the frequent inclusion, in introductions, appendixes or back page commentaries outlining the precise circumstances of the texts' production. The role of interpreters, editors, authors and non-Aboriginal authorities is spelled out for the benefit of the reader. These entrees to the text proper are themselves integral to the production of an assured and confident Aboriginality for the unsuspecting reader.

Roughsey's *An Aboriginal Mother Speaks* (1984) is a recent example. Roughsey's text comes from her own pen, minimally edited, with her supervision, by two white academics whom she 'decided to get help from'. These editors themselves comment on the complexities of editing while remaining true to the original text. A system was devised to do so while simultaneously trying to 'make easy the reading of the text for the non-Aboriginal reader'. Hence the text was structured into paragraphs and chapters, tenses standardised to differentiate more clearly past and present, spellings corrected and footnoted commentaries added where ambiguities interfered with the reading (Roughsey 1984, 241). To what extent does the text remain interpretable to both black and white readers within the bounds of the author's intentions—to educate the reader 'to read with the most interest and learn from it, so we can closely contact with love' (Roughsey 1984, 236)?

To ask whether this text is more or less Aboriginal than the autobiographical sketches of Bropho or Gilbert, or the representations of Stanner or Elkin, is to require an analysis which looks beyond the text itself to its history of production, for by itself it cannot convince us of its authenticity. Ultimately it is Aborigines themselves, the authors, the black readers and all who place themselves within the identity of 'Aboriginal' who must be the judges. The validity of the text becomes a problem of accountability.

It would be naive to expect a homogeneity of opinion within the black community. There is a wide range of opinions and aspirations as well as experiences. Gilbert (1977, 1, 93) has criticised, and directs his work to the correction of, certain myths which Aborigines as well as whites are inclined to perpetuate:

> together with a number of sympathetic whites, they embrace and propogate a number of myths...There are a few vague dreams about...'self-determination', 'land rights', 'we must get back to our Aboriginality', but there is no cohesive drive to achieve any of these things. Because so many of the leaders have no wider vision, no standard and no rules, the black movement at the present time is a game played solely according to their moods.

In speaking in these terms Gilbert is hinting that the next step in Aboriginal discourse is the move toward more direct control of Aboriginal writing, and hence a more guided and intelligent construction of Aboriginality. It is not only white myths which must be debunked, but also inappropriate black ones. In another field, Rob Merritt, on the film production of his screenplay 'Short Changed', commented that his conflict with white director Ogilvie has left him determined to direct his next screenplay himself, to avoid misrepresentation (*Sydney Morning Herald*, 8 November 1986). (It should be noted that neither Merritt's 'Short Changed' nor two other films on Aborigines—the white authored and produced 'Fringedwellers' and 'Backlash'—were successful at the box office. Despite 'Short Changed' and 'Fringedwellers' being critically acclaimed and nominated for awards, none of these films ran for more than a few weeks on the Sydney cinema circuit.) Merritt's position in the Aboriginal Arts Board (AAB) places him in a position of some influence to pursue his ambitions. The role of leading individuals such as Gilbert and Merritt may become more central in the future as this counterdiscursive stage becomes more coherent and articulate.

The ascent of individuals such as Gilbert and Merritt clarifies the political problem of accountability—accountable to whom? Clearly it is the intention of such publicly prominent figures to exert their own judgement more decisively on the issue of selecting and propagating a particular Aboriginality over any other. These figures seek to further clarify, solidify, a politically efficacious Aboriginality. Their success depends on financial allocation (sponsorship for Merritt, or fund allocation to the AAB), as much as more purely ideological issues. It is here that the construction of

Aboriginality becomes an issue of personal as much as community politics—the myth of Aboriginality as community-centred breaks down. Though such individuals invariably feel to some extent representative, accountable to their communities, it is their actions on the personal level that largely determines their success.

The plurality of the Aboriginal community compounds the complexity of the self-determination issue. How much is Merritt's accountability reaching beyond his political ambitions, as an artist and an administrator and organiser to the particular theatre or film group he may be working with, to his tribal identity (eg to the Wiradjuri in the *Cake Man*), to all Aborigines, to all blacks, all oppressed people *ad infinitum*? Can we equate Merritt's sense of accountability with the nebulous nationality and sense of responsibility such as Walker or Tucker alude to? In the latter views Aboriginality is finally subsumed under a general humanism, a concern for all persons regardless of cultural or racial identity.

> White people have many different nationalities in their inheritance too. I am always saying that color is not the issue, it is character that counts (Tucker 1977, 87).

> My love is my own people first
> And after that, mankind.
> I don't see myself as an Aboriginal poet. I see myself as a universal poet who happens to be of Aboriginal descent (see Davis and Hodge 1985, 82).

In counterpoint, Gilbert, long a radical exponent, continues to warn against a too accommodating stance toward the colonial aggressor. In his own poetry Gilbert states (see Davis and Hodge 1985, 85):

> In another time, another age,
> If fate had reversed the play,
> And a hard black boot pressed on your white throat,
> When released what would you say?
> Friends and pals forever together
> In a new fair dawn?
> Or meet like you and I shall meet
> With flames and daggers drawn?

The politics of Walker or Tucker are quite different from that of Gilbert. It is even quite tempting to pass off Gilbert as a discursive eccentric in the continuum of Aboriginal discourse. The heady Black Power rhetoric of the politically charged early 1970s was something of an interference in the discourse which redirected the sychophantic nationalism of the early assimilationist days into a more resistant, separatist discourse more aware and assertive of its otherness. Black discourse adopted self-determination as a means of further constructing this otherness. We are charged with the impression in the 1980s that Aboriginal life is less politically volatile, less violent than the threatened aggression of the 1970s rhetoric, than those early years of self-determination. This impression, imparted by the relative absence in recent years of the political Aboriginal in the media generally, is a result of the increasingly effective appropriation of black political action within the state apparatus. This appropriation has seen the effective retreat of a public political Aboriginality. As power struggles become more firmly located within the state apparatus, the more obvious political machinations of the Aboriginal struggle recedes from public view. What is left is an apparent 'cultural Aboriginality' devoid of an overtly political struggle. Aboriginality as culture, as art, literature and dance emerges as the predominant expression. This apparent teasing of the political from the cultural, I would suggest, is rather misleading. Aboriginal organisation rely more than ever on the allocation of federal and state funds. The financial struggle is becoming a pervasive aspect of Aboriginal life. Perhaps soon the vying for private funds will become a more feasible alternative and new possibilities of struggle and control may emerge.

It is misleading to attempt to separate culture and politics at all in the field of Aboriginal discourse. I do not think Aborigines readily abstract culture from politics, particularly when so much cultural activity today relies on government funding. In many ways the continuing efforts of Aborigines to pursue their social and political integrity is seeing this diversification of expressions, in the areas of literature, dance, film and the visual arts. Such cultural growth is dialectic. Black and white communities are communicating more with each other. Through its entry into public discourse, Aboriginal consciousness is reasserting its own integrity and uniqueness, while non-Aborigines can only find it increasingly difficult not to hear the voice of a people once written out of history. Only by speaking for themselves can that presence be a real force for change. The process of becoming public forces Aboriginal discourse into recognising and taking up (at least the outward) forms of the public cultural stage. Aboriginality becomes contemporary, in literature, film, theatre, in political organisation and action. None of these contemporary forms is recognisably traditional, except in the most nebulous of senses. But they are nonetheless Aboriginal when in the hands of those who identify and seek to assert their identity, as Aborigines, through those media.

References

Barwick, D.E.
1981 Writing Aboriginal History: Comments on a Book and its Reviewers, *Canberra Anthropology* 4(2), 74–86.

Beckett, J.
1986 Uses of the Past in the Construction of Aboriginality, Paper Presented to the Biennial Meetings of the Australian Institute of Aboriginal Studies, 13 May.

Berndt, R.M.
1985 Opening Address. In J. Davis and B. Hodge (eds), *Aboriginal Writing Today*, Australian Institute of Aboriginal Studies, Canberra, 7–10.

Bropho, R.
1983 *Fringedweller*, Alternative Publishing Co-operative Ltd, Sydney.

Coe, M.
1986 *Windradyne—A Wiradjuri Koori*, Black Books, Sydney.

Davis, J. and B. Hodge (eds)
1985 *Aboriginal Writing Today*, Australian Institute of Aboriginal Studies, Canberra.

Gilbert, K.
1977 *Living Black: Blacks Talk to Kevin Gilbert*, Allen Lane, Melbourne.
1985 Black Policies. In J. Davis and B. Hodge (eds), *Aboriginal Writing Today*, Australian Institute of Aboriginal Studies, Canberra, 35–42.

Johnson, C.
1985 White Forms, Aboriginal Content. In J. Davis and B. Hodge (eds), *Aboriginal Writing Today*, Australian Institute of Aboriginal Studies, Canberra, 21–34.

Langton, M.
1981 Anthropologists Must Change, *Identity* 4(4), 11.

McGuinness, B. and D. Walker
1985 The Politics of Aboriginal Literature. In J. Davis and B. Hodge (eds), *Aboriginal Writing Today*, Australian Institute of Aboriginal Studies, Canberra, 43–54.

Merritt, R.
1978 *The Cake Man*, Currency Press, Sydney.

Rabinow, P.
1984 *The Foucault Reader*, Pantheon, New York.

Roughsey, E.
1984 *An Aboriginal Mother Speaks of the Old and the New*, Penguin, Harmondsworth.

Rowley, C.D.
1970 *Outcasts in White Australia*, Australian National University Press, Canberra.

Ryan, L.
1986 Reading Aboriginal Histories, *Meanjin* 1, 49–57.

Sykes, R.
1986 *Incentive, Achievement and Community*, Sydney University Press, Sydney.

Tucker, M.
1977 *If Everyone Cared*, Grosvenor Books, Melbourne.

Walker, K.
1975 Aboriginal Literature, *Identity* 2(3), 39–40.

9. Basil Sansom   The past is a doctrine of person

There are two ways of considering the past, that is, things and beings that have perished: the conservative standpoint, which harks back to the past, implies faith in tradition; and the creative and transfiguring vision which integrates the past in the future and eternity and resuscitates dead things and beings. Only the second approach is in harmony with the present which is inherent in the past; the first merely reflects the actual present which is always becoming the past (Berdyaev 1938).

In human practice, the use of the past must centre around some doctrine of person. Somehow, the authors of past acts must be given character if they are to appear as actors on a scene. The question is: What manner of human actor will be admitted into consciousness by those who would use past human acts and states of being as substance in their discourse? After Geertz, we may note that because the problems posed by this question are existential, they are universally encountered. 'Their solutions [however], being human are diverse' (Geertz 1975, 363).

In language supplied by Kenneth Burke (1969), the issue can be more precisely phrased: To be admitted into discourse, human authors of acts must continually be given character as they apply agencies to some purpose and so appear as volitional agents on a scene. Any style of practice can usefully be analysed through consideration of the way in which its practitioners place emphasis and value on act in relation to scene, in relation to agent, agency and purpose. Always in practice one or more of the relationships among this pentad of terms is stressed to the neglect of the remaining possibilities. Thus the Great Man theory of history (besides being androgenous in its designation), emphatically structures the past around the agent–scene ratio. The heroes of such history are men who make their worlds anew. In contrast, Marxist thinking requires 'the systematic featuring of act' (Burke 1969, 210). This act is the revolution toward which class conflict inevitably tends because opposing class agents are located in a scene (the capitalist system as such), which has its own dynamic and which implacably drives them.

Burke's grammar of the permutations of ratios is as handy for anthropology as it is for the analysis of political constitutions and philosophies. It has promise because it is crafted to comprehend diverse ways (themselves Burkian agencies), of and for imagining the world and those who people it.

This chapter is written to show an antinomy of doctrines. There is, on the one hand, the late Professor CD Rowley's mercantile doctrine of person. It is central to his authoritative trilogy on Aboriginal society and also to his posthumously published book, *Recovery: The Politics of Aboriginal Reform* (1986). On the other hand, I deal with an Aboriginal doctrine of person whose terms were vouchsafed to me when I did fieldwork in Darwin.[1]

The Aboriginal doctrine is religious, grounded in ideas about the creativity of spirit. Each of the two doctrines is at the centre of its own world of discourse. Thus located, each doctrine is entailed in its particular order of practice that brings the past to the present. The task I have set myself is to discuss the effects of the centrality of different doctrines of person—one seated in the practice of a scholar, the other vested in cultural practice among the Aborigines I know.

The past in Rowley's practice

A major device in Rowley's practice is the assimilation of human acts to scene. He makes the past doings of human beings point to conditions for existence which may be eternal but which are more usually defined as time-bound trends that characterise the respective eras of their realisation. In this mode, there are few personalised historical figures. Rather, the world of the past is populated by reified agents. These are class actors, each of whom stands for the exemplary but unheroic instancing of trend, quality or proclivity. Assimilated to scene, typified human agents then figure in Rowley's discourse as a medium for the expression of the tendence of their times.

Consistent in his practice over the years, Rowley's method has been to aggregate the particularities of historical agents to the agencies which contain them. In this, Australian whites feature as the class actors who (as pastoralists, settlers, company men, missionaries, public servants etc), extended the frontier which moved in a phased progression 'round the coastal regions of Australia and into the centre of the continent' (Rowley 1972a, 3). We now live in an era when the activities of class actors have cumulated to produce what I shall call the 'Rowley line'. This represents the once moving frontier in its current state of arrest.

The line is drawn on Rowley's map with reference to a ratio. In regions of the tropical north and the desert centre, 'Aborigines of the full descent' (Rowley 1972a, 1), outnumber the declared part-Aborigines of the 1961 census. In the temperate zones, declared part-Aborigines preponderate. In terms of population, the arrested frontier is thus a divide between zones of contrasting demographic disproportions. In terms of politics, the divide is between colonial and settled Australia. In terms of Aboriginal adaptations, the Rowley line is drawn to separate the colonised but still 'traditionally-oriented' Aborigines from those who are 'outcast in [a] white Australia' (Rowley 1986) of cities, towns and farmlands. Rowley has recourse to the obvious ecological argument to explain the historical arrest and final stabilisation of the once moving frontier. In the northern regions (Rowley 1972a, 4):

> the limits set to possibilities of industrial land use by the nature of the country, and by the requirements of pastoral and agricultural technology at the time, seem to have been more obvious features of a colonial and plural society than the time factor.

This, being interpreted, means that nature in the Australian north is a block to non-labour-intensive expansion of primary industry. The northern reaches are thus fated to underdevelopment.

Historical trends that culminate in an arrested frontier have produced two conditions of Aboriginal entrapment. Further, there are mechanisms for the perpetuation of entrapment of either sort. These are a set of vicious circles—there is the apparent financial irresponsibility of Aborigines which was begotten of the stinting of cash to Aborigines who were paid more in kind than in adequate wages. They were thereby denied the opportunity to learn how to put money to use and so continued to evince financial irresponsibility when cash came to hand and so provided the administrator with a justification for the continued withholding of fiscal responsibility from Aboriginal communities and councils. Similarly, poor health among Aborigines is a result of political and administrative conditions which lead to underprovisioning. But even scant provisioning has further causal effects 'like strictly scheduled feeding of infants, which of course prompted resistance and failure to co-operate with the authoritarian health worker, which led to more infant deaths' (Rowley 1986, 147).

In Rowley's analysis, those Australian developments and emergent states of affairs which bear on Aborigines are subject to four orders of determination. At base, there is a nexus of determination between ecology and technological development. Then there is the presage of frontier movement, internationally true to form. With arrest of the frontier comes establishment and with it the determination visited on Aborigines by instituted vicious circles of perpetuation. Finally, there is situational determination that frames fighting in Aboriginal communities as 'inmate violence' (Rowley 1986), and explains addiction to either petrol-sniffing or alcohol as the outcome of relative deprivation that is situationally induced. There is 'the gap between the implied promises communicated via television, radio and video and the harsh realities' (Rowley 1986, 135). Experience of this gap stimulates the addict's 'escape' into an altered state.

To note the orders of determination which Rowley persistently employs to account for the Aboriginal condition in space and time is also to remark his intellectual debts. His frontier theory is the Turner thesis transported to Australia and vested in Aboriginal studies by Elkin (1951). Vicious circles and spirals are the notions that Myrdal (1944) gave first to the analysis of race relations in *The American Dilemma* and afterwards to development studies (Myrdal 1958). Then there is the sociology of total institutions and inmate reaction; to which add finally Merton's thesis of relative deprivation, especially in its application by Aberle (1966) to those native Americans who instituted a drug-centred religion in the peyote cult. My point is not that Rowley borrowed theory as do we all. It is that his own and particular contribution to Aboriginal studies is in using the past wholly to deny the pertinence of cultural identity to policy science. Rowley's analyses belong to a strict sociology of depersonalised social forces. Once and only once in his writing he invokes 'cultural lag' as a cause.[2] Otherwise, his sociology remains determinedly culture free.

When time is a human condition

Often the ground values of the social scientist are not explicitly set out and so are to be divined by considering the gist of an author's work. My appreciation of Rowley's gist is that, for him, time is a human condition—there is a succession of eras determined by social forces which are law-like in their operation and expressed through the activity of class actors. He eliminates any identity which is culturally constructed in order to allow people of every place and clime to be free to join the human race.

At the beginning of *The Remote Aborigines*, Rowley (1972a, 5) discusses Aborigines as dissidents. His aim is to make native Australians at one with a known class actor—the colonial rebel.

> From the history, one would expect Aboriginal society to be marked by...dissidence. In this context, the intransigence of Aborigines, whether part-Aboriginal or of the full descent, in the southern regions, in the fringe dwellings and more recently in the central areas of the metropolitan cities, has a direct relationship to the intransigence of the colonial rebel. And it may be more profitable for inquiry to be concerned with what is common to all mankind rather than with cultural differences.

Toward the end of Rowley's treatment of *The Remote Aborigines* (1972a, 353), the suggestion proffered in his introduction is made over into an imperative of practice.

> The time seems to have long passed for hope that descriptive research can offer new guidance for governments while history suggests that Aboriginal groups have reacted as other groups have done in similar circumstances. They are as they are, because they are like the rest of us, not because they are different. In overall planning of government action, it is what men share in common which counts, not the differences.

Rowley does not invoke Hobsbawm (1959) who gave us the primitive rebel as social type. However, the first citation provides one of the few instances in which Rowley can give Aborigines as 'primitive rebels' the character of class actors and thereby assimilate their action to sociologically recognised typicality. But the rarity of such attribution can be explained. After 'the destruction of Aboriginal society' (Rowley 1971), Aborigines were denied autonomy and so their self-expression could but be reactive. By definition, the class actor is distinguished by purpose and so can be identified only insofar as there is demonstrated initiative on the part of the collectivity in which the class actor is vested. Hence Rowley's celebration of the unique Pindan strike, of the single reported instance of Gunwinggu protest and, more recently, of the Noonkanbah confrontation. His is not the questioning that provokes anthropologists to puzzle about the absence of cargo cults in Aboriginal Australia or to remark the lack of those syncretistic movements that elsewhere have produced the religions of the oppressed. Yet Rowley's (1972a, 353) emphatic principle is that 'Aboriginal groups have reacted as other groups have done in similar circumstances'.

Apparently unknowingly, Rowley finally reveals what is basic to his doctrine of person when he finds another class actor in Aborigines of the 'homelands movement'—the people who have deserted settlements to return to country. With Wallace's (1956) dicta about 'revitalization movements' uncited but nonetheless apparent between his lines, Rowley (1972a) writes that:

> This movement is a phenomenon of the tribal folk who still prefer to live by the rhythms of the seasons rather than those of the clock; are still engrossed in the ceremonial life; for whom life is a series of climaxes interspersed with periods of preparation and apparent passivity. Gambling engrosses many, as a means of distributing available cash in an adventurous manner, probably still with regard to the mores of gift exchange. The heroic winner who gives back the winnings to keep the game going is the direct antithesis of the careful civil servant, and of the ambitious business-man who is to be the final product of the proposed policy of Aboriginal self-management. Especially

do these groups prefer to settle their differences in their own ways, as far as possible from the white man's law.

The cadences for envisioning an Aboriginal Arcadia then give way to the tones of a prophet of forebodings (Rowley 1986, 134–35).

> In time the attractions of cash and what it can buy may well reduce even these people to the conformity of 'one-dimensional' economic man. For cash poisons the generous mind by opening up possibilities of endless acquisition, not only of goods but of power. Here will come the temptation to leaders like the temptation on the mountain in Christian mythology. In the subsistence economy where the range of choice was small, greed for goods was pointless; and the way to power was through learning and the gift exchange, in which obligations could be used competitively.

Rowley's philosophy of money and its opening up of possibilities of endless acquisition of goods and possessions, is directly related to his advocacy of a policy science of circumstantial determination. The social importance of money is that it creates manifold possibilities for conversion, and conversion on the human plane is in the substitutive ability of human units of like function one for the other. Human actors, in this, are distinguished from one another only by potentialities of function which inhere in them through natural ability which has been modified by the acquisition of skills. And there is a market in functionaries. Further, the substitutive functionary is acquiescent. As Burke (1969, 355) remarks, 'when men respond to the laws of the market and its price system as second nature, the qualities of *scene* are thereby *internal* to the *agent*'.

The envisioning of persons as replaceable and trainable functionaries is taken to a theory of circumstantial determination to reproduce Rowley's principled relegation of the study of cultural difference to practical irrelevance. His message is that given autonomy, allowed access to resources and accorded formal identity as members of incorporated Aboriginal companies, Aborigines will have the chance to learn to function decisively rather than reactively in the modern world. The hope for Aboriginal recovery thus lies in situational conditioning whereby qualities of scene will be made internal to the agent. Rowley's rejection of human particularity engendered by culturally diverse ways for imagining reality means that he does not fully appreciate the nature of Aboriginal intransigence. That intransigence which Rowley admires in his characterisation of the Aborigine as colonial rebel is, in my view, real. It is rooted not in rebellion but in the resilience of cultural practice. In particular, there is a stubborn Aboriginal substantiation of the person which, in the words of Berdyaev (1938, 100), 'integrates the past in the future and eternity'.

Ceremony and the everywhen

Aboriginal ceremony is structured to reproduce the first of Berdyaev's two ways for considering the past. The ideology of the Aboriginal Dreaming is, in Stanner's (1968) apt phrase, the ideology of an 'everywhen' that admits no human acts of creation. Furthermore, the broad organisation of ceremony is something contrived to promote the stabilisation of forms and their accurate transmission. The ceremony life promotes the practitioner as perfect performer of received styles. It is grounded in a tradition which works against innovation and does not generally celebrate originating charisma.

In conscious memory, ceremony is uncreative because it has been made slave to receding time. While I find the detailed experience of ceremony engrossing, its stultification of the transfiguring vision makes the intricacies of its performance intellectually unchallenging. In Darwin, I was told that, despite a good record of attendance, I was 'notta law man really'—no man of dedication in the repetition of myth and rite. This was a considered verdict born of a studied collecting and reading of those signs which bear their witness to the elective affinities of person. My heart was not in it. As always in these considered matters, my hosts were right. But only now have I come fully to understand why.

For the present purpose, the important thing is that the 'notta law man' attribution is one I still evoke. With a set of other positive and negative verdicts on affinities and performance, the attribution plays a part in constituting the particularity of my being for the Darwin countrymen who know me. The attribution is thus one of the clutch that goes to the particularisation of my being into reflexive existence. These attributions accumulate to give meaning to my manifestation of a name.

My big name is not my casually used birth name 'that Basil'. More pointedly, it is the reserved name that attaches me to country and which was endowed upon me through recognition of my affinity as spirit with a Singing Man who bore it and whose capacities were summated in the name to give it, not the reification of the name-as-symbol, but the substantiated significance that comes of a temporally extended witnessing to a name's meaning by its bearer.

Put into English, the logic entailed in Aboriginal name-affinity has oxymoronic form. That in which the Singing Man and I were seen to share is the substance of spirit. Note that the substance of spirit partakes of time as the cumulation of attributions to which a considered series of one's past acts bear witness. One's reserved name, then, is constituted in the present as all the significances of those identified and tellable past times which point to the essence of one's being in its known and arrived at state.

Such a name can have the power to evoke the stories that subtend it. This means, in turn, that the name is seated in a web of shared understandings about persons on the local scene and there it functions as a sign. To ask 'what's in a name?' is to call for its substantiation. Unlike a rose, an Aboriginal name of substance is like a novel in that *Wuthering Heights* is its own story. It is the integrity of each novel that is signalled in its title so all we may be prepared to say of this literary genre is: a novel is a novel is a novel. Read it to know what it is as in Aboriginal Australia, persons are particularised into being through the telling of stories that evidence their signal attributes. The basic relationship between the sign value of a word that names a person or place or thing and the signal value that inheres in the story of that person, that place, that thing, is at the centre of an Aboriginal ontology. To ask about fire is to evoke a regional story about the Dreamtime discovery of right wood and wrong wood for making firesticks. To ask about ol Luke is to be taken to that man's substantiation in the Daly. Let me explain.

The substantiation of the Daly

Ol Luke bore the name of the freshwater reaches of the Daly River. The name could be given in Mullak Mullak, ol Luke's father language. More usually, however, one heard it in English. One could say, 'I'm going to see that Daly' or 'going longa that Daly for a visit' or 'I bin come away from that Daly'. In usage of this sort, there is punning potential. The ambiguity of Daly as river and Daly as ol Luke can also lead to outright misunderstanding.

As an ethnographer of speaking, I want to note that when 'Daly' exists as a conflation of person and place, 'Daly' becomes a noisy name. Noisy names exist as standing opportunities for joking and, in their own right, they provoke exercises in the uncrossing of crossed wires. All this is best realised when noisy names belong to persons of note.

Ol Luke was acknowledged as a Masterful Man at Wallaby Cross, the Darwin fringe camp which I made my base. There he dominated a camp section. In the usage of my time, 'Masterful Man' was employed by those who frequented the camp instead of the more usual 'Boss' of Aboriginal English. I suspect that it was ol Luke himself who originated this substitution. He was, in general, a source of Wallaby Cross style. As such, he originated, promoted, and then legislated words into the local lexicon. Ol Luke policed the convention that Masterful Man was to be used and used only with reference to Aboriginal leadership.

When I knew him, ol Luke was working on 'Gentleman'. Gentleman was defined by him as 'thatfella who always gonna show respect'. Respect had become a central issue of concern because a set of lads was being watched over by ol Luke as they progressed toward impending ceremonies of man-making. Ol Luke would look around camp, pick on someone to serve as exemplar, and then launch into 'thatta Gentleman' and 'that notta Gentleman' stories. Gentleman, however, was only a creature of its brief time. It fell out of use when the man-making was finally accomplished. What remains in the lexicon is the phrase of dispositional attribution applied to 'somefella always showing respect'. This phrase is regional in its distribution and more true to local form. In general, the crystalisation of quality either in an entitlement or in the single noun is resisted in favour of the active and descriptive phrase—'always lookin out for kid', 'always good for ceremony', 'always drinkin' and so on. What is attributed as personal quality is thus given in the form of performative characterisations. Again oxymoronically, these serve as labels for aspects of a person's persistent stance.

Performative attributions are closer to story than are entitlements. They are, in fact, the lines which serve stories as their destination: 'So you see, useta be thatfella always fightin'. With their double function as stimulus to storytelling and culmination of the story itself, performative attributions are like Euclidian theorems. Theorem exists in three moments: in its proof which is its own substantive formulation; as that required to prove; and as that which was to be proved. However, while Euclid's theorems are abstract, absolute and eternal, the performative attribution is personal in its referent, mutable and (because evidences of performance are continuously aggregated to it), it is the daughter of time.

The performative attribution belongs to the second of Berdyaev's ways for considering the past. It is the instrument of the transfiguring vision in that it is the vehicle for the registration of change in personal identity. People change through their acts of re-dedication so that the man who 'useta be always drinkin' can turn into 'that Missionary' (where 'Missionary' means non-drinker). And there are no routine conversions, no standard passages whereby the drinker marches into sobriety. Each transformed one time drinker undergoes his or her particular and circumstantial transformation, and thereby in each instance hangs a tale.

Like 'Masterful Man', 'Missionary' is one of the rare nominal entitlements, and it is rarity that marks such terms in the lexicon of Aboriginal English. Such rare terms are special words of stance. They are always conspectual in that they take to themselves all the departments of personal activity and this makes them words for total ways of being. Notice that Missionary is not a class word like Christian. It comes not from a person's affiliation to a group, but from individuality and spirit. So a pack of wowsers is 'a lotta Missionary' whereas 'that missionary mob' refers to the organisation of the church. A missionary mob is not endowed with collective will, or group purpose. Rather, the fellows who qualify as 'a lotta Missionary' are each and every one of them persons of dedicated abstinence. In this, there is a principle—it is the reservation of purposive dedication to persons, it is denial to collectivity.

The principle of reservation of purpose goes to time to give the lie to corporate identity, perpetual succession and the notion of corporate personality which even we admit is our own grand fiction. Further, the past is disallowed to the establishment of corporate identity so that, in general, Aboriginal mobs do not have histories—it is their members who do (cf Sansom 1985).

Ol Luke and story

In Darwin, ol Luke became the substantiation of the Daly for reasons of history which include a high rate of masculine mortality in his generation. 'Lotta fella bin die', but he was a survivor. He lived a life of activity concentrated in the restricted set of people who own Daly River affiliations. In particular, he had participated in the raising and rearing-up of successive cohorts of youngsters. He had put a lot of boys through the business of man-making. He had been a leading hand when a stockman and had been a drover too. As drover, Ceremony Man and substitute Dad, ol Luke was credited with a stock of contributions to the raising of Daly youth. Over the years, he had established himself as an ever-giving mentor.

A repository of knowledge, ol Luke also ran a small business dedicated to giving town dwelling Aborigines their respective pasts. Those who had been brought up in institutions (usually light-skinned children who had been kidnapped from Aboriginal guardians by welfare authorities), came to ol Luke bearing gifts. In return, he gave them their families. 'Granddad la you fella, bin callim that one Nugget. Face like polish. Man for boot: always Drovin fella that one.' And it was in a time of the drover's absence that the kidnappers struck. The cost of Nugget's droving was that he 'bin losim kid'. Such are the wages of absence.

The kidnapped kids who visited Wallaby Cross brought gifts in supermarket bags. They got words in return. But visiting youngsters of the Daly mobs gave words. They would come up to the Darwin Daly from the river itself and, shortly after greeting ol Luke, they would find an audience for their attestations. The anthropologist was useful because ignorant. His presence provoked stories of great detail thematically dedicated to explain: 'Why I gotta callim this olfella Dad'. 'Notta father really', this 'olfella' nonetheless had been the teller's rearer. Rearing to fish for barramundi, followed by the branding business, first muster, initiation of course, and the time when 'olfella bin fixim up that police trouble'. Ol Luke had put a stop to homicidal fights, and helped youngster after youngster into marriage.

Ol Luke thus lived in a world of tribute by attestation. He was always silent—even mildly abstracted—as the youngsters told their stories. He would often stop the flow by talking not to a person, but to Pimlight his favourite corgie. The dog 'took him for that toilet', lighting the way at night with a torch gripped tight in his corgie jaws. As the youngsters registered indebtedness, affiliation and regard, ol Luke would find occasion to have dealings with Pimlight. 'Youfella Pimlight, you always helpin? I doan know. Kid come here for trouble. I never bin see this kid for years an years. Now he got trouble, he comin this way. Dog more better I reckon.'

I am instancing the insertion of the past in the present with a dog's constancy of devotion constituted as a living reproach to the loyalty of a kid whom ol Luke had helped to rear. My point is to assert that there is no single corpus of Daly River stories to substantiate ol Luke as the Daly. Instead, there is a trend of action that makes ol Luke the Daly. Masie and Hendry and James and Tom, come up to Darwin each to give a particular attestation to celebrate the 'specialness' of the times which each had spent with the old fellow. In this, the stuff of consociate history goes to the grounding of relationship. Then the grounding of relationship goes to identity. To gain recognition as a person who should be fostered, cared for and given a socially acknowledged place in a Darwin encampment, the attestor brings the past into the present in an attempt to project the quality of past association into the future.

As I remarked, there is no actual collection of stories that go to Luke's identity. There is rather, a cumulation of moments of attestation in which the variety of ol Luke's associations with person, place and engrossing business is affirmed and re-affirmed by a plurality of storygivers. When a person becomes a Masterful Man or a Missionary, there is a transcendence of the ordinary. 'Always masterful' or 'never drinking' are stances that are attested in detail by a range of people, each of whom has a particular story to tell. While the stories are diverse both in origin and in ownership, they go to similar conclusions—'always helping', 'rearing-up whole lot' and so on. Ol Luke was thus made the Daly through the cumulation of individually rendered testimonies to the nature of his being.

One day, someone said to me: 'We all lovin that ol fella. He bin gibbin that whole lot.' Well, the Daly name is a 'whole lot' attribution. In life, ol Luke was urgent in his teaching of respect. He was masterful because he legislated respect into the common run of social dealings, demanding from others the conduct of respectful father–son, brother–sister or husband–wife relationships. He himself was not merely respected. A man who neither demanded nor spoke of reverence, yet that is what he won.

Ol Luke died and the Daly was gone from Darwin. Ol Luke could have no successor and to this day there is no Daly save for the flood-prone river. I am, however, waiting in anticipation because I know that sometime there will be a re-emergence of the Daly substantiated in a man. That man will be distinguished as the nodal person in whom the reverence expressed in a clutch of Daly stories is aggregated. He will share in some of the qualities that ol Luke evinced. Maybe he'll keep a dog—but it won't be the Pimlight of toilet and torch.

In Aboriginal society one can live in the sureness of continuity expressed in eventual reassertion. There is, however, no contrived and ensured succession. Continuities are not managed. Rather, they are emergent phenomena born of a way of conceptualising the present in relation to past histories of consociate experience. A consequence is that when people die and once their spirits have been ritually returned to country, there is a collective experience of final loss. With the departure of his potentiating spirit, there are no futures in stories of that Daly. But the Daly will be resurgent when the spirit of place is newly assimilated to a man. Then scene will enter person and the Daly will regain ambiguous assertion as flowing river and a man of serving deeds.

Conclusion: antinomies of doctrine

In this chapter I have juxtaposed what I see as two distinct doctrines of person. They are antinomies. Rowley's doctrine has substitutive functionaries for persons in a world where corporations endure, where there is perpetual succession to position and where persons have assimilated laws of the market to their being. Aborigines have persons who are particularised into existence and are, in themselves, the past emergent in the present. Where identity is thus always emergent, there is no succession but the recognition of the particularity of death's undoing which is symbolised in the prohibition that forbids the calling of the names of dead people. Doctrinal contrasts of such scope cannot be put aside in our appreciation of the position of Aborigines in white Australia. Without cultural analysis all policy science is vain.

Notes

1. Intensive research was carried out in the Northern Territory during my tenure of a Research Fellowship at the Australian Institute of Aboriginal Studies, 1974–77. My thanks to Patricia Baines who introduced me to the writings of Berdyaev and commented extensively on earlier drafts of this chapter.
2. Rowley (1972b, 53) invokes 'cultural lag' as explanation when he cites Beckett's (1964) work on Aboriginal drinking patterns in the northwest corner of New South Wales. In Rowley's interpretation, Aborigines learned to drink on a 'binge-and-bust' pattern decades ago with white frontierism as the role model. Binge-and-bust drinking persists among the Aborigines of settled Australia even though the frontier has moved on. Persistence of the frontier drinking mode is, for Rowley, an unadaptive anachronism.

References

Aberle, D.F.
1966 *The Peyote Religion Among the Navaho*, Aldine, Chicago.

Beckett, J.
1964 Aborigines, Alcohol and Assimilation. In M. Reay (ed), *Aborigines Now: New Perspectives in the Study of Aboriginal Communities*, Angus and Robertson, Sydney, 32–47.

Berdyaev, N.
1938 *Solitude and Society*, Geoffrey Bles, The Centenary Press, London.

Burke, K.
1969 *A Grammar of Motives*, University of California Press, Berkeley.

Elkin, A.P.
1951 Reaction and Interaction: A Food Gathering People and European Settlement in Australia, *American Anthropologist* 53(2), 164–86.

Geertz, C.
1975 *The Interpretation of Cultures*, Hutchinson, London.

Hobsbawm, E.J.
1959 *Primitive Rebels*, Manchester University Press, Manchester.

Myrdal, G.
1944 *An American Dilemma: The Negro Problem and Modern Democracy*, Harper and Row, New York.
1958 *Rich Lands and Poor: The Road to World Prosperity*, Harper, New York.

Rowley, C.D.
1971 *The Destruction of Aboriginal Society*, Australian National University Press, Canberra.
1972a *The Remote Aborigines*, Australian National University Press, Canberra.
1972b *Outcasts in White Society*, Australian National University Press, Canberra.
1986 *Recovery: The Politics of Aboriginal Reform*, Penguin, Harmondsworth.

Sansom, B.
1980 *The Camp at Wallaby Cross: Aboriginal Fringe Dwellers in Darwin*, Australian Institute of Aboriginal Studies, Canberra.
1985 Aborigines, Anthropologists and Leviathan. In N. Dyck (ed), *Indigenous Peoples and the Nation State: Fourth World Politics in Canada, Australia and Norway*, St John's Institute for Social and Economic Research, University of Newfoundland.

Stanner, W.E.H.
1968 *After the Dreaming*, The Boyer Lectures, Australian Broadcasting Commission, Sydney.

Wallace, A.F.C.
1956 Revitalization Movements, *American Anthropologist* 58, 261–81.

10. Tim Rowse — Middle Australia and the noble savage: a political romance

In January 1985 Australian National Opinion Polls (ANOP) presented to the Hawke government the public opinion study 'Land rights: winning middle Australia' (ANOP 1985), purporting to show an electorate fearful and suspicious of land rights. The Department of Aboriginal Affairs (DAA) suppressed this report but its theme had been widely leaked by the middle of 1985. The findings quickly became part of the political elite's folk sociology. By Freedom of Information procedures the federal opposition obtained a copy, and the Premier of Queensland publicly extolled its contents as a confirmation of his views. The Hawke government included individuals with reservations about national land rights legislation; they found endorsement of their conservatism in the ANOP analysis. Supporters of land rights were forced by the leaked report to reassess their mandate. ANOP had constructed a plausible image of what it called 'middle Australia' and had described the very limited version of Aboriginal rights which that constituency might possibly tolerate.

Labor's platform in 1983 had combined the best elements of the Northern Territory land rights law (veto over mining, right to claim unalienated Crown land, protection of sacred sites) with an aspect of the New South Wales legislation required for land rights to work in the southern states—the compensatory purchase of land. Labor's platform was to pass a national Bill to bind the states to the one set of principles from which they would have to fashion their own Acts. But the mining industry wanted no further legislative confinement of their entrepreneurship. The Australian Mining Industry Council (AMIC) and the Western Australian Chamber of Mines campaigned especially strongly in Western Australia in 1984–85, convincing the Burke Labor government that it would lose office if it implemented the recommendations of the 1984 Seaman inquiry (which would have placed unalienated Crown land in Aboriginal hands with veto over mining) or if it consented to federal legislation embodying such principles. The Burke government quickly became an advocate of states' rights within the Labor party.

The extent of national support for land rights has never been tested in the federal electorate. Although the Australian Labor Party (ALP) has had a commitment to land rights in its platform since 1971, no federal election has ever been fought in such a way as to create a nation-wide political debate on the issue. The 1967 referendum, mandating federal powers over the states in matters of Aboriginal policy, had not been an expression of electoral opinion about the substance of any federal policy. If anything, the vote (ninety-one per cent of the national electorate) had implicitly endorsed assimilationist thinking, then the philosophy of all major parties.

Since 1983 the ALP has held office in Canberra and in four states, an ideal moment for the pursuit of a national land rights package. Yet the Hawke government, since the leaking of the ANOP study, has denied any mandate to act on its platform. As we entered the Bicentennial year the government appeared nervous. In September 1987 the possibility of a 'compact' with Aborigines was mooted. A search of newspaper files since then reveals silence, rather than public debate, about how Aboriginal rights to land might be part of any compact, or indeed about the legal status of the compact. The contribution of the new Minister for Aboriginal Affairs, Gerry Hand, has been equally ambiguous. In the second week of December 1987 he outlined a draft preamble to legislation setting up the new Aboriginal and Torres Strait Islander Commission. The preamble will both acknowledge Aborigines as 'original owners' of the continent and reaffirm (as if it were needed) that Aborigines now 'have no recognised rights over it other than those granted by the Crown'.

To the extent that this nervous paralysis is underwritten by ANOP's report of the state of public opinion, it is timely to examine that report closely. Asked, in August 1984, to 'undertake a community attitude research program as the basis for development of a communications strategy which would maximise public support for the federal government's policy on land rights' (ANOP, 1), ANOP obtained data in three stages. It first convened seventeen group discussions composed of adults of both sexes and 'a range of class groupings' who were found to be 'not strongly committed in their attitudes towards politics in general, and land rights in particular'. They also interviewed twenty-eight 'opinion leaders'. Next ANOP conducted a national survey of 2,000 adults. Finally, a number of 'communication themes' were tried out in ten further group discussions. By this mix of methods ANOP generated both qualitative and quantitative data. In January 1985 ANOP summarised the results (ANOP 1985, 5).

> The Australian population can currently be divided roughly into three camps regarding land rights: one quarter implacably opposed and unshiftable in the short term; one quarter firmly supportive; and half in the middle leaning increasingly to opposition and prejudice through fear, ignorance, misinformation, and soft racism. But more importantly, it is not a case of an apathetic, 'couldn't care less' attitude among this half—it is an expression of 'soft prejudice' which has a greater propensity to harden than to turn to sympathy.

It does not distort this paragraph to paraphrase it by saying that only one in four Australians supports land rights.

Polling and politics

In March 1985, a few days after Hawke's Cabinet dumped party policy, a journalist at a National Press Club lunch challenged the Prime Minister with the observation that it was the job of parties of reform to lead public opinion in a progressive direction. Hawke's reply encapsulated his conservative populism: the Australian people, he observed, were particularly able to resist the manipulations of politicians. While Hawke professed regret at what appeared to be a declining tolerance of Aboriginal rights, his substitution of 'manipulation' for 'lead' suggests deep sympathy with the electorate's alleged immobility.

Since Whitlam's political demise such pragmatism has drawn confidence from a bipartisan perception that the electorate's horizons are severely limited. Labor Senator Robert Ray recently said that,

> You can have two attitudes if you're in a political party. One's a vanguardist one which says it's your role to lead on issues, to educate your own supporters, and there are absolute black and white morals. A lot of people in the Labor Party, especially in the Left, take that view. Whereas I take the view that's intellectual arrogance. I'm only a representative of the Labor movement, and I should represent their attitudes in the Parliament and in politics generally. The thing they want is as near to full employment as possible, a safety net around those that are disadvantaged; they want opportunities for their family, and they want basically a peaceful world. Summed up in a couple of words: progressively higher standards of living.[1]

ANOP Director Rod Cameron is the author of a portrait of the electorate with which Ray would agree.[2] It is ANOP's business to give representations of 'public opinion', to create substantial political figures called 'the public' (or subdivisions of that public) and to give these figures personality and attitude so as to make them a comprehensible and predictable Other of the political elite. A statistical idiom, in which facts which are numbers appear as the sole and objective determinant of analytical statements, lends enormous plausibility to pollsters' constructions of the public. Yet these constructions are fanciful in two senses: the methods for turning the complexities of behaviour and consciousness into quantifiable units of opinion or attitude are notoriously frail; and a body of quantitative data may support a number of competing interpretations—it may be quite tendentious to offer one as definitive.

So artificial is the usual result of these two mediations of 'public opinion' that Pierre Bourdieu has claimed that 'public opinion does not exist' (Bourdieu 1979).

Opinion polls make a number of related assumptions which Bourdieu questions. Firstly, they posit that everyone can have an opinion attributed to them. Accordingly, polls often fail to report and consider the significance of 'no reply', as substantive a result as a stated opinion, says Bourdieu. Secondly, polls assume that there is a consensus about what the issue is. Political elites set an agenda of issues and test people's opinions on the issues as they have framed them, ignoring differences of 'class ethos' in the ways issues are understood, and treating lack of engagement with the issues defined in the poll as unworthy of analysis. Thirdly, polls treat all opinions as of equal weight, overlooking that (Bourdieu 1979, 129),

> there is, on the one hand, mobilised opinion, formulated opinion, pressure groups mobilised around a system of interests; and on the other, certain inclinations, opinions in an implicit state which, by definition are not really opinions, if by opinion we mean a formulated discourse with a pretention of coherence.

In the light of Bourdieu's critique ANOP's work at first seems sophisticated. The report is sensitive to the difference between mobilised, articulate opinion and 'opinions in an implicit state'. On the one hand ANOP singled out opinion leaders (the churches, in favour of land rights, and the miners and pastoralists' organisations in opposition) for special investigation. On the other, ANOP sought to investigate what it called 'middle Australia', those whose opinions were not at first forthcoming in the administration of a questionnaire but who were probed in group discussion to find any sentiment at all, for or against. ANOP were aware that 'no reply' or notable reticence in response was significantly different from readily offered opinion.

Indeed ANOP's principal claim was to have identified this reticent group, 'middle Australia', and to have definitively explored its attitudes. Rather than overlook the silent ones, ANOP promoted them; in the report's phrasing, 'middle Australia' became a collective actor, a crucial but reluctant interlocutor with government, made to speak via ANOP's representation. In constructing 'middle Australia' ANOP carried out what Bourdieu (1979, 125) sees as opinion polls' most important function, 'to impose the illusion that a public opinion exists, and that it is simply the sum of a number of individual opinions'.

I will argue that ANOP's 'middle Australia', hardening against land rights, is an empirically dubious construction which panders to Labor's populist pragmatism. But note, that my argument is sceptical rather than affirmative. I do not pretend to know the state of public opinion better than ANOP, or better than anyone else. Rather I wish to undermine the seeming reality of this entity 'middle Australia', by showing how it was produced and by pointing to its strategic consequences.

Nation, community, electorate

Notwithstanding the weaknesses of public opinion research, there is some value for political parties in attempting to survey connections between issues, opinions and voting intentions. But ANOP's work was not, on this occasion, strategically nuanced. ANOP paid no attention to the way the machinery of political representation fragments the nation into electorates of greater or lesser political importance. Nor did it measure the salience of the land rights issue to that small proportion of the voting public whose votes would decide the contest in marginal seats.

ANOP's study formulated the government's political problem in terms which recalled a notion of national consensus and undisrupted community, reminiscent of the populist rhetorics of such politicians as Paul Everingham (former Chief Minister of the Northern Territory) and Bob Hawke. The report concluded that the Labor government would become alienated from the heart of the Australian community which it called 'middle Australia'. The nation was therefore at risk (ANOP 1985, 35):

> Black rights generally, and land rights in particular, represent the most divisive and potentially explosive issues we have ever dealt with—and we suspect that this country has faced in the post war period.

ANOP adopted a theme used tirelessly by Paul Everingham—that the future of community (the Territory or the nation) is at risk when people disagree about the relative merits of Aboriginal and non-Aboriginal claims to resources. Qualifying its prognosis with the word 'potential', ANOP implied that land rights was becoming a more salient issue. No evidence was offered to support this claim.

I have already quoted Senator Ray on the importance of not straying too far from the concerns of 'ordinary people'. To know the disposition of the 'ordinary Australian', to speak confidently of the wishes and views of a silent majority, has become a powerful rhetorical position in contemporary Australian politics. Geoffrey Blainey has claimed this tribunal stance; columnists such as *The Australian's* Des Keegan peer weekly into the hearts of 'middle Australia' and find confirmation of Blainey's divining. Katherine West has authored a similar position from which to speak of the exclusion of the concerns of the common people from the Accord, which she describes as elitist. Some Liberal leaders, such as Jim Carlton, have taken to contrasting the prominence of 'big' unionism in the Labor government's consensus-oriented economic policies with a more authentic 'consensus' of citizens disenchanted by their remoteness from the corridors of power.

With the currency of such rhetoric on both sides of politics, public opinion research can offer governments and oppositions more than just an instrument of electoral strategy; it can clothe populist representations of policy formation in the garments of scientific fact, precipitating a new criterion of 'statesmanship'. Published or leaked opinion research can index governments' fidelity to popular will: it can appear to document, in this case, the fragility of consensus, nationhood's need for a steady, preserving hand. By dishonouring its platform to introduce national land rights, the Hawke government, once the ANOP results were summarised by the media, could claim to be honouring democracy and preserving community.

ANOP has its own interests. 'Land rights: winning middle Australia' not only tried to convince the government of the urgency of campaigning for land rights, it sketched a campaign in which ANOP (1985, 8) itself might play a part.

> We have never recommended so strongly before that a government campaign is needed in any area...The Federal government must bite the bullet in 1985 and start to wear down the prejudice and resentment of middle Australia...Unless the government is prepared to spend a great deal of money, the chance to influence white attitudes will be greatly diminished.

But because DAA did not have the necessary resources for this 'major ongoing PR and advertising campaign', it would be better to spend a 'great deal of money' on a 'high level unit with political, journalistic and PR skills', ANOP (1985, 8) suggested. However, the Cabinet subcommittee on government advertising, chaired by Senator Peter Walsh, turned down DAA's submission outlining the strategies and expenses of such a campaign. For the right wing of the ALP the urgent pessimism in ANOP's claims to know the mind of 'middle Australia' was a statesmanlike basis for doing nothing at all.

A profile of 'middle Australia'

Throughout the ANOP report we are given far more information about those 'leaning increasingly to opposition and prejudice through fear, ignorance, misinformation, and soft racism' than about either of the other two sectors of opinion. Three questionable features of their analysis produced (as 'fact') this grouping.

Firstly, ANOP treated as a single group those who at first declined to express an opinion. What is the character of such reticence? Apparently it was not based on acknowledged ignorance of the facts of the issue—only forty per cent of 'middle Australia' confessed they had no idea what land was in question, the same proportion confessing ignorance as in the sample as a whole.

It is possible that the reticent people were unforthcoming because land rights was of low salience to them. ANOP could then have disregarded their views, on the grounds that, whatever made them vote for or against the government, it was hardly likely to be ALP land rights policy. Without discussing this possibility, ANOP presented the reticent respondents as strategically crucial because of their apparently unformed views. They became the citizens the government must work hardest to reach. In the course of the report government willingness to stretch itself into this empathic posture becomes a test of the quality of its leadership of the nation as a whole.

Secondly, and in keeping with the above, ANOP preferred to homogenise 'middle Australia'. The survey acknowledged that an undisclosed proportion of the fifty-two per cent, when probed, 'tended to be in favour' of land rights with reservations. However the small group discussion apparently revealed that those same reservations were voiced by 'middle Australians' who tended to oppose land rights. Accordingly, ANOP refers to the group as a whole as the 'softly prejudiced', highlighting their common stock of reservations rather than their opposed, if tentatively stated, opinions of land rights.

Thirdly, in developing a model of 'middle Australia' ANOP (1985, 3) paid 'special attention' to 'rural and provincial town dwellers; residents of North Queensland and North West Western Australia; and farming and mining communities'. The report never reveals what 'special attention' amounted to, but there seems an implication that these locales are among the heartlands of 'middle Australia'. We are left wondering whether ANOP may have treated these three regional populations as non-Aboriginal Australian's quintessence.

Each of these three moves is questionable enough to prompt a cautious reception to all of ANOP's generalisations about 'middle Australia'. Indeed, on ANOP's own evidence, 'middle Australian' opinion is heterogeneous. Sixty-two per cent assessed federal government assistance to Aborigines as 'too much' or 'about right now–not much'. Forty-one per cent perceived (with only partial accuracy) land rights to affect the use of valued land ('very large areas', 'good pastoral land', 'mining land', 'Ayers Rock'). Fifty-nine per cent wanted land rights, if it were introduced, to apply only to certain categories of Aborigines ('full bloods only' and 'tribal, rural, outback

Aborigines'). Fifty-two per cent would not like Aborigines to have 'the right to stop mining on land they own', but forty-three per cent said Aboriginal owners should have this veto (twenty-seven per cent on sacred sites and living areas only, and sixteen per cent on all land Aborigines owned). However, sixty-four per cent of 'middle Australia' wanted white land owners to be able to veto mining on their land. Such discrimination in favour of white land owners, evident in the same proportion, among the sample as a whole, particularly alarmed ANOP and the government.

These statistics tell us of the reservations which some 'middle Australians' entertained about land rights. But notice that the proportions given in the preceding paragraph do not suggest that 'middle Australia' is of one mind on any question asked. In what way is 'middle Australia' a coherent grouping? If your answer to this question by now is as sceptical as mine then let us ask it of the other two alleged groupings of opinion, those for and those against land rights.

Though ANOP gives little comparative data on the reservations about land rights expressed by all three groups the results presented are intriguing: almost one third (thirty-one per cent) of those 'strongly in favour' of land rights said they thought that government was doing too much for Aborigines, or said 'about right now–not much'. Of course the proportion of those opposed to land rights who expressed this view was much higher (eighty-one per cent), but the result for those in favour is remarkable.

Three interpretations of this unexpected result are possible. The first, that the supporters of land rights include many ready to defect to the opposition, is implicitly rejected by ANOP's choice of the term 'strongly in favour'. The second is that its supporters see land rights as a means for Aborigines to free themselves of dependence on government. ANOP does not consider this possibility. For the third interpretation we should remember that public opinion researchers have long known that people's agreement or disagreement with very general propositions is not systematically connected to their opinions on issues which apply concretely those propositions. In other words, in answering a questionnaire, people who support land rights may also support propositions implicitly hostile to land rights when those propositions are couched in a very general way. In this interpretation we can then choose whether to weight responses to general propositions or those on the specific issue polled.

My point is not that we must plump for one interpretation or another. Rather I insist that it is artificial to present ambiguous results as meaning one thing only. The relationship between pollsters and their government clients inhibits tolerance of ambiguity, however—there is a product to be sold, an answer to be given.

Middle Australia and the noble savage: a political romance

What ANOP did not tell us about the two opinionated quarters of the population is very important if we are not frightened of an ambiguous 'answer'. What proportions of those strongly in favour and those strongly opposed: declared themselves to be ignorant about what land was involved?; saw land rights as affecting lands of value?; wanted to limit land rights to certain categories of Aborigines?; agreed with the inclusion of a mining veto, to all or parts of Aboriginal land?; discriminated in favour of non-Aboriginal land owners' mining veto? In not answering these questions ANOP hopes the client will infer that those in favour of land rights are well informed and of one (progressive) mind on questions related to their view of land rights, that those against are of the opposite single mind and also well informed, and that 'middle Australia' is distinguished by its messy, inchoate attitudes.

ANOP does not allow us to examine the hypothesis that opinions about land rights, whatever their direction and however forthrightly enunciated to interviewers, are formed relatively independently of their assent or resistance to a background noise of cliches about the limits of government responsibility, about authentic and inauthentic Aborigines, about the rights of land owners to privacy, about the national importance of the mining industry, and so on. To entertain that hypothesis is to admit to doubts about our ability to 'know' the three sectors of opinion presented by ANOP.

In the one table in which ANOP does compare the three groups' assent to propositions about the pros and cons of land rights, this dangerous hypothesis gets some support.

Though there are undeniable consistencies within the three groups, these results are surprising. Those in favour of land rights can stomach apparently negative features of the policy: half of them think (wrongly) that some people could lose their private land; one fifth think Aborigines should have to buy or work for land; one tenth think land rights unfair to whites; a quarter are willing to countenance the risk of racial tension and a separate Aboriginal state; fifteen per cent believe Aborigines will own too much of Australia; and two out of five consider Aboriginal land use unproductive.

On the other side, roughly one in four of those strongly opposed to land rights don't agree that private land might be lost; that Aboriginal land use is unproductive; that Aborigines will own too much of Australia; and that there is a risk of racial tension and a separate Aboriginal state. A significant number (fourteen per cent) opposed to land rights reject the view that land rights is unfair to white land owners. And, most bizarre of all, if the wording in the table is taken seriously, more than one in ten of those opposed to land rights do not agree that Aborigines should be sold rather than given land. ANOP did not comment on these counterintuitive results.

Table of responses to land rights propositions (ANOP 1985).

LAND RIGHTS ARGUMENTS	MIDDLE AUSTRALIA	STRONGLY OPPOSED	STRONGLY IN FAVOUR
		(per cent agreeing)	
PRO			
Land rights will help Aborigines keep their culture and help the survival of their race	53	21	96
Aborigines should get land rights because it's important for their traditional way of life	50	22	93
Land rights will help Aborigines improve their lives and help solve some current problems.	41	16	81
Aborigines should get land rights because they were here first	31	4	93
Aborigines should get land rights because land has a special meaning for them	30	12	84
We should compensate Aborigines for the way they've been treated by giving them land rights	26	6	74
CON			
Giving land rights to Aborigines is unfair to white Australians	65	86	11
Aborigines shouldn't be given land rights; they should have to buy or work for land	64	88	21
Giving land rights means that some people could lose their private land	59	77	52
Giving land rights to Aborigines means that a lot of land won't be used for productive purposes	59	78	42
Land rights for Aborigines means that they would own too much of Australia	55	76	15
Land rights may lead to racial tension and a separate Aboriginal state	48	75	26

There are several alternative readings of ANOP's data to be made. For example, there seem to be four identifiable sectors of public opinion on land rights (in favour and against, strongly and weakly asserted). If so, then the number in favour is much greater than the 'one quarter firmly supportive'. Secondly, the four sectors also seem to share many attitudes. The two quarters that, in ANOP's view, are polar opposites are apparently riddled with 'defectors' to each other's position. Thirdly, and I will deal further with this below, each of the ANOP's three sectors contains a majority ignorant enough to think that land rights would alienate private land from non-Aborigines. Why didn't ANOP formulate the principal political problem as one of combating ignorance? The answer appears to be that ANOP is suspicious of information and disinformation as weapons of political struggle.

Ignorance and 'good vibes'

ANOP asked an open-ended question: 'Do you happen to know what the Federal government is actually proposing regarding land rights for Aborigines? I mean here, what sort of land will be involved if Aborigines get land rights?' Forty-two per cent admitted ignorance, and many others displayed it. Eleven per cent mentioned 'good pastoral land', which no government bill or policy has included. Land in private hands could pass into Aboriginal ownership only through sale on the market, but many respondents (sixty per cent of sample) thought such land at risk of 'loss' under land rights. ANOP (1985, 24) concluded that:

> There is virtually no knowledge of the following aspects of land rights policy: type of land to be granted; proposed tenure; provisions for public access; mining—access, veto provisions (Western Australia is an exception here) or allocation of royalties.

Nor could many respondents say much about Aborigines. Thirty-three per cent of the sample were stumped when asked to name an Aboriginal man or woman with whom they were 'impressed'. Thirty per cent could not name any aspect of Aboriginal life which 'impressed' them. No doubt there is some negative evaluation, not just ignorance, in these failures to answer.

Another question was not loaded with such evaluative elements. Respondents were asked to choose one of four descriptions (comfortable, not too bad, fairly bad, very bad) of Aboriginal life in five different categories of living style or place of residence. More than one fifth of the sample were unable to choose a description for 'Aborigines in tribal conditions' and 'Aborigines on reserves'. The lowest non-response rate (nine per cent) occurred in relation to 'Aborigines in country towns'.

It is interesting that respondents were least able to characterise precisely those groups of Aborigines who have benefited most from land rights.

But to overcome such ignorance would need more than information, argued ANOP. Positive images of Aborigines ('good vibes') must be generated by government so that people would be willing to listen to the information supplied. For ANOP, 'attitudes' seem to be the currency of the political market place. Accordingly they recommended a two-pronged campaign to generate support for land rights: 'general image-building—a period of "softening up"', followed by information and persuasion about land rights itself. Their suggestions about what themes would 'soften middle Australia' and what 'information' would then fit in with their favoured attitudinal framework were disturbing.

ANOP (1985, 42–43) first listed the themes that must be avoided in any government campaign.

> Egalitarianism—land rights as a way of achieving equality for Aborigines; Aborigines need to be compensated for historical misdeeds;
> Self-help through land rights;
> Land rights have worked in the Northern Territory;
> Aborigines have a stronger, more significantly different relationship with the land.

Discussion groups composed of 'middle Australians' apparently rejected these arguments, demonstrating to ANOP that the anti-land rights campaign has incontestably captured them. The meaning of 'equality' is thus no longer at stake, it now means only what the AMIC wants it to mean.

The reports of the discussion groups cannot be inspected in the way that statistics can be; we are almost at the mercy of ANOP's intuitions here. But there are at least two reasons to wonder at the ANOP researchers' judgements.

Firstly, the compensation argument, we are told, would not work because 'middle Australia' felt no guilt. Yet it is surely possible to persuade many Australians of the justice of compensation without arousing guilt. Contemporary Australians are entitled to feel no guilt for others' actions, but they can still be invited to assess the damage caused by those actions, as they assess the claims for compensation made by accident and crime victims. By linking compensation with 'guilt' ANOP put the argument ineptly and perhaps revealed the prejudices of their own staff.

Secondly, ANOP seems to have forgotten the importance of maintaining existing support, as well as adding to the numbers of land rights supporters. The arguments which ANOP would have the government abandon have been important in building support for land rights. Would it not be dangerous for the government to distance itself from them altogether?

Wishing to start afresh, ANOP (1985, 44) searched for 'a credo which the Australian community will accept already but which is broad enough to have attached to it related information or image aspects important to the aims of the campaign'. They were guided by the marketing belief that public opinions must never be contested: 'to expose the ludicrous fallacies implicit in white Australia's stereotypes of the Aboriginal people will be resented and rejected as an insult' (ANOP 1985, 50). Although it is easy to understand why the makers of Lux don't spend their advertising budget denigrating Rinso, this marketing nostrum prescribes the end of political debate.

ANOP field tested four themes in discussion groups. That 'Aborigines have a right to preserve their spiritual and cultural heritage' apparently got heads nodding, but ANOP warned that it would be necessary to establish that land was part of Aboriginal heritage; and the land rights of urban Aborigines, insofar as they are seen to have lost their culture, would not be upheld.

The second theme, that Aboriginal identity, dignity and self-respect required land rights, also failed to bridge the gap between the 'legitimate' Aboriginal identity of rural Aborigines and the suspect Aboriginality of urban blacks. 'Middle Australia', reported ANOP (1985, 46), sees the future of urban Aborigines as 'integration and acceptance in white society as wage-earners and home-makers'. Did the ANOP researchers point out to discussants that there was nothing in this scenario incompatible with making grants of land to such Aborigines? Or was it, again, too close to the researchers' own flawed perceptions of land rights to be challengeable?

The third theme defensively took note of 'middle Australians' preference for 'real Aborigines'—'land rights provide the opportunity for tribal Aborigines to live their chosen life style, away from Australian values and society'. But this theme, though supported in group discussions, was thought to apply to very few Aborigines. And it 'smacked of separatism' and 'apartheid'. Another problem was that many people could not see how Aborigines so traditional as to be still nomadic could need title to a particular locality.

The final theme tested in group discussion was that land was needed for Aborigines to re-establish ties of family and community. ANOP reported that only a minority appeared to 'grasp' this argument, and that many thought it entailed massive physical relocation of Aboriginal people, a disruptive and threatening implication.

Assuming that 'middle Australians' were not only reticent but immoveably dim, ANOP concluded that the first theme was the best for Labor to use as long as 'spiritual and cultural heritage' was made to include more than the protection of sacred sites, and as long as the Aboriginal heritage was seen not just as 'theirs' but as the heritage of 'all Australians'. Ruling out the compensation argument ('guilt'), ANOP concluded that land rights could not be promoted as a solution to the problems of urban Aborigines. ANOP was willing to sacrifice the land needs of an unspecified number of 'inauthentic' Aborigines in order to capitalise on the image of the 'noble savage', making the land rights case a hostage of a colonial ideology which is romantic in inspiration and capricious and arbitrary in application.

The romance of the primitive

Frantz Fanon has argued that colonising cultures construct idealised, ahistoric images of the indigenous cultures they subjugate. Part of the 'high culture' of the colonists is the scholarly study of the pre-colonial culture through custody of material culture in museums and through ethnographies of remnant enclaves of the pre-colonial society. Adaptations made by the subjugated peoples are regarded as the adulteration and decay of a pristine culture. Controlling the definition of what was essentially characteristic of the subjugated culture, the colonisers reserve the power to distinguish authentic and inauthentic aspects of the living traditions of the colonised. If the colonised argue political demands by reference to their culture, the colonisers are quick to adjudicate what is genuine in such claims (Fanon 1967, 180–81; 1970, 44).

ANOP revealed that many Australians distinguish the rights to land of Aborigines who are 'tribal' and 'traditional' and inhabit parts of the 'outback' from the rights of those whom they see in, or on the edges of, cities and towns. ANOP would have the government abide by this distinction, rather than override it or confront it. Yet the former New South Wales government, as moderate as Labor governments can be, survived legislating land rights for Aboriginal people who, in these terms, have 'lost their culture'. ANOP's poll did not find New South Wales to be an atypically enlightened state, so must the land needs of urban blacks be so undersold?

There is another problem. From ANOP's own data, and from my own historical observation, the approved 'authentic' Aborigine is a fantastic entity, a Loch Ness monster much discussed but hardly ever sighted with certainty. Symptomatically, this figure is identified with the 'outback', not a region or even a number of regions, but one metaphorical side of a mythical partitioning of nationhood into primeval and civilised aspects.

Elsewhere I have noted a convergence between lay and professional perceptions of central Australian Aborigines between the wars—that Aboriginal culture was so fragile that it rapidly disintegrated when adapted to a novel material culture. The evidences of disintegration were the visual incongruity of 'stone age' people dressed in trousers and shirts, and the nuisance of Aboriginal mendicancy (Rowse 1986). Professional and some lay opinion has more recently accepted that Aboriginal use of introduced material culture can help the adaptation of their social structure and belief. But it is likely that, just as many Australians still use the discredited metaphors of eugenics ('full blood' or 'half-caste') to conceptualise cultural change, so they cling to notions of similar vintage that Aborigines exposed to European goods quickly 'spoil'. The number of Aborigines with a culture left to conserve may, in this perspective, be very few in number; and, like the outback, they may be so far away, both spatially and psychologically, that they are beyond acknowledgement.

ANOP disclosed but failed to comment on evidence pointing to instability in respondents' concepts of the 'authentic Aborigine'. Remember that fifty-five per cent of the entire sample wanted to limit land rights to either 'full bloods only' or 'tribal, rural, outback Aborigines', and that 'maintaining their culture' was a popular argument for land rights. How then are we to understand the strong support for the statement that much Aboriginal land would not be used for 'productive purposes'? Hunting, foraging and the ceremonial use of land are not perceived as 'productive' by forty-two per cent of those in favour of land rights, the same group that almost unanimously (ninety-six per cent) agreed that 'land rights will help Aborigines keep their culture'. This suggests that even those most sympathetic to land rights have yet to come to grips with some of the ways Aboriginal land use is productive. Is this the positive understanding on which ANOP wants to build?

The needs of 'tribal' people also seemed to be out of focus for many. When asked to describe the conditions of 'Aborigines in tribal conditions', one fifth were unsure, and half said these conditions were 'comfortable' or 'not too bad'. 'Aborigines' closer to home (in capital cities, country towns or on the edge of towns) were placed in a descriptive category by a higher proportion of the sample and were twice as likely as 'tribal' Aborigines to be described as living in 'fairly bad' or 'very bad' conditions. In other words the Aborigines whose image would spearhead the ANOP campaign are those least known and most often thought not to need help.

Conclusion

'Land rights: winning middle Australia' reproduced two sentimental strands of Australian culture: the conservative populism, now so embedded in our political elites and in managers of the media, in which Australians are held to be implacably modest in aspiration and narrow in horizon; and a colonialist romance of the primitive. The report attempted to ground a campaign to perpetuate that romance in a 'researched' calculation of the likely limited trajectory of popular thinking.

Some DAA officers with whom I spoke in mid-1985 were intimidated by the report and rued that they were not able to exploit the limited public relations potential ANOP perceived. All they were allowed to do was promote the handing back of Ayers Rock (Uluru). I think we should be grateful, in one sense, for Senator Walsh's reserve. Would not the promotion of the 'noble savage' also have consolidated the ideological system which produces 'him' and which divides Aborigines into those with a spiritually-based land grievance and those too deracinated to be land claimants? ANOP's 'good vibes' strategy would have conceded too much to the reactionary arguments sanctified as the unshakeable sentiments of 'middle Australia'.

It is a premise of my argument, not a critique of it, that the reception of polls is inevitably partisan. Those against land rights have no motive to challenge ANOP's January 1985 report. But it would be disastrous if those in favour of land rights took the poll as an authoritative description of what Aborigines are up against. There are good reasons for both doubting and denouncing 'Land rights: winning middle Australia'. Its data and methods are not sufficiently open to scrutiny. Its political reasoning is ludicrously shallow and naively mired in the rhetoric of land rights opponents. Those who make such nonsense the basis of their political judgements only line, with populist excuses, the coffins of their erstwhile idealism.

Notes

1. *Sydney Morning Herald* 24 September, 1986. The same easy distinction between 'elitist' criticism and 'mass' satisfaction is common in contemporary public discussion. It was recently invoked by Mr Robert Smith, Pizza Hut's national marketing manager for restaurants when he was asked to comment on gastronomic critics of his product. 'They account for a microscopic amount of our customer profile. Quite frankly, we're all tired of a vocal minority claiming that "the masses" are forced to buy our products' *Sydney Morning Herald* 13 January, 1987.

2. See Mills (1986, 21–25). Mills also comments (1986, 52): 'The Hawke government is the most extensive and most successful user of public opinion polling of any Australian government—and not just to determine electoral strategies.'

References

Australian National Opinion Polls (ANOP)
1985 *Land Rights: Winning Middle Australia, An Attitudes and Communications Research Study*, ANOP, Crows Nest, Sydney.

Bourdieu, P.
1979 Public Opinion Does Not Exist. In M. Mattelart and S. Siegelaub (eds), *Communication and Class Struggle*, Bagnolet, New York, 124-30.

Fanon, F.
1967 *The Wretched of the Earth*, Penguin, Harmondsworth.
1970 *Toward the African Revolution*, Penguin, Harmondsworth.

Mills, S.
1986 *The New Machine Men: Polls and Persuasion in Australian Politics*, Penguin, Ringwood.

Rowse, T.
1986 Evidence and Inference: Aborigines as Historical Actors, *Historical Studies* 87(22), 176-98.

11. Lenore Coltheart — The moment of Aboriginal history

I do not want to deny that there is a space in our knowledge of the human experience of this continent which is usefully addressed by the writing about the last 200 years of the Aboriginal past. If there ever was a 'cult of forgetfulness' or a 'great Australian silence' (Coltheart 1984a), I am not advocating a re-run. The problems with which I am concerned are the very concept of Aboriginal history and the notion of writing on the other side of the frontier as missionaries of liberal scholarship and a magistracy of democratic politics. The very idea of a past silence has produced the currently urgent need to speak and the writing of history is a response to that need. It is that idea which has helped bring about the moment of Aboriginal history by creating a demand for writing about Aborigines.

A perspective in which anthropology and history are discrete disciplines is singularly inappropriate to the study of the Australian past and the problem inherent in the concept of Aboriginal history can only be clarified from a transdisciplinary perspective. In this way, the disciplinary borders are no barrier and as well, the boundaries of liberal scholarship might be transgressed. The immediate difficulty for Australian historians in the rush to end their silence is not merely the apparent fence between history and anthropology, although that apparition must be dissolved. A more stubborn obstacle is presented by the limitations of liberal scholarship, the built-in assumptions about the nature of knowledge which support a framework of inquiry and therefore are not subject to questioning themselves. The specificity of the liberal notion of time and the liberal notion of what constitutes knowledge are thus blurred and those notions universalised.

The problems discussed here first, concern the significance of differences in European and Aboriginal conceptions of time and knowledge. History is our familiar blend of the European ideas of time and knowledge and a 'natural' product of our system of thought (Smith 1983, 166). History is our second nature, the context of experience for our praxis, as for our contemplation; the source of explanation for us as political agents in public and in private. To Hegel, history was the necessary resolution of the tension between temporal change and eternal truth (Lloyd 1984, 5). If we did not conceive of the 'night of the past' nor an absolute knowledge, we might not need history. It is only by maintaining an indifference to the possibility of distinctions in conceptions of time and knowledge in an Aboriginal system of thought that we can ignore the paradox of the term 'Aboriginal history' and thus fail to acknowledge our own epistemological boundaries. The philosophic problem of the possibility of an equivalent Aboriginal theorisation about time and knowledge has not been addressed. Where are the non-Aboriginal anthropologists, political theorists, lawyers and historians, and the Aborigines who have seen the need? Most have seen a more immediate and incompatible need.

Our sense of history depends on a linear notion of time, though anthropologists have produced evidence of Aboriginal sense of time as a vital aspect of difference. This evidence has not been received as a challenge by historians, who disregard the implications of, for instance, funerary rites and conception myths which reveal an understanding of life and death as aspects of a continuity. The notion of events as fundamentally repetitive, the capacity for neutralising the novel, the idea of the Dreaming and ritual participation in the Dreaming are all part of the currency of historians' knowledge about Aborigines. This is not to suggest that we should have recourse to a simple alternative explanation such as the notion of cyclic time, nor to consider the problem one of different counting, nor of a curious use of grammatical tense. We must start from our problem with time, that is our concept of time as linear, of the past as finished, of mortality, even of progress. It is our opportunity to problematise our concept of linear time which brings to light the idea of history as contingent on that concept.

Indeed, we need history because we see our civilisation as constantly progressing—we study the past from our need to learn from the past, explain the present and predict and prepare for the vast novelty that is the future.

A function of our need to record the past is as a validation of that one immutability—the criterion of positive knowledge. Although I am treating the problem of time and knowledge in the context of liberal thought, so that the criteria of knowledge are Cartesian, we could trace other influences, and even double back to question the role of European history in the Cartesian formulations, as Sahlins (1983, 526) indicates in pointing out that: 'Thucydides initiated the western historiography of the Unvarnished Truth, or the triumph of *logos* over *mythos*.'

The modern emphasis on positive knowledge might be the culmination of that historic practice and that historic explanation. The understanding that we are beneficiaries of a progressive process of thinking and understanding with Plato as the starting point, the Renaissance and the Enlightenment as markers, and a cumulative set of truths our legacy, is now seriously challenged. One of the most powerful critiques (see Smith 1979) of this comfortable view is that developing in feminist philosophy (another is the theory of quantum mechanics). The goal of positive knowledge, of the universality of European philosophy and of the reign of a bi-valent system of logic have been questioned both as a limiting system and as the product of male thinking (see Salleh 1982, Lloyd 1984, Zukav 1980).

When we consider, for instance, the thirteenth century systematisation of knowledge received into the tradition of western thought, it is clear that the very possibility of such work depends on an understanding of an ordered and logical universe in which everything made sense and everything is accessible as knowledge. The shift from the immutability of divine law to the immutability of scientific fact was not such a large step, logically, for men. Sahlins (1983, 519) uses the example of Fenimore Cooper Indians moving in single file, in the same footprints, giving the impression of one giant Indian, to illustrate the underlying dynamic of 'heroic history'. The progress of 'heroic knowledge' has been much the same. Not much alternative exploration has been done nor other paths made in order to form the impression of authenticity, power and authority along the way and thus reinforcing the tradition of Cartesian thinking. A system of knowledge based on mathematics as the model for logical reasoning, the establishment of the secure premise and the doctrine of falsifiability is self-perpetuating—it ensures its own validity by no more complex means than placing alternative modes of thought out of bounds and is thus referred to as a limiting system (see Zukav 1980, Jones 1983, Sebba 1970). The contemporary feminist critique is directed toward the problem of justification of Cartesian knowledge outside the 'law and order' system of which it consists. There lurk the metatheoretical assumptions devalorising forms of knowing other than the ethnocentric and androcentric epistemology referred to as Cartesian thought. The process of identifying and questioning those assumptions is vital to women's explanations of their experience—and to our recognition of the idea of Aboriginal subjectivity.

Most critical is the current feminist theorisation of difference, which highlights the structural reinforcement beneath the notions of sex equality and race equality. Racial identity, like sexual identity, is not a problem of socialisation, to be neutralised by resocialisation. This view (Gatens 1983, 147) is 'implicitly, a Rationalist account, an ahistorical account and an account which posits a spurious neutrality of both the body and consciousness'. To be Aboriginal is not of itself a problem at all, only if the power of philosophic definition, like the power of social control, is in white and not black hands. Historiography is part of the process of definition, so that a distinction emerges between history about Aborigines and Aboriginal history. It is the former we have begun to do so well, but the explanatory potential of the dominant canons of reason falters before the paradox of the Aboriginal subject. Is Aboriginal experience of the past available for historical interpretation? Clearly, much remembered experience is providing a valuable corrective to historiography based only on the European records of the bicentennium of European contact. Nevertheless, the question of an Aboriginal system of thought, and of the relations of time and knowledge therein, must be kept open to avoid the writing about Aborigines having the same neutralising potential as the equality-through-resocialisation view. The clarification of difference turns the theoretical notion of racism on its head—if we can imagine difference without connotations of inferiority. Aborigines, like European women, are devalued by their association with nature where nature is seen as inferior to history: some strategies for exploring the possibilities of such associations rather than being equalised out of the association have been offered by feminists (Salleh 1984); others have been practised by Aborigines. Alexander states (1983, 88):

> From a position of nothingness, which was assigned to them by our discursive practice, (Aborigines) now cut into the white discourse...The right to be different...is a political answer to the claim of whites to know what is good for them.

Is historiography good for Aborigines? The proposition that Aborigines 'have' history, like the one that they 'have' politics has only recently been taken seriously, and there are those who still reason that without written records there is no history; without leaders and property to protect, no politics. It was, indeed, a significant historical practice to have reduced these propositions to curiosities; maintaining the dominance of the liberalist construct of history and the liberalist construct of politics and sustaining the notion that civilisation was being brought to the wilderness. This practice operates by excluding the idea of the Aborigine as historical subject, and it even worked in abstraction, as Stanner (1960, 74) observed in the Northern Territory in the 1930s:

> In capital and province the sense of history was shallow; there was no grasp whatever of the chaos of the past; and there was no understanding of the welter which contemporary life had become for surviving Aborigines.

That writing history about Aborigines is essential to our understanding of the chaos of the past and the condition of the present is not in question. Neither can there be any doubt that much of the current writing is an important resource for Aborigines— if Aboriginal identity is to be developed from a characterisation as 'other', then the evidence of the extent of colonisation, massacre, of clearing, pacification, dispersal, resistance or compromise, is necessary to that development. As Ann Curthoys (1983) argues, the effect of writing history from the other side of the frontier can be to reinforce the values of the dominant tradition. The quaint idea that a white male image struts this stage of Australian history underlies the most scholarly attempts to retrieve historical evidence of the Aboriginal past where the notion of one historical understanding is implicit, because that one understanding has been white, and male. The problem underlying Curthoys's critique of the work of Reynolds is an epistemological one, and will not be resolved by writing more history.

The function of the annexation of the Aboriginal past to Australian history is ironically, powerfully and tragically analogous to the colonisation process it records. Writing history about Aborigines is, necessarily, the imposition of an alien explanatory framework on Aboriginal experience and Aboriginal understanding. A construction of Aboriginal identity by non-Aborigines, no matter how sound the intellectual foundation, must remain suspect to the logician at least (Thiele 1984).

I have referred elsewhere (Coltheart 1984b) to a genre of Australian historiography as 'Arcadian' history, the Australian variant of 'Whig' history. This is a way of presenting Australian history as a linear story of progressive land settlement. The substantial evidence of forcible expropriation of Aborigines and of the extermination of whole populations is important and unavoidable in increasing our historical knowledge as well as our sense of political responsibility. Unless we escape the dynamic of Arcadian history we ultimately reinforce the progressive land settlement interpretation in which Aboriginal land use is replaced by European land use. This is simply the constant echo of the view enshrined in the work of historians publishing in the period Reynolds refers to as 'the Great Australian Silence'. Surely it is a serious underestimation of the political power of that work to disregard the function of the view that Aborigines did not own the land because they did not use it according to European methods and that this (Collier 1911, 129–30):

> was the capital offence, and it was irredeemable...Their disappearance was a natural necessity. It came about in obedience to a natural law. It was affected by natural processes, and followed on the lines of the substitution of vegetal and animal species all over the world.

The use of 'natural', 'law' and 'necessity' recur (Haydon 1911, 281):

> that Aborigines are steadily decreasing is the natural consequence of conflict with civilization; it is only in accordance with the general law that governs the contact of a black race with a white one.

The same effect is achieved without referring to the owners of the land in subsequent major histories by treating as inevitable, or good, the European use of Aboriginal land. Hancock (1966, 23), Roberts (1924, xiii; 1975, 9) and Bolton (1975, 108, 339) provide some examples. The valorisation of the European method of cultivating knowledge has the same effect as the explicit and implicit endorsement of European occupation of the Australian continent.

The central problem here is a theoretical one, and it is our problem. One way of addressing the difficulty of writing history about Aborigines is to listen to Aborigines, and to Aboriginal evidence, and to be open to the challenges to our practice and our perspective which this entails. Ethnographic research has recently shifted the notion of Aboriginal society as static and organised by 'tradition'—this presents new possibilities, and new problems, for historians and for political theorists, as for anthropologists (Sutton and Rigsby 1986, 156).

This research largely depends on the accumulation of anthropological work for Aboriginal land claims under the Northern Territory legislation, whereby claimants must establish ownership by detailing their traditional, inherited tie to the land. The sum of these anthropological proofs ironically leads to a questioning of the possibility of transplanting this juridical concept at all. The complex and fluid arrangements for succession in Aboriginal land owning groups, the management exercised in some areas to restrict the size of such groups, the processes involved in changing relationships to land (Sutton and Rigsby 1986, 157–66) and the significance of 'wrong events' (Yengoyan 1976, 122), cannot be accommodated by the legal notion of 'traditional ownership', which is a pre-emption of the concepts of ownership in Aboriginal thought.

Unfortunately, need for knowledge about Aborigines is rendered more acute by this pre-emption, and our practice in writing about Aborigines is impelled to production without the accompanying reflection in which at leisure, as scholars, we turn over and toy with the problems of this process. Without that reflection we all too readily participate in a kind of epistemological expropriation—thus history about Aborigines becomes 'Aboriginal history'. Our practice will always turn up evidence of these difficulties as long as we remain open to the possibility of different, Aboriginal, criteria of knowledge. For instance, the practice of writing history about Aborigines is appropriately located in the landscape, if it is not Aboriginal to succumb to the idea of this separation (Alexander 1983, 86).

An opportunity to develop this practice as critical, and reflective, is provided by the exploration in feminist theory of the epistemological status of the liberalist split of nature and history (Salleh 1984).

An historiography in which an ordering principle emerges from a dialectic of experience and environment, and history and nature have parity, will enlighten us about Aborigines and about Australian landscapes, and about writing history. This is a unique, and momentous, opportunity for an Australian contribution to an historical understanding which moves beyond the 'self-contemplation of the European past as the history of "civilizations"' (Sahlins 1983, 534).

My acknowledgement of these problems arose from a study of a particular region of the Northern Territory in the nineteenth century (Coltheart and McGrath 1980). The country of the Port Darwin hinterland south to Pine Creek, from the Finniss River in the west to the Daly Ranges in the east was the subject of this study. Until recently, the areas either side of the Stuart Highway were largely bush, in many places not accessible to ordinary vehicles. Some of the land was held under pastoral or agricultural lease, and there were townships at Pine Creek and Adelaide River—not much of a contribution to the history of civilisation. The experience of the region was intriguing, for the bush in most places was subsequent vegetation, covering the scars of landscape reduction on a massive scale. Material evidence of the gold and tin mining activities of the late nineteenth century abounded, as did excavations in the sides of hills and the gaping holes of vertical shafts. As gold mining was never very profitable for Europeans in the Northern Territory in the nineteenth century, this by-product of the industry had not been judged of historical importance. Because the Finniss River region did not display the symbols of a transformation of wilderness into civilised landscapes it was not of interest to historians.

The region was, however, the most intensively occupied and the most extensively used in the Northern Territory in the nineteenth century. Examinations of evidence of land survey activities, the construction of the overland telegraph line in the 1870s, road and bridge building, the establishment of townships and transport networks to service the extensive mining population, reef and alluvial mining, grazing and plantation enterprises, railway construction, operation and maintenance, had never been directed to the question of the actual lasting effects of these activities. There was no creation of new landscapes in celebration of the progress of land settlement, but a broad scarification of terrain and bush, which permanently altered lagoons, scrub, trees and hills. JL Parsons, the Government Resident, wrote of Mount Wells, site of tin mining, in 1884:

> Two years and a half have wrought strange changes in that conspicuous mountain: when I was there in the early part of 1882, with the exception of the 'trig' station on its summit, it lifted itself up with no marks of man's interference with the wild disorder of nature; once the creek which flowed round its ample base was full of clear, bright water overhanging with trees and bushes. Now the sides of the mountain are scarred and seasoned where the lodes have been found and laid bare, and the creek in the dry season had disappeared. But though the wild natural beauty was gone the evidence of mineral wealth and the prospect of development for a large mining population was a material compensation.

There was no continuous development of the region as 'material compensation' and thus no validation of Europeans' activities or the consequences.

The landscapes of this region were substantially changed by these activities in the decades 1870–1900; but the altered landscapes were instead, symbols of *Abbau*, or land reduction and deterioration (Mumford 1974, 97).

The owners of this country were the Kungarakany, Warrai and Parlamanyin people: a reconstruction of their experience over these decades from official reports indicates a second aspect of the historiographical lapse of attention to 'uncivilised' regions. The widespread use by Aborigines of opium, the frequency of the practice of inducing abortion by crude methods, the epidemic proportions of venereal disease, the ill-health and mortality of Aboriginal women (Dahl 1926, 146; Elder 1979, 52), provide the answer to an unasked question in Northern Territory history. Although the small numbers of non-Aboriginal women have been acknowledged, and the high proportion of Chinese to European men, the distribution of the Chinese men has never been examined. A survey of records shows that over the decades of Chinese mining (from 1874 until the 1890s) most of these men were engaged in alluvial mining in the Finniss River region—approximately 5,000 Chinese men and a calculated 200 European men were there in 1888 (Coltheart 1984c, 207–08).

The Aboriginal explanation of events, neutralisation of novelty and accommodation of change, might be referred to as 'historiology' if we suspend our dependence on the criterion of falsifiability in a system of positive 'truth'. Aboriginal historiology was at a point of crisis for Kungarakany and Warrai people in these decades of 'wrong events'. The effect of the unexplained, unpropitiated and unpunished loss of landscape was profound, and may have been a more significant factor in the deterioration of their society than the specifically economic impact, or even the savagery of conflict under European and Chinese occupation. In this country that was the profound and initial detriment—the events were too swift for the sanctuary of historical explanation. The essential precondition to the regeneration of life was lost to the Kungarakanay and Warrai—the scoured landscapes were the ultimate symbols of the decades of impious use. Clearly, an historical examination of Stanner's (1960) interpretation of a 'voluntary' aggregation of Aborigines from this country in European or Chinese centres, or of McGrath's (Coltheart and McGrath 1980) interpretation of the 'consent' of Aboriginal women in sexual 'contracts' with European or Chinese men, must proceed from the recognition of the vital effect of loss of landscape. Similarly, the important role of Aborigines in pastoral and agricultural and mining activities in the Northern Territory must acknowledge whether loss of landscape was an indicator, or accessibility to country was a reinforcer, of that role. Otherwise, all of these interpretations of Aboriginal experience attach that experience to assumptions about goods, or sexual relations, or labour which are not Aboriginal, and split that experience from the land to which ontologically it is always tied.

The historiological explanation proceeds from the essential integration of people and country. The widespread reduction of landscape in this area could be expected to constitute a profound challenge to the understanding of the Kungarakany and Warrai people, as the impious use of resources on a massive scale should have incurred the obvious displeasure of the spirit *Kurduk* on a similar scale. The detriment of the extensive changes to their country was evidenced in accounts of the reduced numbers of people, their state of health and the mandatory destructuring of their economic life. Although I am concentrating on the landscape changes in the last decades of the nineteenth century, the process of disruption of Kungarakany and Warrai activities continued. Mining, especially at Bamboo Creek and Rum Jungle and Mount Finniss, the construction of airfields and other army works during World War II and the evacuation of coastal people to army control camps on the Stuart Highway decreased the possibility of a restoration of Aboriginal political and economic structures in this region. These experiences would seem, cumulatively, to pose an impossible obstacle to this restoration or indeed to a continued Aboriginal tie to the changed landscapes.

Though none of the Aboriginal owners of the area lived there, many having moved to Darwin, Humpty Doo and Adelaide River, the determined efforts of some families to gain recognition of their traditional rights and to obtain legal title to any part of this country were notable (Layton and Williams 1980, 6). The considerable efforts made by Kungarakany and Warrai people to remain together as families and to perform their obligations in their country is a remarkable phenomenon given the significance of landscapes in the tie to land and the extensive reduction of these landscapes. The processes by which matrilineal and patrilineal links were given parity because 'we can't throw away coloured kids', and naturalisation and adoption principles were used for the incorporation, as land owners, of certain other people, are historiological processes. Similarly, when the Parlamanyin died out as an identifiable group the Kungarakany succeeded to their lands as if they were Kungarakany—that is, the belonging of people in these landscapes was the same kind of link as with other Kungarakany landscapes (Layton and Williams 1980, 24).

An important aspect of the spiritual responsibilities of the land owners is the transmission of the body of traditional knowledge, of which the framework is the general charter of association of the people with the country whether expressed in mythological terms, in the form of anecdotes in the remembered experience of the speaker, in design, song, or ritual expression. The knowledge, authority and fidelity of people such as Alngindabu, the Kungarakany woman who accompanied her children when they were taken to live in Kahlin Native Compound; her daughter, who succeeded to her mother's important role in the transmission of knowledge; and Abalak, the Warrai man forced to leave the Rum Jungle area with his people when mining began there, are clearly a potent force in this historiological function. The privacy, rather than universality, of Aboriginal knowledge, as well as the non-linear sense of time, provides flexibility. An example of the problem of confrontation, in historiography, of historiological explanation is the competing evidence of occupation of an area of land by Kungarakany and Maranunngu people. The Maranunngu evidence appears in conflict with earlier anthropological and linguistic analysis, which placed their country to the south of the area in question. Yet Maranunngu display an intimate knowledge and association with these landscapes, and transmit spiritual knowledge as the charter of this association (Layton and Williams 1980, 49–51, 82–90). There appears to have been no problem for Kungarakany and Maranunngu people in this, but there is certainly a problem for historians and anthropologists writing about Aborigines.

Just as the regeneration and regrowth of subsequent bush vegetation covers much of the reduction of landscapes in this region, so a regenerative explanation of experience in those landscapes provides the historiological ameliorative to the destruction of belief, and Aboriginal propriety is sustained. That process cannot be defined in historiography because it defies historiography. The step to consider historiology may allow us to know more about Aboriginal experience but it is not about that experience, it is about the propriety of liberal scholarship.

References

Alexander, C.
1983 Power and the Australian Aborigines: The Aboriginal Effect. In J. Allen and P. Patton (eds), *Beyond Marxism? Interventions After Marx*, Intervention Publications, Leichhardt.

Bolton, G.
1975 *A Thousand Miles Away*, Australian National University Press, Canberra.

Coltheart, L.
1984a The Breaking of the Great Australian Silence: Aborigines in Australian Historiography 1955-1983, Trevor Reese Memorial Lecture, Australian Studies Centre, University of London.
1984b Arcady: An Idea and its Australian History, Paper Presented to Australasian Political Studies Conference, University of Melbourne.
1984c Australia Misere: The Northern Territory in the 19th Century, PhD thesis, Griffith University.

Coltheart, L. and A. McGrath
1980 Research Notes on the History of the Finnis River Region, typescript.

Collier, J.
1911 *The Pastoral Age in Australasia*, Whitcombe and Tombs, London.

Curthoys, A.
1983 Rewriting Australian History: Including Aboriginal Resistance, *Arena* 62, 96-110.

Dahl, K.
1926 *In Savage Australia*, Phillip Allen, London.

Elder, P.
1979 Northern Territory Charlie: Charles James Dashwood in Palmerston 1892-1905, BA thesis, Australian National University.

Gatens, M.
1983 A Critique of the Sex/Gender Distinction. In J. Allen and P. Patton (eds), *Beyond Marxism? Interventions after Marx*, Intervention Publications, Leichhardt.

Government Resident's Report
1884 *South Australian Parliamentary Papers*, Government Printer, Adelaide.

Hancock, W.K.
1966 *Australia*, Jacaranda Press, Brisbane.

Haydon, A.
1911 *The Trooper Police of Australia*, Melrose, London.

Jones, R.
1983 *Physics as Metaphor*, Abacus, London.

Layton, R. and N. Williams
1980 *The Finniss River Land Claims*, Northern Land Council, Darwin.

Lloyd, G.
1984 History of Philosophy and the Critique of Reason, *Critical Philosophy* 1(1).

Mumford, I.
1974 The Impact of Industrialism. In W. Thomas et al (eds), *Man's Role in Changing the Face of the Earth*, University of Chicago Press, Chicago.

Roberts, S.
1924 *History of Australian Land Settlement 1788-1920*, Macmillan, Melbourne.
1975 *The Squatting Age in Australia*, University of Melbourne Press, Melbourne.

Sahlins, M.
1983 Other Times, Other Customs: The Anthropology of History, *American Anthropologist* 85(3).

Salleh, K.
1982 On the Dialectics of Signifying Practice, *Thesis Eleven* 5(6), 72-84.
1984 Contribution to the Critique of Political Epistemology, *Thesis Eleven* 8, 23-43.

Sebba, G.
1970 What is 'History of Philosophy', *Journal of the History of Philosophy* 8, 251–62.

Smith, D.
1979 A Sociology for Women. In J. Sherman and S. Torton Bech (eds), *The Prism of Sex: Essays in the Sociology of Knowledge*, University of Wisconsin Press, Wisconsin.

Smith, S.B.
1983 Hegel's Discovery of History, *The Review of Politics* 45(2).

Stanner, W.E.H.
1960 Dumurgam, a Nangiomeri. In J. Casagrande (ed), *In the Company of Man: Twenty Portraits by Anthropologists*, Harper, New York.

Sutton, P. and B. Rigsby
1986 People with 'Politiks': Management of Land and Personnel on Australia's Cape York Peninsula. In N. Williams and E. Hunn (eds), *Resource Managers: North American and Australian Hunter-Gatherers*, Australian Institute of Aboriginal Studies, Canberra.

Thiele, S.
1984 Anti-Intellectualism and the 'Aboriginal Problem'. Colin Tatz and the Self-Determination Approach, *Mankind* 14(3), 65–178.

Yengoyan, A.
1976 Structure, Event and Ecology in Aboriginal Australia: A Comparative View Point. In N. Peterson (ed), *Tribes and Boundaries in Australia*, Australian Institute of Aboriginal Studies, Canberra.

Zukav, G.
1980 *The Dancing wu-Li Masters*, Fontana, London.

12. Jeremy Beckett

The past in the present; the present in the past: constructing a national Aboriginality[1]

> Yet even if the discovery of the other must be assumed by each individual and eternally recommenced, it also has a history, forms that are socially and culturally determined.[2]

The construction of Aboriginality in Australia has been achieved through a variety of processes, in various places and at various levels of society, giving rise to a complex interaction between the loci of construction. At the local level, the most striking line of tension may seem to lie between what Aboriginal people say about themselves and what others say about them. But crosscutting this is another field of tension between the ideas of Aboriginality (and non-Aboriginality) that people of all kinds construct and reproduce for themselves, and the constructions produced at the national level by the state in its various manifestations, the mass media, science, the arts and so on. This is what Weaver (1984) calls public ethnicity. The tension persists despite the commanding position of the public construction, or rather because of it. Tending toward the global and the uniform, it is finally alien to those for whom Aboriginality is also behavioural, situational and heterogeneous (cf Weaver 1984).

This second line of tension is localised, in the sense that it occurs only in those relatively few places where Aboriginal people live together and in some kind of relationship with other Australians, which is to say under conditions conducive to the production of private Aboriginalities. However there are large areas from which Aboriginal people have been 'missing' since the early days of settlement. Their 'disappearance' is a direct consequence of colonisation, not simply the killings, introduced diseases and starvation that the records affirm, but the officially instituted removal and segregation of 'tribal remnants', as well as social and cultural practices that have rendered Aboriginal people 'invisible'. As a consequence, while Anglo-Australians have continued to know about Aborigines, those in the coastal cities (the majority), have known them only by report. Even in the rural areas, local Aboriginal people have been ignored in favour of 'the real Aborigines', supposedly living a 'tribal' life 'in the bush'. This public has been largely dependent on representations of Aborigines to be found in the statements of various 'authorities', the work of painters and photographers, the printed and recently the electronic media, or even in artefacts aimed at the popular and tourist markets.

These productions construct Aboriginal people in their absence. Even those that have been the outcome of direct contact cannot be understood simply in these terms. Nor is it sufficient to allow for prejudice, as used to be done in studies of race attitudes. We need a clearer understanding of the context in which the construction is made, the audience which receives it, and the discourse of which it forms a part—in other words, of the nature of the 'Aboriginal absence'. It is, for example, a mistake to assume that a painting of Aborigines, a scientific study of their social or physical characteristics, or a television documentary about their life, is about Aboriginal people. Bernadette Bucher in her *Icon and Conquest* (1981) has shown how sixteenth century European artists ordered and reordered according to their own logic the symbols of aboriginality that travellers brought back from the Americas. Hayden White (1978, 152) reviewing the archaeology of the idea of wildness in the western tradition, observes that 'when men were uncertain as to the precise quality of their sensed humanity, they appealed to the concept of wildness to designate an area of subhumanity that was characterized by everything they hoped they were not'. In Australia likewise Europeans have found Aborigines 'good to think' about quite other matters (cf White 1981, 9–13).[3]

These constructions have nevertheless had consequences for Aborigines, in the sense that they have provided the cultural context in which Europeans have acted upon them, and in which Aborigines have been required to respond. To elucidate this statement, something must be said about the way in which Aboriginal people have been incorporated into Australian society.

Michael Taussig (1984, 495) has interpreted the atrocities committed by Peruvian rubber companies in the headwaters of the Amazon, early this century, in terms of what he calls 'the colonial mirror—the mimesis between the savagery attributed to the Indians by the colonists and the savagery perpetrated by the colonists in the name of...civilization'. Atrocities associated with the Australian frontier suggest parallels (see Evans 1975), but subsequent events indicate another kind of mimesis between the state in its various manifestations and its Aboriginal wards, in which power of the former has been used to bring the latter into at least external conformity with its constructions.

Recognition of this process is critical, since the prevailing mode of incorporation has been governmental for at least a century, and the place of Aborigines in Australian society—that of a minority managed through specialised institutional structures must be termed colonial.[4] An explanation for this can be found in the marginal status of Aborigines in the labour market. They have at times played an important role, particularly in the pastoral industry, but employers have generally preferred to import labour from elsewhere when they could, while organised labour has often excluded them from its ranks. Time and again the state has been called upon to take charge of unwanted, indigent Aborigines. However it has not only brought the indigent into institutionalised dependence, but at times included those capable of living independently. In part this must be explained in terms of the dynamic that is set in motion when bureaucratic agencies are established. One must also take into account the concentration of Aborigines (and Torres Strait Islanders) along Australia's poorly defended northern coastline, and the tendency for Australia's international critics to seize upon instances of Aboriginal deprivation and oppression with the aim of embarrassing her. At home also Aborigines have sometimes constituted an embarrassment to official versions of the Australian way of life.

Managing Aboriginal people under one guise or another, the state has been in a position to influence their public constructions. Not only has it determined who should have access to them, but it has played a major role in the assembling of information about them, has commissioned much of the research conducted by experts on them, and has acted as patron for artistic representations of them. When, as in recent years, Aboriginal people have taken a hand in the process of public construction, the state has been quick to incorporate them, if not co-opt them, into its structures. The mass media remain formally outside its orbit, but their treatment of Aboriginality almost invariably takes the form of a dialogue with the state, as the agency responsible for what happens to them. If there has never been complete agreement on the matter of Aboriginality, there has been a degree of consistency in the debates.

This suggests that an understanding of public Aboriginality in Australia cannot be achieved simply in terms of the particularities of the Aboriginal condition. Nor, however, can it be achieved simply in terms of practical reason or realpolitik. The state also acts within an ideological context, not merely in the sense of manipulating ideas to legitimate what it does in relation to Aboriginal people, but in creating and recreating the society as a whole. The construction of public Aboriginality must thus be understood in the context of the formation of a British colony of settlement in an age of European imperialism, and of the building of a small, semi-peripheral nation state in an age of superpower politics, transnational business and mass culture.

No one has yet attempted comprehensive cultural criticism of public Aboriginality, as it has been constructed since the beginning of European settlement in Australia. Leaving aside attitude surveys, conducted to gauge the extent of race prejudice in the non-Aboriginal population, or critiques of official policy toward Aborigines which do not take cultural analysis very far, attention has been focused on the early years of settlement. Historians, attracted perhaps by the 'noble savage problem', have tended to concentrate on this period (Smith 1969, Mulvaney 1964, Dixon 1986, White 1981). WEH Stanner's historical work is likewise devoted to this period, while the recent collection, *First Encounter* (Donaldson and Donaldson 1985), is, as its name suggests, primarily concerned with the nineteenth century. Healy (1978) has attempted to cover the period from the beginning to the present, but only with respect to novels and poetry. This chapter is mainly concerned with the twentieth century, but even this must be preliminary and selective. Its principal concern is that of the uses of the past in the construction of Aboriginality. This topic is itself complex, for the past is both a remote past of prehistory and a recent past of living memory. More the idea of a past is only meaningful in relation to an idea of a present and of a future, and the supposed links between them such as are found in notions of progress and devolution on the one hand, and the continuity of essences on the other.

Such notions are of particular importance in colonies of settlement such as Australia, where civilisation has confronted not just untamed nature, but notionally its own beginnings. While this encounter has been re-enacted continuously over the 200 of settlement, the frontier, or the outback, has long been an idea rather than a reality for the coastal city dwellers who constitute the majority of Australians. Perhaps for this very reason it has assumed a symbolic importance in the construction of Australian nationality (cf Ward 1964, White 1981), with the antiquity of the landscape contrasted with the newness of the European settlement. The Aborigines have been an integral part of this metaphorical frontier, 'an ancient people in an ancient land', as one scientist called them.[5] Indeed, the 'antiquity' of Australian Aboriginal culture, if not its human bearers, has rarely been absent from constructions of Aboriginality, whether popular or official.[6]

The location of 'the real Aborigines' simultaneously in the remote past and the outback (see Rowley 1970), bring together time and space within a unitary concept. The link between the prehistoric Aborigines and the outback Aborigines is made through the idea of heredity, concretised in metaphors such as blood and family likeness. But whereas among westerners the succession of generations is coordinated with history, if not the advance of civilisation, that among 'real Aborigines' entails no such progression. Compared with, and at times comparing themselves with, the 'real Aborigines', Aboriginal people are caught between the attribution of unchanging essences (with the implication of an inability to change) and the reproach of inauthenticity.

What follows is an exploration of some of the ways in which European and Aboriginal people have attempted to construct Aboriginality around this contradiction. The mode of presentation is loosely chronological, focusing on the dominant construction of a particular period. But it must be emphasised that there has never been unanimity. Nor has one construction ever been completely erased by its successors—unpopular ideas linger, to reappear at another time, perhaps in a different context. Indeed Lattas's study suggests that many of the ideas were formulated within the first few years of colonisation. Their transformation, modification and substitution have taken place in the course of social and political processes, themselves embedded in material processes. They have not, however, been mere epiphenomena, for culture is not made *de novo* but from what there is.

Aborigines in history

Almost twenty years ago Stanner (1968) drew ABC radio listeners' attention to the absence of Aborigines from the work of Australian historians up to that time. The omission is not surprising, given the historians' preoccupation with the formation of a British colony of settlement and its subsequent transformation into an Anglophone nation state, for Aboriginal people were not the heroes of these events. The Aborigine was likewise an embarrassing ghost at feasts celebrating the forging of the Anzac spirit in the mateship of bush workers (cf Ward 1964). But Stanner might have added that a scholarly division of labour had assigned Aborigines to anthropologists, the earlier generation of whom had relegated their culture to prehistory, while many of the next seemed to want to suspend it in the timeless vacuum of structural-functionalism.[7]

In the high age of imperialism, Britain saw the world in terms of a hierarchy of races: rulers and ruled; masters and servants. In colonial Australia, first the Irish, later the Kanakas and Chinese seemed destined to be the work fodder of progress, but not the Aborigines. The first administrators of New South Wales had hoped to (Robinson cited in Dixon 1986, 37):

> call these Wand'rers to the 'promised Fold',
> And from the Dawn o' Reason's genial Day,
> Bid their Night yield—to intellectual Day.

But the early explorers had remarked that Aborigines on the one hand did not respond to overtures of exchange, and on the other failed to respect property (quoted in Stone 1974, 15–20). Not only did they go naked, but when given clothes either rejected them or wore them in ways that seemed more like an aping than an acceptance of civilisation. On the pastoral frontier they appeared as savages in the popular sense of the time, inimical to civilisation in their 'treachery', even bestial, and so unworthy of humane consideration (see Evans 1975). Behind it they were once again *sauvages*, children of nature, doomed to disappear as the wilderness was brought to order, and meanwhile useful devices in poetic and graphic compositions. Dixon (1986, 57-58) notes:

> Almost all of the native groups appearing in topographical views from the early decades of the nineteenth century were based upon a few familiar models...[and]...No matter what the period of society depicted—whether it be the commercial heart of the empire at Sydney, the rural and pastoral frontier society of the outlying villages or the more primitive society of the frontier regions—the natives provide a constant standard against which the philosophical reader may measure the progress of colonization.

As the discoveries of archaeology in Europe gave scientific depths to popular notions of progress, the Aborigines became a 'stone age people', a metaphor that was readily metonymised to make them one with Early Man.[8] Their displacement by settlers could thus appear as a process that had been prefigured in evolution. Fusing the principles of cultural and biological evolution, Aborigines became an anachronism whose extinction was a natural even if pathetic fact of life. They belonged to another time and would not be staying long. While they lingered they might be used for rough work, as trackers or even to exterminate their fellows, as in the Queensland Native Police (Evans 1975). It seemed that they need not be included within the normative framework of society, though they might become the objects of charity, scientific research, amusing anecdote or artistic representation.

The half-caste problem and some solutions

During the early years, Australia reproduced the structures of the British society on the frontier, only substituting convicts for a free proletariat. Thus while the colonists might have identified Aborigines with nature and characterised their behaviour as brutish, they could also apply the term to convict and other disorderly elements. The doctrine of degenerationism, current in the early nineteenth century, enabled Europeans to accept the original humanity of Aborigines, as descendants of Adam, while assigning them to a lower order in the present. And since a similar fate could overtake Europeans, it also, as Andrew Lattas (1986) observes, provided the dominant class with a 'conceptual weapon' against the lower orders, who could become as the Aborigines were.

Later in the nineteenth century an Australian-born settler population began constructing an identity in terms of British origins and participation in British Imperial hegemony (White 1981, 71–72, 111–12). These sentiments gained scientific status through racist theory, enunciated by an educated elite, but also embraced by a lay audience through popularising mediums such as the periodical *Science of Man*, published in Sydney. While assuming the new authority of science, racism also made sense to a popular wisdom that already explained human differences and similarities in terms of heredity. Thus understood, inequality could be made to appear natural by reference to those most natural of events, reproduction and birth. And just as people perceived physical likenesses between parents and children, so they believed that qualities and capabilities were transmitted in the same way. Just as they expected no good to come from a bad family, so those who were 'no good' could be presumed to have come from a bad family. Thus the *Science of Man* (21 July 1899) could write of 'families of hereditary criminals'. Similarly, shared physical characteristics were taken as evidence of shared mental capacities and behavioural propensities, and scientists looked for physical likenesses in persons to whom particularly behavioural propensities were ascribed. Since these qualities were immutable they presented society with a choice—either to contain them through strict control or to terminate their physical reproduction.

The reality of interbreeding was subversive of this kind of reasoning, particularly in the case of racial miscegenation, so that the 'half-breed' or 'half-caste' constituted an anomaly if not a danger. According to the *Science of Man* (22 September 1900), hybrids either showed increasing signs of degeneration, eventually dying out, or reverted to one or other of the 'original race types', depending on climate and the races in question. Somewhat inconsistently, the same writer suggested that hybrids showed the bad qualities of both races, adding that 'In Australia the children of black women by white fathers are worse than the pure blacks in many particulars.'[9] Such theories were safe from scrutiny, since it would be several generations before their predictions would be realised—thus what might seem to be a successful hybrid remained under the shadow of atavism in some later generation.

These problems assumed added complexity in the Australian context. In particular, while British descent remained the colonial population's principal mode of identification, the severing of intergenerational kin ties through emigration required that the idea be generalised and elevated to the status of a scientific fact. Given primacy, the idea of race could transcend notions of hereditary criminality (otherwise implicit in such thinking) and suggestions that superior northern stock degenerates in tropical climes (White 1981, 70–71). The Aboriginal-European population, which was making its presence felt by the second half of the nineteenth century, thus posed a national problem.

Conditions on the frontier were such that white males would gain sexual access to Aboriginal women, but rarely acknowledge any relationship with their 'half-caste' children. Raised by their Aboriginal mothers, and often acquiring Aboriginal step fathers, these children became in practice and were often officially classified as 'natives'. Although authority sometimes drew a veil over these offspring of doubly illicit unions, it was not easy about abandoning children with 'British blood' to 'the blacks'. But when the state or its mission surrogates assumed the role of the missing white father, it also severed the connection with the black mother. Attributing to Aboriginal society the rejection practised by Europeans,[10] it set about 'rescuing' the many children who had not in fact been rejected 'from the degradation of the blacks' camp'. Their destination was not, however, white foster parents or even public orphanages, but government or mission institutions established specifically for part-Aboriginal children. Assuming the legal authority of the parent, without transmitting 'blood', the state turned its wards into orphans, cut off from their Aboriginal kin without acquiring European kin. Uncertain about what it was creating, and fearful of atavism, it often repeated the separation of parents and children in subsequent generations, while limiting the scope of relationships that were allowed to exist. Such practices seemed to envisage a population of perpetual orphans. (In northern Australia, this intermediate stratum corresponded to, and was evidently intended to fill, positions such as domestic servants and overseers of native workers which employers had difficulty in filling from either the European or the Aboriginal population.)

Xavier Herbert's *Capricornia*, first published in 1938, took as its subject matter the plight of the offspring of Aboriginal mothers and European fathers in the Northern Territory. Herbert later insisted that the novel's 'deep motive was the father–son relationship' and one critic has interpreted it in terms of Herbert's relations with his parents (Heseltine 1973, 11–13; cf Healy 1978, 154–68). In terms of its subject matter, however, it must be understood as proposing the recognition of the submerged relationship between white father and half-caste son. In Herbert's story, social pressure, human frailty or tragic circumstance, always result in this tie being severed. Since the Aboriginal mothers are either dead, absent or ineffective, the offspring are consigned either to a brutish life among Aborigines or a scarcely less degrading institutional limbo. (Aboriginality is represented as a romantic if finally unrealistic alternative for the anti-hero Norman, but as degradation and death for the girl Constance.) At the conclusion of this chronicle of failed conjugal and parental relationships, the story reunites Norman with his scapegrace father in a partnership of doubtful prospect. (Although the question is not directly addressed, his prospects for reproducing himself will presumably depend on once again replacing his dead black mother with the fictitious Javanese princess, his step father had invented for him.)

Contemporaneously, the Commissioner for Native Affairs in Western Australia, AO Neville, was formulating his own plan for absorbing the 'mixed blood' population into the white majority. As he explained in a book written after his retirement, this was to prevent the undesirable possibility of the 'coloured' population becoming an 'ethnic group' like the Negroes in the United States (Neville 1947, 56; Jacobs 1986).[11] His solution was the application of bureaucratic power to secure planned breeding. Throughout Australia, officialdom had the power to prevent sexual contacts between white and black, and commonly discouraged the rare European who wished to establish a legal relationship with an Aborigine. Neville proposed to take these powers very much further. Central to his plan was the removal of girls of 'lighter caste' from their families to orphanages for white children, where they would be strictly trained in the domestic arts and married to working class males. Insisting that the remote common origins of Aborigines and Europeans ruled out the risk of atavism (1947, 63), Neville included photographs 'proving' that his eugenics was a means of 'breeding out the colour' in the space of a few generations. The other arm of his strategy is worth quoting verbatim (1947, 56):

> It is to the benefit of our own race that the full-blood be rigidly excluded from any association likely to lead to any other union. It would be contrary to our view of assimilation to do anything which might force our coloured people back to the black, and moreover their continued mating with full-bloods is liable to prolong the process of absorbtion until after there are no more virile full-bloods remaining alive.

Neville's (1947, 68) understanding of the effects of 'coloured' marrying back is reminiscent of the *Science of Man*:

> Thirty or forty years ago there existed a better type of half-caste. These were robust, meat-eating people—the women big like the men and as vigorous. The family heads were mostly first-cross people...They were a people apart, and intermarriage was inevitable. The offspring were not equal to the parents; they ran to seed through intermarriage and became lethargic. But with the admixture of further white blood

> they recovered some of the original traits, acquiring part of the good qualities of both races; the physical improvement being notable.

At one end of Neville's asymmetrical connubium are light-skinned females marrying Europeans, and light-skinned males marrying darker women, at the other—although he never admits this—are the darkest males, left without sexual partners and so unable to transmit their unwanted heredity. However, the parents of the 'lightest' girls transmit only their genes, while the state assumes the parental role, until the point at which a white male becomes father, in law as well as in nature, placing his children in Australian society and enabling them to become parents of Australian children.

Albert Namatjira and the assimilation policy

Although Neville's colleagues in other parts of Australia were not unsympathetic to his proposals and sometimes used their power to regulate marriage in the same direction, they stopped short of implementing his eugenic solution in any throughgoing way. And while their conception of assimilation for 'part-Aborigines' may have been largely genetic in 1937 (Rowley 1970, 320), the emphasis shifted to the sociocultural in 1939, when the Federal Interior Minister, J McEwan declared that in the Northern Territory the aim would be (Rowley 1970, 329):

> The raising of their status so as to entitle them by right and by qualification to the ordinary rights of citizenship, and to enable them to help them to share with us the opportunities that are available in their native land.

Interrupted by war in Europe and the Pacific, this became the national policy thereafter.

Although explicit racism was no longer acceptable in the post-Holocaust west, it seems unlikely that either officials or politicians had abandoned racist assumptions. AP Elkin, who as scientific expert, clergyman and publicist, had done much to achieve the acceptance of the assimilation policy, would in 1947 advance no more than the cautious conviction that, 'apart from individual variations, all human beings, irrespective of skin pigmentation and ancestry, are born with like potentials for living worthily, intelligently and happily' (see Neville 1947, 15–16).[12] Younger anthropologists including the author, continued to use the term 'mixed blood' into the 1960s, no doubt in conformity with official usage, but nevertheless perpetuating a confusion between genetics and culture. Despite these survivals of racism, however, the operative definition of Aboriginality had shifted from biological to the cultural, in the sense that the Aboriginal heritage could be terminated without the termination of its bearers.

The assimilation policy must be understood as a statement about the nature of Australia in a post-depression, post-war, post-colonial world. In 1951 the Minister for Territories addressed the following words to the Native Welfare Conference (see Stone 1974, 195):

> On the one hand we in Australia want to give the chance of a happy and a useful life to all our people; on the other hand, we want to build a society in which there shall be no minorities or special classes and in which the benefits yielded by society shall be accessible to all.

This vision turned its back on the past and proposed a new beginning in the form of an affluent, classless, monocultural society: the poor would forget their former privations; migrants would forget Europe; and Aborigines would forget their past. In return all would enjoy the 'Australian way of life' which, as White (1981, 158) remarks, had replaced race and national type as the basis for Australian identity.

While Australia was told that Aborigines were not going to die out, it was also given to understand that Aboriginality was doomed. Timeless and unchanging, Aboriginal culture was incapable of co-existence with the modern world: 'the old Aboriginal cultures are collapsing everywhere under the impact of white settlement, mining exploitation, pastoral expansion and the effects of Government "assimilation" policies' (Strehlow 1963, 455). With 'the old Aboriginal world...now facing its final twilight' (1963, 456), anthropologists would at last be generously funded through the Australian Institute of Aboriginal Studies to study Aboriginal culture 'before it was too late'. What could be retrieved at such a late stage was to be preserved for 'science' and incorporated in the 'national heritage'.[13]

Such constructions left the bearers of this 'non-viable' culture alive, if not very well. Living on borrowed cultural time, their future then was to 'attain the same manner of living as other Australians'. Meanwhile, their predicament justified an intensification of official intervention in their daily lives—even the familial function of providing meals was usurped on Northern Territory settlements. Government reports of the period featured improvements in housing and health care, but the basic emphasis was pedagogical. This is particularly apparent in a late refinement of the official objective, to the effect that Aborigines would 'choose to attain' a similar manner and standard of living.

Where previously governments had had little to say about their management of Aborigines, they now publicised their activities in illustrated reports, booklets and films. In these the policy that required the disenfranchisement of Aborigines as a group was validated on the one hand by the provision of material benefits, and on the other by individuals who distinguished themselves at doing the things that other Australians did—painting, singing, soldiering, playing sport, studying, housekeeping. While Aborigines remained outside the framework of Australian history, the Blairs, Saunders, Nichols and Namatjiras were appropriated by it.

Albert Namatjira became a national celebrity, in the literal sense of the term. The 'primitive' Aranda from the central Desert, who could paint 'like a white man' pictures that ordinary Australians (if not the directors of public galleries) liked to hang in their homes, seemed to span the chasm between stone age and modernity. His muteness, whether structurally determined or, as his interpreters suggested, part of his 'natural dignity' (Batty 1963), made him the perfect vehicle for the constructions of the patrons, protectors, promoters and experts who mediated his creativity to the public. As Burn and Stephen (1986, 11) say, the Aranda painters were 'spoken for'. Although his advocates stressed his achievements 'as a watercolourist, not an Aboriginal' (Batty 1963, 41) and cast him in the role of the artist-hero, Namatjira's Aboriginality was an intrinsic part of his celebrity. As such it must be taken as proving the assimilationist point, that a 'full blood' with talent and ambition could win public recognition and material success. Correspondingly, his fall when arrested for giving alcohol to relatives, and his subsequent death, brought the whole strategy into doubt. Finding the legal disabilities to which Namatjira was subject as an Aborigine—specifically in relation to alcohol—incompatible with his achievement as a national artist, the state had granted him citizenship. This, however, required that he become an isolate, severed from his past, in the form of his kin. Supplying them with alcohol, in recognition of his continuing relation with them, exploded the fiction.

For some Namatjira's demise confirmed the idea that it would take Aborigines 'years to catch up' with white people.[14] Others found an explanation in the withholding of the citizenship that should be a right of all Australians, regardless of race or colour or culture. This was the view that prevailed. Aborigines gained the franchise and legal access to alcohol before the 1960s ended, and there was a general scaling down of legal restrictions throughout the country.

The idea of citizenship had taken on a central importance in the 'national reconstruction' of the war years. During the Cold War it acquired a new importance as a counter to ideas of class struggle. In what was also a period of decolonisation, when discrimination on grounds of colour or race could embarrass attempts to make friends with the new nations, it also provided an appropriate policy for Aborigines. The struggles against *apartheid* in South Africa and the civil rights movement in the

United States, both widely reported in Australia, not only structured Australian's perceptions of their own situation, but gave them a language with which to describe it. Thus on southern campuses and increasingly in the media, Queensland became Australia's 'deep north', where 'apartheid' was practised, and protestors undertook 'freedom rides' through New South Wales country towns.

In this discourse, Aboriginal people were assimilated, not into the community, but into the ranks of the oppressed, the colonised, coloured people, the 'wretched of the earth'. Frank Hardy (1968, 25), feeling himself a 'rebel without a cause' had his 'ancient fire' of compassion for the underdog rekindled by the Gurindji strike:

> There was a time when I would intervene if a shopping mother slapped her tired child in the street. Now I would turn my back on the horror of Vietnam, because white Australia disgusted me with its complacency, it racism, its philistinism. White Australia could go to hell by its own road. But white Australia's greatest crime was its debasement of the Aborigines. Those near them didn't care; those far from them didn't want to know. Well, let white Australia beware. The NT Aborigines were ready stand and be counted; and I would stand and be counted with them.

In keeping with this mood, Hardy called his book *The Unlucky Australians* in ironic reference to Donald Horne's *The Lucky Country*. Organised around the strike and the support campaign in the south, it is also an account of his personal discovery of Aborigines, who, however are presented through these events. There is little about Aboriginal culture, and reference to land rights (just then emerging as an issue) only in passing near the end (cf Healy 1978, 223–40). For the most part, liberal and left critiques of the period located Aboriginal people within broader categories rather than defining them in terms of a unique Aboriginality. If there was a sense of history in all this, it was that the world was, or should be, moving toward greater justice, equality, toleration and harmony.

Aboriginal voices were able to make themselves heard during the 1960s for the first time since the 1930s.[15] The Federal Council for the Advancement of Aborigines and Torres Strait Islanders, which gave a national platform to Aboriginal as well as European critics, also focused upon civil rights issues until the late 1960s. Likewise, the formation of separate 'black' organisations—including a Black Panther Party— toward the end of the 1960s was generally seen as paralleling developments in the United States. The slogan Black Power, taken up at this time, suggested a capacity for decisive, if not violent action, such as had occurred in the ghettos—although the public attention that it attracted proved of uncertain value. Soon after the liquidation of the Black Power leadership in the United States, the slogan fell into disuse in Australia.

'Black', commended by Sykes (Bonner and Sykes 1975) as a way of including people of Aboriginal, Torres Strait Island and Pacific Island descent, remained in currency for somewhat longer. However, governments retained the established usage, and terms such as 'Aboriginal people'. 'Kooris' and 'Murris', or 'Islanders' for Torres Strait people, have been more usual in recent years. In the meantime, Aboriginality was once again acquiring some internal content, rather than being defined in terms of externals (cf Sansom, Chapter 9).

The return of the native

The 1967 referendum, in which ninety-seven per cent of voters endorsed a proposal for national action on Aborigines was both the culmination of the movement for Aboriginal citizenship and, paradoxically, the basis for the construction of a special Aboriginal status. As such it prefigured the Tent Embassy of 1972, an event constitutive of the new Aboriginality, that became in this sense an event (in other words reified), as a result of its diffusion through the national media. Appearing in photographs and on the screen, the protagonists came to stand for the unseen remainder.[16]

The Tent Embassy also reconstituted as the other event, the referendum of 1967, making it a charter for a new Aboriginality.[17] Onto its bland mandate for unspecified action, the enfranchisement of Aborigines (in fact occurring in 1961) and the recognition of land rights (not in fact made law until 1976) were now grafted. More to the point, the embassy transformed the bland expression of concern on the part of non-Aboriginal Australians into a declaration of identity on the part of the objects. By calling the tents an embassy the protestors made a claim to nationhood; by selecting land as their central demand, they claimed a territory in which to practise their nationality. Land rights also proposed common cause across long established divisions among Aboriginal people, southern and northern, traditional and non-traditional.

The McMahon coalition government evicted the embassy after some months, but the Whitlam Labor government reconstituted it as a representative body called the National Aboriginal Conference which, maintained some kind of existence until 1985 (Weaver 1984). The new Commonwealth Department of Aboriginal Affairs also formulated and implemented a national policy, including the fostering of a multiplicity of Aboriginal organisations, to provide for the medical, legal, cultural, economic and housing needs of Aborigines and Torres Strait Islanders. However, land rights remained the constitutive issue.

The past in the present; the present in the past: constructing a national Aboriginality

Our Aborigines

The acceptance of land rights by a broad section (albeit, mainly urban) of the non-Aboriginal population is partly to be understood in terms of primitivism, which Hayden White (1978, 170-71) defines as the seeking to 'idealize *any group* as yet unbroken to civilizational discipline'. White (1978, 171) characterises this tendency as radical since it is based on 'the conviction that men are really the same throughout all time and space but have been made evil in certain times and places by the imposition of social restraints upon them'. Taken in these terms, primitivism can be understood as part of the decolonisation process. Similar assumptions underlay melioristic social programs and sexual freedoms of the west of the 1960s and 1970s.

After the demise of the 'noble savage' at the end of the eighteenth century, primitivism re-emerged at the beginning of the twentieth, in the beginnings of modern art in Europe, in the cultural relativism of between-the-wars North American anthropology. In Australia, as Healy (1978, 168-77) writes, writers 'used' Aborigines in the course of constructing a new nationalism around a 'timeless land'. Following World War II an ever increasing flow of travel books introduced a mainly urban readership to the bush. What they celebrated as 'the real Australia' was no longer hostile, so much as a stimulating challenge to the resourceful traveller, and far from being a wildness to be tamed, it was a wilderness to be preserved. In the old natural history mode, but in anticipation of the ecology movement of the 1970s, Aborigines were included along with the flora and fauna, as part of a seamless web of life.

An outstanding example of this genre is *Brown Men and Red Sand: Journeyings into Wild Australia*, by the self-taught anthropologist and photographer, CP Mountford. First published in 1948 and reprinted in 1961 and 1981, it exhorts the reader to 'leave civilization behind' and, braving 'the terrifying desolation' of the 'dead heart' (1948, 19), discover the 'fascination' and 'wonder' of the country and its people. The culture of the Aborigines is not only 'the simplest in the world' (1948, 17) but representative of the beginnings of human life. They live close to nature, particularly the children; 'open air, the joy of song and bodily movement' (1948, 42) 'naked brown skinned children, like bronze statues' (1948, 34), though there are also 'magnificent specimins (sic) of manhood'. Mountford undertakes a sustained apology for the Aboriginal way of life. Far from being cannibals, they are a 'simple and kindly people (1948, 110), with a medicine that is seemingly effective (1948, 53), an intelligence producing 'simple yet wise' ways for survival in a harsh environment (1948, 72), a respect for the land, ceremonies that leave one with 'the sensation of having seen something beautiful'. In Ayers Rock the 'grandeur' and 'majesty' of the scene, the 'strangeness' of Aboriginal mythology, and the antiquity of both, create a sense of 'mystery' that is indivisible (1948, 86–88). Although Mountford is at pains to emphasise the 'strangeness' of his subjects, he has nevertheless assimilated them into the national culture, to be 'our Aborigines'.

In the years that followed, desert Aborigines were to be put to work as a national emblem. In postage stamps, travel brochures, art catalogues and assorted tourist merchandise, the Aborigine was represented as black, male, bearded and scantily dressed, holding a spear and with his eyes fixed on some distant object—all against a background of scenic splendour. Such an icon suggested that the conjunction of these features was necessary and natural.

While such writings might incorporate Aborigines into contemporary national ideology, they did not envisage the incorporation of their culture or way of life. Mountford represents civilisation as not merely irrelevant to their way of life but inimical to it. Clothing 'disfigures...a slim lovely body', obscuring 'natural dignity' and bringing disease (1948, 180); education curbs the untrammelled freedom of childhood to inculcate irrelevant knowledge. The implication, albeit regretful, is that Aboriginality lives on borrowed time, preserved only through an accident of geography.

While, as we have seen, scientists and laymen alike expected the passing of Aboriginal culture, academic anthropology was beginning to undermine the idea that this fate was inevitable. The early scientific writers had located Aborigines firmly in prehistory. Elkin (1945), though not free of such thinking, had also been exposed to the comparative religionist, Andrew Lang. Speaking with the combined authority of scientist and minister to a great diversity of lay audiences, he discussed Aboriginal religion in the same terms as Christianity, and drew comparisons between the feats of Tibetan lamas and those of Aboriginal Men of High Degree. WEH Stanner, trained in an anthropology that compared societies in a timeless frame, also explored the comparison between Aboriginal Judaeo-Christian doctrine in his essay for the layman, 'The Dreaming' (1958), while Ronald and Catherine Berndt delivered similar messages in forms accessible to the intelligent lay audience.[18] The ground was laid for Aboriginal religion to take its place in an emerging religious pluralism. Progress, if not history, had lost its linear form, to be folded back upon itself in the search for the 'primitive' spirituality that 'civilisation' had lost. In somewhat the same way, Aboriginal art moved from the museum to the art gallery, as something of contemporary significance, and Aboriginal foraging became a model for the ecology movement.[19]

Through the 1960s, the Commonwealth's formulations of the assimilation policy were increasingly qualified by the recognition that Aborigines should not be prevented from practising their tradition as long they wished to do so (Department of Territories 1967, 40–44). With the establishment of the Council for Aboriginal Affairs in 1967, the possibility was posed of actively assisting Aborigines to practise their culture. Land rights became the means by which they might do so. With the reformulation of Australian nationality as multiculturalism, in the 1970s, taking the Aboriginal option became compatible with citizenship rather than an alternative to it. Nevertheless, the Aboriginal claimant for land was cast in the role of *homo religiosus* rather than *homo economicus* and the case presented in terms of sacred sites rather than hunting grounds. Intended or not, this emphasis meant that subsequent conflicts between Aboriginal and mining interests were conducted in non-comparable terms, although the latter sometimes implied that Aborigines were inventing sacred sites for material gain, and eventually government imposed a monetary value on sites as a means of securing an agreement between the two.

Reconstructing Aboriginality

In formulating a national policy for Aborigines, the Commonwealth avoided making distinctions among people of Aboriginal descent, opting instead for self-identification and/or recognition by a community. The remote Aborigine nevertheless remained the touchstone of Aboriginality: the point of ultimate reference in definitions of Aboriginality by descent; and the source of fetishised forms of Aboriginal culture, enshrined in museums, galleries, demonstrations and institutionally framed 'sites of significance'.[20]

Such representations of Aboriginality called into doubt the special status of those who called themselves Aboriginal, but lived in urban settings, practised no traditional arts or ceremonies, and generally failed to 'look the part'. Such people had constructed their Aboriginality in other modes, as Lyndall Ryan (1986) has noted, primarily by reference to proximate ancestors and living kin. Sansom (1980), similarly, has identified it as a major component of what he calls 'the Aboriginal commonality', implying as it does a continuous network embracing all Aboriginal people throughout the continent. However, in practical terms each individual occupies a particular position on the network, and while it may be possible to push outward along a series of links to discover 'new kin', it is not possible to jump several links and pick up the threads. It is thus questionable whether such notions have the potential to construct Aboriginality on a national scale. There has been, however, a similar problem in relation to land rights, which consists of a series of local claims brought by small groups of traditional owners, and which has been politically fractured through the institution of different legislation in different places.

If the Gurindji and their friends brought land rights before the Australian public (Hardy 1968), it was the urban Aborigines who made it a national issue. In the early 1970s they 'enacted' their Aboriginality in dramatic demonstrations and projected themselves through the media as spokespersons for the Aboriginal 'cause'. By these means they have been able in some degree to shift the emphasis away from the ungeneralisable particularities of tribe, country and kinship. Of recent years, land has become not just an economic or a spiritual resource, but the means by which the Aboriginal past is substantialised in the Australian present, and the locus in which Aboriginality can be realised through self-determination.

The idea of ownership, that among traditionally-oriented Aborigines is expressed through mythology and in ritual, is here condensed in the principle of descent, so that the special relationship with, and entitlement to land are represented as instrinsic to anyone who is descended from the original inhabitants of the continent. For those with some non-Aboriginal ancestry, descent is—in anthropological parlance—ambilineal. But what counts is that one lives as an Aborigine and participates in the struggle for land rights.

The cultural processes at work are by no means peculiar to the Australian situation. What Janet Dolgin (1977, 61–62) has written about the New York Jewish Defence League (JDL) bears so close a resemblance that I have adapted by simple substitution one of her most insightful passages:

> Through descent and political activism, urban Aborigines made the Dreamtime contemporary, and the means by which this occurred was backward metaphorisation of the present. While the blood tie between the Aboriginal and his or her parents, the tie which makes them Aboriginal, is a 'natural' tie, the link to the Ancestors is a tie of metaphoric blood; the mediator between the 'natural' blood of the family and the metaphoric blood of History is 'code for conduct' (conceived by urban Aborigines as activism).[21]

Aboriginality on the rock

In 1986 the federal government withdrew its support from two structures which gave most substance to the idea of Aborigines as a national minority, the National Aboriginal Conference and the promise of a national program of land rights. Though

The past in the present; the present in the past: constructing a national Aboriginality

the results of the 1985 ANOP poll were never made public, their reputed content effectively terminated the mandate that the 1967 referendum had become during the 1970s (Rowse 1986, also Chapter 10). Preceding these events, however, were not only the well financed campaign of the mining lobby, but a series of media events. Possibly the first of these was the edition of the *Sydney Morning Herald* (12 November 1983) which gave central position on its front page to the headline 'Land rights clash over Ayers Rock'. In the same issue was a report of a plan to Aboriginalise the Arts Board and a letter from Minister Holding under the heading: 'Give the Aborigines a fair go'. There was also an account of the enquiry into the death of John Pat in police custody, which had received coverage earlier in the week along with the court hearings into the shooting of an Aboriginal man in Moree. The conjunction of these discrete items, remarkable in itself, announced an end to consensus in Aboriginal affairs. Special treatment for Aborigines now seemed not merely divisive but a cause of violence in the community. Not long after, 'backlash' came into currency as the response of the hitherto voiceless rural and outback whites to the special status accorded to Aborigines.

In the campaign against Aboriginal land rights mounted by the mining lobby and the governments of the Northern Territory, Western Australia and Queensland, the rhetoric of earlier years has reappeared in two modes: either the remote Aborigines are to be attached to the past while the rest are severed from it; or all Aborigines are to be brought into the present, in other words to be assimilated. In the latter mode, land rights is subjected to a liberal critique. It is equated with apartheid—a trope borrowed from the civil right campaigns of the 1960s—and rejected as subversive of the equality that must prevail among Australian citizens, regardless of race, colour or creed. This equality is defined in terms of formal legal, political and economic rights, and without recognition of the inequalities created by conquest, dispossession and institutionalisation. In the words of the Australian Mining Industries Council, 'Whatever injustice may have been perpetrated on the Aboriginal People in the past, Australia is now one nation with one community of people' (see Rowse 1986, 65). If Aboriginal people qualify for assistance it must be like other Australians, disadvantaged through isolation, poverty, ill-health and the like.

There has also been at least one move to detach Aboriginal people from an Aboriginal past, once again located firmly in prehistory. Thus sacred boards are withheld from the descendants of those who made them, on the ground they are not ritually qualified to see them (McGregor 1987). Mining executive Hugh Morgan, writing in the *Sydney Morning Herald* (19 March 1985) and several other major newspapers, has depicted Aboriginality as not only a thing of the past but irredeemably savage. The Aborigines, we are informed, had 'no historical sense of time', and no technological achievements. He characterises their culture in terms of practices calculated to repel the reader, such as warfare, cannibalism, subincision, polygyny and brutal punishments. Morgan critises some Europeans—missionaries and others—who believe that they can pick and choose among Aboriginal practices selecting what they approve and suppressing what is unacceptable; echoing the structural-functionalism of an earlier anthropology, Aboriginality is indivisible; we must take it or leave it as a package—and we will be much better off leaving it, since it has no future. There is no recognition of Aboriginal culture as adaptive and changing: indeed the article begins with the assertion that it 'had changed very little, perhaps not at all, for many centuries, if not for milennia', prior to 1788. History is once again what the settlers did to and for Aborigines.

Against this background, the return of Ayers Rock (Uluru) to its traditional owners in 1985 assumes a certain ambiguity. With the federal government's abandonment of a national land rights program, it can seem like the final act in the sequence of events that began with the 1967 referendum, a settlement of accounts with the remote Aborigine. Uluru, however, is not just another piece of anonymous land. Annette Hamilton (1984) writes that it has become a 'unique cultural symbol' for Australians of European descent as well as Aborigines. Those who opposed the transfer, including the Northern Territory government, questioned whether the handful of Aborigines involved should, or would be capable of, looking after what was part of the national heritage. Yet the bitter controversy that ensued was over form rather than fact: the Aboriginal owners were to return the rock to federal authorities, with uncertain rights of control over its use. Recent reports suggest that the owners are having difficulty in resisting the endless succession of demands from commercial and media interests—even including a proposal to sell chips of the rock as souvenirs (*Sydney Morning Herald* 19 April 1986).

Recalling Annette Hamilton's (1984, 377) observation that the visitor to Uluru expects to have access to Aborigines as part of the touristic experience, we might conclude that the transfer of ownership, rather than attaching the rock to them has attached them to the rock, as part of its primeval allure. However, it is remarkable that as this meaning becomes increasingly generalised through use in advertising and as a backdrop for media happenings, Aboriginal people are being literally left out of the picture.[22] After all, if Uluru pre-dates human occupation, the Aborigines were as much immigrants as the Europeans who came after them! (At this point,

The past in the present; the
present in the past: constructing a
national Aboriginality

scientific attempts to establish the origin and point of entry of Aborigines takes on a new significance.)

While the critics of land rights have turned back to the doctrines of assimilationism, there is no question of returning to the 1950s: too much has happened in the meantime so that Aboriginal people have a history in which Aboriginal people are the actors. Aboriginality may, however, undergo further redefinition. Now that the campaign has been largely contained within the Northern Territory, land rights may lose their effectiveness as a national focus. The media have seized upon the twentieth anniversary of the referendum to point up the lack of 'results' and to ask whether the fault lies with the state or with Aboriginal people. Urban Aborigines have made killings in police custody their issue for 1988. But there is no certainty that politics will remain the most important means of construction.

While Aboriginal 'activists' no long seem able to attract the attention of the mass media as they did in the early 1970s, Aboriginal writers, artists, cinematographers and musicians are finding a public of a more limited kind. Coming from Australian education institutions and working through Australian editors, publishers, technicians and agents, they have to negotiate the institutionlised constructions of Aboriginality if they are to 'write black' (cf Ariss Chapter 8). At the same time, their position as Aboriginal artists or writers gives them a licence to reappropriate these constructions.

Hailing the work of some senior Aboriginal writers as 'the underpinning of a newly conceived Aboriginal heritage', Ronald Berndt (1985, 9) has urged that the distinctiveness of Aboriginal traditional cultures and societies should not be lost, and regretted that no one had yet 'thought themselves into the traditional, *uniquely Aboriginal scene*'. In fact, Colin Johnson's *Doctor Wooreddy's Prescription for Enduring the Ending of the World* (1983), begins this way, albeit as a vantage point for describing the end of the Tasmanian Aborigines. In the earlier *Long Live Sandawara* (1979), Johnson presents the past in the person of Sandawara, who led a long struggle against European invasion, but mediated through the wine sodden memory of an old man, long exiled from his country, to take on new life in the imagination of a young urban Aborigine. In the film *Short Changed* (1986), scripted by Robert Merritt, the Aboriginal past is mediated through the land itself and Aboriginal parentage. In another mode, Kevin Gilbert (1977) and Bropho (1980) have preferred to draw upon living memory, seeking to generalise the experiences of particular Aboriginal people, if only by bringing them together within the one book. The remote Aborigines are left out of account, however. Again, Gerry Bostock (1985) has realised a history of black theatre through the experience of Aboriginal actors and playwrights such as himself over recent years. Rather than linking it with an Aboriginal past, however, he establishes it in the lineage of Sophocles and Shakespeare, in other words in the history of humanity.

The present in the past

Ethnicities and the 'others' that they entail are typically constructed around a triadic structure: an 'original' culture, located in the more or less remote past; a living 'folk' which is the repository of this culture, perhaps in an impure form; and a 'modern' population who are its heirs. The linkage of these three elements is achieved through notions of physical and cultural inheritance and through location in particular places. Thus the past can be said to exist in the present. Equally, the present can be said to exist in the past, in the sense of being a realisation of what was already there—a potentiality, a destiny, whether noble or ignominious.

Nations are not made out of archaeological remains, half-forgotten languages or folk customs: these 'dead' elements only come alive in the course of political, social and cultural conflict, which is then represented as a realisation of a destiny prefigured in that past. Their importance lies in their capacity to generalise and give historical meaning to the experiences of particular individuals in particular places. Correspondingly, an attack on nation building requires that if the present be not severed from the past, then it must be trapped within it.

Nations that become nation states move on from imagined communities to political institutions, and national struggle becomes objectified in official history. The nations of the Fourth World, however, have not become nation states and are unlikely to do so. Encapsulated as the internal colonies of nation-states, the cultural struggle remains vital and for long periods may be all that they have. Aborigines, like native Americans and others, face the unending task of resisting attempts, on the one hand to cut them off from their 'heritage', and on the other to bury them within it as 'a thing of the past'.

Notes

1. My thanks to Tim Rowse, Jan Larbalastier and Sheila Shaver for ther comments on various drafts of this paper.
2. Tzvetan Todorov *The Conquest of America: The Question of the Other*, 247.
3. As Smith (1969, 22), notes what Cook and Banks said about the Australian Aborigines was later used to describe the Fuegians.
4. While almost all Aboriginal people have shared this relationship with the state, forming since the 1950s a unitary group, they have over the longer run been subjected to separate legislation and administrative apparatuses in the various states and the Northern Territory. Instituted at different times and operated at different degrees of intensity, the policies were not essentially divergent, and they were subject to unifying pressures from the 1930s, long before the Commonwealth government made Aboriginal affairs a national matter in 1973. Nevertheless, changes and variations in the definition of who was Aboriginal had important consequences for families and individuals.
5. A Swedish scientist, Knut Dahl (1926, 8) wrote of Australia, 'Everything in it is "old fashioned"—it is as though it had stopped in a stage which the rest of the world has long ago passed.'
6. A newspaper feature discusses 'the failure of 199 years to reach equality between cultures 30,000 years apart' (Robert Haupt, *Sydney Morning Herald*, 26 May 1987).
7. Although most social anthropologists of the time worked in colonial situations, some Australians seemed to believe that valid research was no longer possible among Aborigines. Thus the author of one of the best monographs written on Aborigines remarked that, '*none* of the Australian fieldwork with which I am acquainted (and I include my own) has produced data upon which can be based what I take to be a valid structural-organization analysis of Aboriginal society' (Meggitt 1963, 216).
8. Dahl (1926, 9, 11) observed, 'Among living races few if any parallels will be found. Recourse must be had to finds and excavations of very distant ages in order to find a human race comparable with the Australian aboriginal...[and later]...Life among these aborigines becomes a series of revelations of the life of pre-historic man.'
9. Joseph Conrad, in his novel *Victory*, casts two Colombian 'half-breeds' in the role of mindless brutes, doing the bidding of the villain. A Queensland writer of the same period, used the South American example as a warning of what would eventuate if Australia produced a half-breed strain (Evans 1975).
10. Although it may be that some infants were killed, many survived to take their place in Aboriginal society, acquiring as fathers the Aboriginal men with whom their mothers lived. The belief that Aborigines rejected half-castes seems to mirror the European practice. An anthropology that emphasised social placement through the father gave scientific authority to the idea of the displaced half-caste.
11. Neville does not admit to a practical reason behind his plan, but his repeated references to extreme deprivation among Aborigines in the southern part of the state suggests that their plight—and the public burden of relieving it—may have outweighed the advantage of an intermediate group of half-castes in the cattle raising north in his strategy.
12. Elkin during the 1930s declared an open mind on the matter of racial equality (cf

Markus 1982), notwithstanding his campaign on behalf of Aborigines. After the war he refrained from comment on the matter.

13. In Stanner's words (1963, xvii–xviii) 'Time did not seem to be a problem when scores of thousands of Aborigines were living by a tradition we might have understood in all its fullness had our resources and methods of study been better. When methods improved, public interest was at its lowest ebb, and traditional life could be found only in the remote outposts. Now that there has been a revolution of public interest, and more precise methods of study are at hand, only a few years remain in which to bring together, as best we can, our new respect for the native Australians and the preservation for posterity—theirs and ours—of a true and competent record of their way of life.'

14. Only a few years earlier, Australians had flocked to see the film 'Jedda' (made in 1955) which depicted an Aboriginal girl brought up by whites succumbing to the 'call of wild' in the person of an outlaw Aboriginal called, appropriately, Marbuck!

15. After the highpoint of the 1930s in Victoria and New South Wales (Horner 1974), Aboriginal protest languished through the 1940s and 1950s, sustained mainly by the survivors of that era, and isolated outbursts in Western Australia (Bandler 1983).

16. See Kevin Gilbert (1973), also Marcia Langton's photographic collection *After the Tent Embassy* (1982).

17. The referendum has been used ironically to contrast the hopes of 1967 with the disappointing realities of 1987.

18. A partial exception was TGH Strehlow (1947, 6) who, while locating Aboriginal religion among world religions, stressed its rigidity and conservatism.

19. A new generation of interpreters have also discovered 'timeless symbols' in the watercolours of Albert Namatjira (Thomas 1986, 26), and suggested that the Aranda painters 'played a significant role in preparing a groundwork for the popular acceptance of land rights' (Burn and Stephen 1986, 13).

20. Morris (Chapter 5) defines fetishised culture as 'culture presented as an aspect of the past separated out from everyday existence'. The means of this separation deserve closer examination.

21. Dolgin's (1977, 61–62) original reads as follows: 'Through "blood" and through "code for conduct" JDL made that "too remote" past contemporary, the means by which this occurred was backward metaphorization of the present. While the blood tie which makes a person a Jew, is a "natural" tie, the link to Moses and Abraham, to Judith and Deborah, is a tie of metaphoric blood; the mediator between the "natural" blood of the family and the metaphoric blood of History is "code for conduct"' (conceived by JDLers as 'action').

22. This may be due in part to Aboriginal resistance to the intrusive cameras of tourists (*Sydney Morning Herald* 19 April 1986). However, a survey of tourist brochures selected at random from the Northern Territory Tourist office and a Sydney travel agency revealed only two photographs of Aboriginal people.

References

Bandler, F.
1983 *The Time Was Ripe: A History of the Australian Aboriginal Fellowship (1959–1969)*, Alternative Publishing Cooperative Ltd, Sydney.

Batty, J.D.
1963 *Namatjira: Wanderer Between Two Worlds*, Hodder and Stoughton, Melbourne.

Bonner, N. and R. Sykes
1975 *Black Power in Australia*, Heinemann, Melbourne.

Bostock, G.
1985 Black Theatre. In J. Davis and B. Hodge (eds), *Aboriginal Writing Today*, Australian Institute of Aboriginal Studies, Canberra, 63–74.

Bropho, R.
1980 *Fringedweller*, Alternative Publishing Cooperative Ltd, Sydney.

Bucher, B.
1981 *Icon and Conquest: A Structural Analysis of the Illustrations of de Bry's Great Voyages*, University of Chicago Press, Chicago.

Burn, I. and A. Stephen
1986 Traditional Painter: The Transfiguration of Albert Namatjira, *Age Monthly Review* 6(7), 10–13.

Dahl, K.
1926 *In Savage Australia: An Account of a Hunting and Collecting Expedition to Arnhem Land and Dampier Land*, Phillip Allan, London.

Department of Territories
1967 *The Australian Aborigines*, Commonwealth Department of Territories, Canberra.

Dixon, R.
1986 *The Cause of Empire: Neo-classical Culture in New South Wales*, Oxford University Press, Oxford.

Dolgin, J.
1977 *Jewish Identity and the JDL*, Princeton University Press, Princeton.

Donaldson, I. and T. Donaldson (eds)
1985 *Seeing the First Australians*, George Allen and Unwin, Sydney.

Elkin, A.P.
1945 *Aboriginal Men of High Degree*, Australasian Publishing Co, Sydney.

Evans, R.
1975 'The Nigger Shall Disappear' Aborigines and Europeans in Colonial Queensland. In R. Evans, K. Cronin and K. Saunders (eds), *Exclusion, Exploitation and Extermination: Race Relations in Colonial Queensland*, Australia and New Zealand Book Co, Sydney.

Gilbert, K.
1973 *Because a White Man'll Never Do It*, Angus and Robertson, Sydney.
1977 *Living Black: Blacks Talk to Kevin Gilbert*, Allen Lane, Melbourne.

Hamilton, A.
1984 Spoonfeeding the Lizards: Culture and Conflict in Central Australia, *Meanjin* 43(3), 363–78.

Hardy, F.
1968 *The Unlucky Australians*, Nelson, Sydney.

Healy, J.
1978 *Literature and the Aborigine in Australia*, University of Queensland Press, St Lucia.

Herbert, X.
1938 *Capricornia*, Publicist Press, Sydney.

Heseltine, H.
1973 *Xavier Herbert*, Oxford University Press, Oxford.

Horner, J.
1974 *Vote Ferguson for Aboriginal Freedom*, Australia and New Zealand Book Co, Sydney.

Jacobs, P.
1986 Science and Veiled Assumptions: Miscegenation in Western Australia 1930-37, *Australian Aboriginal Studies* 2, 15-23.

Johnson, C.
1979 *Long Live Sandawara*, Quartet Books, Melbourne.
1983 *Doctor Wooreddy's Prescription for Enduring the Ending of the World*, Hyland House, Melbourne.

Langton, M.
1982 *After the Tent Embassy: Images of Aboriginal History in Black and White Photographs*, Valadon Publishing, Sydney.

Lattas, A.
1986 Savagery and Civilization: Towards a Genealogy of Racism, unpublished manuscript.

Markus, A.
1982 After the Outward Appearance: Scientists, Administrators and Politicians. In B. Gammage and A. Markus (eds), *All That Dirt: Aborigines 1938*, Australian National University, Research School of Social Sciences, Canberra, 83-106.

McGregor, A.
1987 The Strehlow Collection, *Age Monthly* VI, 11.

Meggitt, M.
1963 Social Organization: Morphology and Typology. In H. Sheils (ed), *Australian Aboriginal Studies*, Oxford University Press, Oxford.

Mountford, C.P.
1948 *Brown Men and Red Sand: Journeyings into Wild Australia*, Robertson and Mullens, Melbourne.

Mulvaney, D.J.
1964 The Australian Aborigines 1606-1929. In J.J. Eastwood and F.B. Smith (eds), *Historical Studies:Selected Articles*, Melbourne University Press, Melbourne, 1-56.

Neville, A.O.
1947 *Australia's Coloured Minority*, Currawong Publishing, Sydney.

Rowley, C.D.
1970 *The Remote Aborigines*, Australian National University Press, Canberra.

Rowse, T.
1986 Land Rights, Mining and Settler Democracy, *Meanjin* 45(1), 58-68.

Ryan, L.
1986 Reading Aboriginal Histories, *Meanjin* 45(1), 49-57.

Sansom, B.
1980 *The Camp at Wallaby Cross: Aboriginal Fringe Dwellers in Darwin*, Australian Institute of Aboriginal Studies, Canberra.

Smith, B.
1969 *European Vision and the South Pacific 1768-1850*, Oxford University Press, Oxford.

Stanner, W.E.H.
1958 The Dreaming. In W.A. Lessa and E.Z. Vogt (eds), *Reader in Comparative Religion: An Anthropological Approach*, Row, Peterson and Evanston, Illinois.
1968 *After the Dreaming*, The Boyer Lectures, Australian Broadcasting Commission, Sydney.

Stone, S.
1974 *Aborigines in White Australia*, Heinemann, Melbourne.

Strehlow, T.G.H.
1947 *Aranda Traditions*, Melbourne University Press, Melbourne.
1963 Anthropological and Ethnological Research. In H. Sheils (ed), *Australian Aboriginal Studies*, Oxford University Press, Oxford.

Taussig, M.
1984 Struggles of the Nation-State to Define Aboriginal Ethnicity: Canada and Australia. In G.L. Gold (ed), *Minorities and Mother Country Imagery*, Social and Economic Papers 13, Institute of Social and Economic Research, Newfoundland.

Thomas, D.
1986 Albert Namatjira and the Worlds of Art: A Re-evaluation. In N. Amadio (ed), *Albert Namatjira: The Life and Work of an Australian Painter*, Macmillan, Melbourne.

Ward, R.
1964 *The Australian Legend*, Oxford University Press, Oxford.

Weaver, S.
1984 Struggles of the Nation-State to Define Aboriginal Ethnicity: Canada and Australia. In G.L. Gold (ed), *Minorities and Mother Country Imagery*, Social and Economic Papers 13, Institute of Social and Economic Research, Newfoundland.

White, H.
1978 *Topics of Discourse: Essays in Cultural Criticism*, Johns Hopkins University Press, Baltimore.

White, R.
1981 *Inventing Australia: Images and Identity 1688–1980*, George Allen and Unwin, Sydney.